YAZ
· · ·

DOUBLEDAY

NEW YORK LONDON TORONTO SYDNEY AUCKLAND

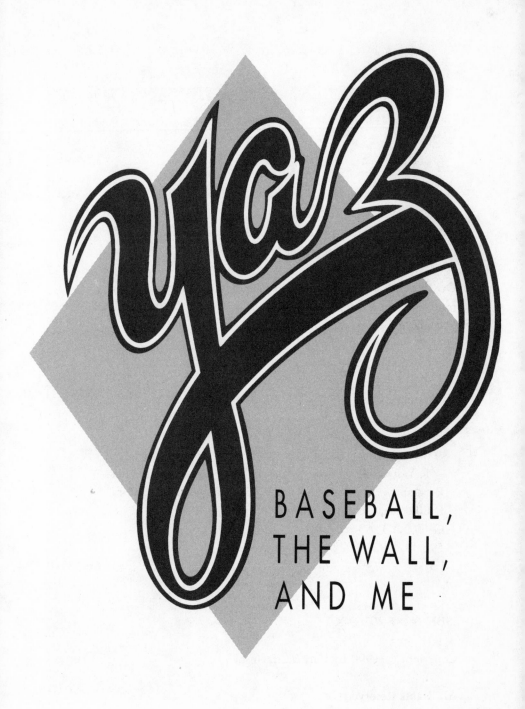

BASEBALL,
THE WALL,
AND ME

CARL YASTRZEMSKI   GERALD ESKENAZI

PUBLISHED BY DOUBLEDAY
a division of Bantam Doubleday Dell Publishing Group, Inc.
666 Fifth Avenue, New York, New York 10103

DOUBLEDAY and the portrayal of an anchor with a dolphin are
trademarks of Doubleday, a division of Bantam Doubleday Dell
Publishing Group, Inc.

Library of Congress Cataloging-in-Publication Data

Yastrzemski, Carl.
    Yaz : baseball, the wall, and me / by Carl Yastrzemski and Gerald
Eskenazi. —1st ed.
        p.   cm.
    1. Yastrzemski, Carl.   2. Baseball players—United States—
Biography.   3. Boston Red Sox (Baseball team) —History.
I. Eskenazi, Gerald.   II. Title.
GV865.Y35A3   1990
796.357'092—dc20
[B]   89-38910
                                                                          CIP

ISBN 0-385-26769-X

THIS BOOK IS DEDICATED TO THE MEMORY OF MY
MOM, HEDWIG YASTRZEMSKI,
AND TOM YAWKEY.

A life that includes twenty-three major league seasons cannot be recalled with the snap of a finger. To help us remember those days and nights, on and off the field, at the farm and in Fenway, special thanks go to:

Baseball Hall of Fame and Bill Guilfoile, associate director, and research staff; Jay Acton, whose foresight and ideas saw the project through; Dave Gernert of Doubleday, who had the first requisite for an editor: enthusiasm; Dick Bresciani, Boston Red Sox vice president of public relations, and Josh Spofford and Jim Samia; Stew Thornley, Minneapolis Millers buff; Bob Hercules of the Media Processing Group, Inc.; Roger Valdiserri of Notre Dame; Steve Keener of The Little League; attorney Bob Woolf, and Kathy Campanella, Jill Leone, and Stacey Woolf of Bob's office; Laurence K. Goodier and Dave Mugar of Mugar Communications Corporation; Elias Sports Bureau and the great Seymour Siwoff; Major League Baseball and Rich Levin of the commissioner's office; the American League and Phyllis Merhige and John Maroon; Jon Levine and Farrell Shapiro, baseball experts.

THIS PAGE IS FOR ELLEN, MARK, AND MICHAEL.

CONTENTS

• • •

PROLOGUE
. . .

I liked the plaque.

The first time I saw it was when I turned around on the platform of the Hall of Fame to see it unveiled. I could hear the fans shouting, "Yaz!" In a funny way, in the same way it had always been when I came to bat in the clutch, those fans, that cheering, calmed me. It gave me confidence to go on. This time, on this warm, beautiful July day in 1989, it gave me the strength to make my speech. The jitters disappeared.

I had made it, along with Johnny Bench, as the newest players to be inducted at Cooperstown.

Behind me the old ballplayers sat, guys I had worshiped. Now I was joining them. Ted Williams was there in the front row, without a tie and wearing an open-necked shirt as usual, and there were Campy and Stan the Man, Harmon Killebrew, Willie McCovey, Bob Feller, Ernie Banks.

Funny, I was fifty, the Hall was fifty, the Little League was fifty. We all were born the same year and I was now part of all of them.

If baseball really wasn't invented in Cooperstown, it should have been. Everywhere you looked there were kids wearing baseball shirts and caps—just like their moms and dads. Outside of town, people played catch along the side of the road. Teenagers played pickup baseball games in the field. This was baseball and it was America at the same time. It was almost as if this was where I was supposed to be; it was a place where I felt comfortable.

When I finally got a chance to read the plaque, it told of

how I had played twenty-three seasons with the Boston Red Sox, how I had set the American League record of performing in 3,308 games, how I was the only player in American League history with 3,000 hits and 400 home runs. And yes, it spoke of the Impossible Dream season of 1967, when I became the last Triple Crown winner and helped the Sox win that wonderful pennant.

Dad didn't say much that day. He never does. But, God, was he ever proud when he stood up after I introduced him as the man who had sacrificed his own baseball career to help his family during the Depression. I was worried that when I mentioned my late mom I'd start to break down, but I didn't. And Carol and the kids and brother Rich and Mrs. Yawkey completed the picture. There were also more than three hundred people to take care of that magical weekend. My longtime colleagues at Kahn's had arrived one hundred and sixty strong. Add to that a hundred and fifty friends and relatives, all needing a place to stay in a town geared to once-a-year activity, and it was a busy three days I'll never forget.

You'd think after all these years, after all the at-bats in the garage back at the farm in Long Island, after 11,988 official at-bats in the big leagues, I'd know how to handle a small crowd on hand to hear me make a speech. Not me. Not yet. I'm still intense. I had worked on the speech for two weeks. But on Sunday morning I spent two hours at breakfast going over it with my fine friends Dick Gordon, Vinny Quealy, and Vinny's son-in-law Paul Bartkiewicz. I wanted this speech to be perfect, just as I had always sought the perfect swing.

"It was a long five years waiting, I'll tell you that," I ad-libbed as I broke through the cheers after Commissioner A. Bartlett Giamatti introduced me.

This is how nervous I was about getting into the Hall. The night I waited for the phone call, I was so sure I wouldn't get in on the first try that I wouldn't allow reporters in the house with me. I asked Dad to be there, all right. But that was his bowling night. "You know I don't miss bowling," he said.

So I waited alone that January night until the call came. I was so flustered I didn't even say, "Thank you." I just hung up the phone.

Now here I was, being introduced by the commissioner of baseball. He couldn't resist a quip either as he said, "I remember it well," when he read the plaque and got to the line about the Impossible Dream. Bart was an old Red Sox fan himself. How he loved reminiscing! His sudden death soon afterward left us all sadder, but I treasure his memory—a true fan and gentleman.

In my speech, I stumbled slightly when I spoke of "my dear mother, whom I miss today." But I was warmed by the applause when I introduced my father. In fact, whenever I mentioned "Boston" or "Red Sox," it would trigger a rousing burst of applause. I heard someone call out, "We love ya, Yaz!"

I still recall bits and pieces of what I said that day:

> *To have played my whole career for one team and in one city, Boston, doesn't happen to many major league ballplayers . . .*
>
> *The debt of gratitude I owe Tom Yawkey and his widow, Jean, who has honored me by being here today, can never be repaid . . .*
>
> *Why am I here in Cooperstown? I was never blessed with superb physical strength. I had to work twice as long and twice as hard as many of my peers . . .*

The theme I tried to convey was the line of Grantland Rice's:

When the One Great Scorer comes to write against your name—
He marks—not that you won or lost—but how you played the game.

I told the crowd:

> *I can stand before you today and tell you honestly that every day I put on that Red Sox uniform I gave 100 percent of myself. I treated it with dignity and respect in deference to our fans, my high regard for my teammates, coaches, and management. Anything less would not have been worthy of me, anything more would not have been possible . . . The race doesn't always belong to the swift . . . It belongs rather to those who run the race, stay the course, and who fought the good fight.*

That night there was a quiet party, at least quieter than the two days of fun that had preceded the induction. Those were glorious times, laughing and reminiscing with Bob and Anne Woolf, with Tip O'Neill, with Joe Moakley (head of the Rules Committee of the House of Representatives) and fellow Congressman Sil Conte, with uncles and cousins and a new little grandson.

But Sunday night was extra-special. In a way, I felt I was now officially a member of the Hall. It was a dinner just for the members. That's when I got my Hall of Fame ring. Each of us made a little speech. I told my new colleagues how "I'm so happy to join such an elite group." I pointed out how ironic it was that Johnny Bench and Red Schoendienst, who had been elected by the Veterans' Committee along with umpire Al Barlick, had each played a role in the two World Series I appeared in. Bench was a star of the Cincinnati Reds in 1975, of course, and Schoendienst had managed the St. Louis Cardinals in 1967.

"I really gained respect for you that year, Red," I told him. "You ordered Nelson Briles to hit me after Jim Lonborg had nailed Lou Brock. That's the way the game should be played." A couple of old-fashioned guys had a good laugh over that.

Ted was still the same. He talked about when I was a

young kid and how he knew I'd be okay if I just got over my nervousness. One thing Ted never let me forget, though. He thinks my autograph isn't neat enough.

"Hey, look, no one could even recognize your signature," he bellowed one day in Cooperstown. He took a ball with my name on it and went over to a fan and asked, "Whose signature is this?" The fan said, "Carl Yastrzemski's."

"Well, maybe it's not so bad," the Thumper grumbled.

So I guess he finally thinks I can sign my name after all these years.

1
REFLECTIONS

Thanksgiving 1958. Fenway Park. Snow was on the ground. It was gray and cold and I shivered in my jacket as I took my first look at this old ballpark in Boston.

But where's right field? I thought.

It looked so far away. And the field . . . covered with snow. This was not the place I had dreamed about every night through my teens—all those years of practicing, day in and day out, with just one goal: to play baseball. Fenway Park was not what I had in mind.

My dream was to make it to the majors, yes. It was a dream launched by my father, who had been reluctant to leave the potato fields of Long Island to try baseball during the Depression. He had groomed me to get out of the potato fields, and he had taught me well. I couldn't wait to begin a career of my own. But I wanted to make it to a place where I could be happy hitting.

"Carl, this is a great place for you to hit!"

I looked at my father as if he was crazy. Cripes, I couldn't even *see* right field.

"Are you looking at the same ballpark I am?" I asked my dad.

I stood in Section 26, on the third base side of home plate. Right next to me was Johnny Murphy, the farm director of the Red Sox, beaming. He was so proud of Fenway, so happy to be impressing a nineteen-year-old kid.

But I stared out to right field. It was 380 feet away—380 feet. Oh yeah, you only needed to hit it 307 feet to the right field foul pole—if you could pull it right down the line. But that fence made a quick 90-degree left turn toward center, and suddenly you were staring at a moon shot, at least for me. I was five feet eleven inches tall, but I only weighed 160 pounds.

I was a student at Notre Dame. But I knew that if I was going to play baseball, I'd have to leave school. The weather was bad in Indiana. You couldn't get enough practice in, and with those wintry conditions, there was always the risk of an injury. Now, though, at Fenway Park, I was standing in the snow, humoring the Red Sox farm director. The Red Sox brass had wanted me to see their park. Some first impression. *No way* was my career going to start in this crazy place in Boston.

I had been working out at Detroit, Cincinnati, and Philadelphia. Until Dad killed the deal, I had even hit at Yankee Stadium. Places with short porches in right. I was not a dead-pull hitter and I was looking for all the help I could get. Even though I hit .650 one season in high school, I was more like a Wade Boggs type than a power hitter. I could spray the ball to all fields. But my father made the decision for me. We went back to the hotel that night. He told me that he had been talking to the Red Sox and that they all thought Fenway was the place for me.

If anyone had asked me, though, I really didn't want to sign with them because of that right field fence. I probably would have picked Detroit. Jeez, that would have been perfect for me, a left-handed hitter. But I had too much respect for my father—and, anyway, no one ever changed his mind—and so I went along with him.

I came to love Fenway. It was a place that rejuvenated me after a road trip: the fans right on top of you, the nutty angles. And the Wall. That was my baby, the left field Wall. The Green Monster. You know, when I started playing it that Wall had rivets sticking out of it, it had two-by-fours, it had tin. It had a concrete base that rose about twenty-five feet or so. And you had to know that a ball hit by a left-handed batter would spin off it differently from a right-hander's shot. I'm not even taking into account now what would happen when it hit an exposed rivet. Or the two-by-fours. Or the tin. Or the holes in the scoreboard.

Thirty years later, I sat by the telephone waiting for the call from Jack Lang, the secretary-treasurer of the Baseball Writers Association of America. Mr. Good News. Or Mr. No News. He's the man who counts the votes by senior writers and then lets you know if you've been elected to the Baseball Hall of Fame.

It was very important for me to be elected on the first ballot. Crazy thoughts were going through my mind. I thought, *Maybe I won't get in the first time.* I found myself dwelling on that possibility, and I really started to worry and wonder.

For the last few seasons of my twenty-three-year career, I had become very proud of what I had accomplished. And in the five years I had to wait to become eligible, what I managed to achieve during my career grew in importance in my mind.

I wanted to go in real bad on the first ballot because only seventeen players had ever made it on their first try. There was a tremendous amount of pride involved in doing that. I had gotten the most out of my ability. I didn't have the size most of the guys in the Hall of Fame had. It was just hard work, hard work, hard work.

I had 3,000 hits and 400 home runs. I was the only player in the history of the American League to produce that combination. That was the source of special pride. I didn't have the grace of DiMaggio, and he didn't do it. I didn't have the power and switch-hitting ability of a Mantle, and he didn't do it. Cobb, Ruth, Williams—none of them did it. They got one or the other. But none of them got both. Some people might say, "Yeah, but this guy was injured or that guy was in the service." We all had the same shot.

My size has always been my obsession. That's why the fact that I went to the plate more often than any player in the history of the American League still startles me.

For twenty-three straight seasons—from 1961 to 1983—I wore a Red Sox uniform. I became only the second player in the history of major league baseball to play that long with one club. My years really were the wonder years, when you think about it, encompassing generations of change in the game, the people, even the country. My link went back to the 1930s and extends to the 1990s: I shared a locker room with Ted Williams, with Jim Rice and Fred Lynn, with Wade Boggs. I played for a man, Tom Yawkey, who owned the club for forty-four years, longer than anyone before or since. When I started, you didn't say hello to the veterans unless they spoke first. When I quit—having second thoughts, even though I was forty-four years old—we were in the era when a player got mad if someone brushed him back with an inside pitch, an era when a ballplayer left his club for the highest bidder.

Along the way, I won three batting titles, I was the last man to win the Triple Crown for leading the league in batting average, home runs, and runs batted in, and I played in fourteen All-Star Games. I also batted 11,988 times and had 1,845 walks.

I wish I had enjoyed all of them more. I was so intent on my next at-bat, my next play, my next throw, that the fun of what I had just done never lingered more than minutes or hours. Sometimes, after a hitless day, or a game that we lost in a season going nowhere, I would have such dark thoughts that they frightened me.

Yet, now I think about that fun. I think about the Impossible Dream, the 1967 season, when we leaped from ninth place the season before to the pennant. And we carried all of New England with us, a year people still remind me of and that brings smiles to their faces even now. Or 1975, when we beat Oakland in the playoffs and made it to the World Series again and nearly won it with a goofy cast of characters, when I was at my peak in leading the players in locker room pranks. There was 1978, when we blew a fourteen-game lead over the Yankees, only to tie them on the final day of the season, and then meet them in that one-game playoff. These were part of sixteen straight winning seasons on the Sox.

Maybe it was because I never took anything for granted, that my swing always had to be perfect—if not, I was so damn sure the ball would blow right by me. So after all that, after all the years and the awards, I sweated out that Hall of Fame vote. Yet, when it was over, I got in with more than 94 percent of the ballots—sixth-best average in history.

Me, a nineteen-year-old kid, who went to bed that night unhappy after his first look at Fenway, how could I see down the road that far? Not that night, certainly.

2
THE POTATO FARMER

That wasn't the first time I was shocked at a decision my dad made. Nothing ever topped the time he kicked the Yankees' scout out of our house while I shouted, "Dad, what the heck are you doing?" But my father not only kicked him out but would never talk to him or the Yankees again. But I'm jumping ahead. To understand the way my dad thought about life, and the way I learned about life and baseball, I have to go back.

The work—really, labor—of trying to be my best would eventually pay off, I had always hoped. The thing is: *You're never quite sure.* At least, I was never sure. It was work that started in the potato fields back in Bridgehampton, Long Island. The Island is about a hundred and twenty miles long, and we were about a hundred miles from New York City on the South Fork. That area is more like the Northeast than New York, though—small-town, family-owned farms. You might even think of it as a series of small New England towns. At least that's the way it was when I was growing up there. Bridgehampton had about three thousand people in the 1950s.

I was born in 1939 during the Great Depression, and my mom and dad lived their lives never forgetting how hard it was then. The Depression hovered over their decisions for themselves and for me: "Don't spend, don't spend. Ya gotta put it in the bank." If we had extra money, that's where it went. That was drummed into me, so much that even today I don't think I could go out and buy myself a red sports car—unless, that is, I knew I could sell it eventually for what I paid for it. It may have been a reason, too, that I never really looked elsewhere once I made it to Boston. I got offers from Japan. Clubs in Seattle and Toronto were also after me during the time of free agency. The Yankees even made a backdoor offer. But once I had put my roots in Boston, that was where I wanted to stay—even if I believed in only signing one-year contracts. Heck, Mr. Yawkey and me, we *knew* I'd be back there the next year. I always was.

My mom and dad were part of a large Polish community that farmed the Bridgehampton-Southampton area. Dad and his brother, Uncle Tommy, owned a seventy-acre farm in Water Mill, not far from where our house was. Tommy had his own house on the farm. We had our own place a few miles away. Potato farming was a legacy from Poland, folks coming over here and doing what they knew in the old country.

There were just the four of us in our house: Mom, Dad, me, and my brother, Joseph Richard, who was four years younger than me and who everybody called Rich.

But that was just for starters. The house was always filled with Yastrzemskis and Skoniecznys (pronounced *Sko-nez-nee),* Mom's family. We worked together and, just as important, we played together.

My father loved baseball. After the long hours we all put in on the farm, athletics were our relaxation, and we worked hard to relax. All the Yastrzemskis and Skoniecznys were on a baseball team, run by my dad, called the Bridgehampton White Eagles.

I started out as bat boy, of course. Everyone I knew played some sport—football, baseball, basketball. I know I was young when my dad got me involved. I was so young, I don't even remember posing for the picture my folks used to show me, dragging a bat. Or there were other photos showing me with a bat and ball in my hands. The house was filled with these pictures of me with a ball or a bat.

It probably wasn't too long after those photos were taken that I came to realize how important baseball was to my dad. That was all we heard about and talked about after the business of farming was over at the end of the day.

During the Depression, Dad could have signed with the Dodgers. Can you imagine, the Brooklyn Dodgers! They wanted him, and so did the Cardinals. But he decided not to. He wanted to wait a while. They were only going to pay him $75 a month to play in the minors. He didn't want to leave the farm and take a chance giving up the land, where he knew he could make a living. This was a hard time, remember. He was worried about his next meal.

When Dad finally decided that, yes, he would take a chance on making the majors, it was too late. A few years after he had turned down the Dodgers, he hurt his shoulder. When he tried out for them again, he had lost that extra playing edge.

He never told me, but I always sensed that he was determined that the hard times, the chance that slipped away, the difficult farm life . . . none of that was going to happen to me. I was going to get every opportunity to play baseball—even to the extent that he would control my well-being. He would always know what was best for me. I may have doubted him, but I was so accustomed to his presence that I always went along with what he wanted.

But I, too, had dreams beyond the farm. How many of us are lucky enough to realize them? My dream was the same as so many millions of other good little American boys—to make it to the major leagues. Like so many of the others, I worked at making it from the time I was six or seven.

I practiced playing baseball every single day of the year. Our garage wasn't like a modern attached garage. You could get a truck in this one. It was about a hundred feet from the house, but it didn't matter what time of year it was. Late in the afternoon was my practice time.

How did the dream begin? Maybe when I was eleven or twelve and read about one of those bonus babies, you know, with the $100,000 bonus. His name was Paul Pettit, and I think he was the first ballplayer ever to get a six-figure bonus for signing. I had this feeling, this drive, that I would become the highest-paid bonus player ever. Why that bonus stuck in my mind, I don't know. Maybe it was because they were just teenagers, and I related to them. Maybe it was a symbol, the money, of making it to the big leagues. But that's when I started using my gimmicks.

I'd rig them up in the garage, homemade contraptions I designed to increase my strength, my speed, my ability to do things with a baseball that I just couldn't do up to then. It was all to play with the Yankees. I had seen the Yankees doing great things. We were fervent Yankee fans, my dad and I, and three or four times a year we'd make the two-hundred-mile round-trip to Yankee Stadium to see DiMaggio and Mantle and Ford and Skowron. But with all the brothers and cousins and uncles, we were always bickering because New York had three teams then. There were also the Dodgers and the Giants. Who was better? To me, it was Mick and the Yanks. But someone else would shout for Duke and the Dodgers. And, of course, an uncle or two would root for Willie and the Giants. Let them. I couldn't get enough of the Yankees. It would take three hours just to get to the park. Once I was there, I just knew I was going to be back one day—in uniform.

To get there, I had my gimmicks. I'd take a baseball and drive a nail through it, then attach string to it, and I'd hang the ball from the ceiling. I'd have a lead bat, because of the extra weight, and I'd just swing at the damn ball for an hour. *Whack!* Then another *whack.* And another. In the summer, when I moved outdoors, one of my contraptions was a ball attached to a thirty-foot cord. When I hit it, I could follow the flight of the ball, making sure it was a liner, that each shot was exactly the same height off the ground.

Wintertime? Snow? It didn't matter. I cleared a path from the house to the garage. I'd have on a huge parka, put on a pair of big gloves, and I'd go out there for two hours every day in the wintertime. My mom would call me in for dinner, but afterward I'd do all sorts of drills, trying to strengthen my hands and arms. It was cold in the garage, but I would constantly drill.

During the summertime, when I worked, I didn't pass up any chances to hit balls, or at least swing a bat. Whenever I got a break on the farm, I'd take a bushel basket, pick up some rocks, fill up the basket, and take a bat and just throw the rocks in the air and hit them. *Bing*—one after the other—till the bushel was empty or they called me back to work. While I was batting, I'd play a game. I'd go down the lineup of my favorite players. The late 1940s and early '50s were a great time for players. Take Musial. I'd go into his crouched stance and hit left-handed. He was one of my favorites because he was Polish. When I'd choose DiMaggio, I'd open my stance and hit right-handed. I just hit bushels of rocks. Hit them, go pick them all up, and bring them back, and go back to hitting them again.

At night when I went to sleep, I'd dream about playing in the big leagues, especially when I got to be about eleven.

That's about the time I realized the work was paying off. I actually could compete against older guys. I was surrounded by uncles, and if they were passing the house they'd see me outside and they'd stop the car, and pitch to me. We'd have a little game of stickball. I'd take a stick and saw it off and I'd stand in front of the garage door with a bat in my hand. My uncles would pitch to me, but they wouldn't use a baseball. Instead, they'd take a tennis ball and stand twenty-five or thirty feet away. And they'd try to strike me out. They couldn't. These guys were all good ballplayers, and a tennis ball was soft. You could make it dip and curve and screwball and spin by squeezing it. That didn't matter. They'd move up even as close as fifteen feet and throw as hard as they could and try to strike me out. None of them—Uncle Mike, Uncle Tommy, Uncle Jerry, Uncle Ray, Uncle Chet—could ever strike me out.

I was always competing against people at a higher level. I joined the White Eagles when I was fifteen. Then, after my sophomore year in high school, when the White Eagles just sort of dissolved, I started playing semipro ball, where I got paid, in Lake Ronkonkoma.

In the back of my mind, I always believed that Dad had kept the White Eagles going just so he could play alongside me. By then he was in his forties, and so were many of my uncles. Some of my cousins were in their thirties. A couple of them wanted to quit, but Dad kept the whole thing going. He was the second baseman and he put me at short. I loved his spirit and intensity when I played alongside him. Once in a while, if a cousin or an uncle complained about what position he was playing, Dad would shift the other players around to keep him happy. He didn't want anyone quitting on him. Luckily, he kept me out of the outfield, which I hated. Maybe if I had played in parks that had fences I would have enjoyed it better. But the outfields stretched forever in some of the fields we played in and you'd be chasing balls so much it felt more like a track meet than a baseball game.

In my mind's eye, Dad was the greatest hitter I had ever seen. He would hit close to .500 over a season, a dead-pull hitter who hardly ever struck out. He was so stubborn at the plate, though, that he refused to hit the ball anyplace but the left side, even though all the other teams overshifted on him. Funny, in that way he was like Ted Williams, who refused to hit to the opposite field. The other teams shifted the second baseman to the third base side of the infield, but Dad never would hit the ball to the right side.

And strike out? Never! Even those rare times he was called out on strikes, he would stand at the plate and refuse to leave, insisting the umpire was nuts, that if the pitch had been any good, why, he would have swung at it.

The last years on the club had become a chore. The fields were in awful shape, since the kids that played on them during the week never took care of them. Before we got to the field, though, we'd go to church, which was on Montauk Highway. Since Father Joe Rapkowski was a White Eagles fan, he'd keep his sermons short on the days we were playing at home. He knew we had to get to the field. We'd comb it with a mat we attached to the back of a pickup truck, and do the best we could with the field. Then we'd outline the batter's box and foul lines with lime, and be ready to play. It was obvious, though, that the Eagles' days were numbered. Dad couldn't keep it going just for me anymore.

The Lake Ronkonkoma team was more serious. We faced teams like the Bushwicks, a club from the Brooklyn–Queens border that had it's own stadium, Dexter Park. Or we played the House of David team. I was fifteen, and competing against guys who were thirty-five. In earlier years, my Ronkonkoma team had even played Negro League teams. Dad and I would play down there two nights a week and on Sunday afternoons. We'd each get $20 a game. It wasn't the money so much. We just wanted a game against good competition. Lake Ronkonkoma was sixty miles from home, and the night games were a grind. We wouldn't get done on the farm until about five o'clock. Then we'd get into the car—Mom, Dad, Rich, and me—for the hour and a quarter drive. We wanted to get there early enough to make batting practice. When it was over, Dad would drive home while Rich and I slept in the back.

I've always felt that Dad was doing all this for my sake. He was over forty by this time, but he loved the fact we were in the lineup together. He was always the cleanup hitter and I always was the number three batter. He played second, I played short. The putouts on force plays would read: "Yastrzemski to Yastrzemski." I liked that.

It wasn't easy for me, though. At least, I would not allow myself to think it was. Even when I was slamming the ball, I constantly adjusted. In hitting, you must have physical ability, of course. But I always thought the key was more mental. I thought that after every pitch, whether you swung at it or took it, you had to make that adjustment right there, right then. I knew every single time, whether I swung at a pitch or not, if I was ready to hit, whether it was a ball or not, whether there was something else I should have done or should have prepared for differently. *Did I jump out too hard on it? Not enough?* So I was constantly talking to myself. I didn't stop, even when I got to the majors. Mel Stottlemyre says that when he was a Yankee and pitching against me, he could hear me talking to myself at the plate when he was on the mound. I knew I was thinking something like *Gotta be quick, gotta be quick,* but I never realized I was saying it out loud. Then again, I was so intent on concentrating and repeating these instructions to myself that I probably did talk out loud but never knew it.

Corrections, adjustments, complaining to myself. They were what I always did, an obsession with me as much as worrying about my size. In high school I pitched a lot as well as hit, and even at pitching I had to be the best at it. I guess I was. We played Little League and the Babe Ruth League and we won major tournaments with me playing shortstop or pitching. Although we had a small base of players to draw from, we made it to the state finals of the Little League. But we won the state championship in the Babe Ruth tournament, with me pitching a no-hitter along the way, but we got beat in the regionals by a team from Maryland. They had a couple of Charlie Keller's kids on that team.

The national Little League was created the same year I was born, 1939. In a strange coincidence, so was the Baseball Hall of Fame. When I got voted in, they told me that I was the first Little League player to ever make it to the Hall. Ironically, 1989 also was the fiftieth birthday for all of us.

Dad was never a stage father. He didn't like to put pressure on me. At least, I don't remember him doing that. He'd never get on me about my hitting. We'd discuss batting, but the only thing he'd ever correct me on was swinging at bad pitches. Right from Little League, he'd say to me, "You swung at a bad pitch, out of the strike zone." He never told me anything else, except "Attack the ball." He didn't believe in defensive hitting. He didn't correct me, but he certainly practiced with me. How many hours in the backyard—tennis balls, baseballs? Sports were as much a part of my life as school or working the farm.

My approach to pitching was the same as my approach to batting. It started when I was only six or seven. I'd draw a square, the same size as the plate, on the back wall of the garage. The garage was about twenty-five feet long, so I stood outside. I'd take a tennis ball and I'd throw to spots on that plate. If I threw it down the middle, it was a ball. I had to hit the corners. I had to throw the perfect pitch. I'd just throw that damn tennis ball half an hour day to spots.

One of my best friends was Billy DePetris, an outstanding ballplayer who got signed by the Giants. Billy had a knuckleball that dropped. That was another challenge to me, a chance to overcome an obstacle. Billy's father owned a restaurant, so his dad wasn't excited about Billy playing ball with me all the time. But I'd go over there and wash the dishes, just so Billy could come out and play stickball for half an hour. I had it all figured out. There was a little open area right behind the restaurant. We'd line up twenty feet apart and burn the hell out of each other. You could really do a lot with a tennis ball, and Billy's knuckle-drop pitch would dip like mad. If I just hit it anyplace, I felt as if I had accomplished something.

Despite my meddling with hitting, I always thought I'd make it as a pitcher in baseball. But when I got to be about sixteen, Dad had other ideas. I had gone to major league tryout camps strictly as a pitcher. The Braves had a tryout and brought all the top players in from the New York area. The Braves asked me to pitch to them. I pitched three innings and I struck out all nine guys.

The Braves wanted to sign me to a big bonus right on the spot.

"Nope, he's not going as a pitcher. He's got too much of

a chance to hurt his arm. He's going to go as a hitter," my dad said. It was the first I knew of it.

I had developed physically and as a batter. With the White Eagles I was an opposite-field hitter. But as I approached my senior year, moving up a level with the Lake Ronkonkoma team, I started pulling the ball and hitting home runs. My .650 average—which included a streak of fifteen straight hits at one point—along with Billy's pitching led us to consecutive county high school championships—not bad when you consider the whole school only had about eighty students. They even named a scholastic baseball award for me out in Suffolk County. A few years ago, a left-handed pitcher named Boomer Esiason won it. One year I was the catcher, but I tried to grab everything with my gloved hand, since I was afraid of hurting my right hand.

Dad also was a worrier. Looking back, I see now that he planned my career. Nothing was going to stand in the way of me becoming a baseball player—and a slugger at that. That's why he was so careful of my arms. It was why he growled when he'd see me playing football or any other sport.

By the time I got to Bridgehampton High and started playing football, Dad really became concerned. We didn't have regular varsity football, since we didn't have enough players. This was six-man football, but you could get banged up. In fact, guys were going down with broken collarbones because on every play there was open-field tackling. A play would begin with a lateral in motion. So one day Dad just forbade me to play football when I was a senior. I was really ticked off. I enjoyed playing quarterback.

Without him knowing about it, I went out a few times and practiced with the team, even though you were supposed to get your parents' permission. I started practicing before the season started, and somehow Dad found out about it.

He got pissed off. When he did, he wouldn't rest until he had done something about it. So one day when I was practicing I suddenly saw Dad marching onto the field. He grabbed me.

"Take those goddam shoulder pads off! I never want to see you put them on again. You're not going to break no collarbone playing football."

Then he went over to the coach, Merle Wiggin, who ran all the sports at Bridgehampton High, and said, "I don't want to see him out here again playing football. If I do, you won't see him playing basketball and baseball."

That was a heck of a threat, because I was good enough in baseball then to have received under-the-table offers from big league teams, and I was also the star of the basketball team, about to set a Suffolk County scoring record. Goodbye, football.

There was enough to keep me busy.

I loved basketball. I guess in today's terms I would have been a jump shooter from the three-point circle. I had to be. I was only about five-nine when I tried out for the team at Bridgehampton. I also wasn't fast enough. Because of my size, I practiced shooting from twenty-five, thirty feet out. I couldn't be an effective driver under the basket because I was too small.

Coach Wiggin told me I'd be more valuable to the team if I could be a scoring threat from the outside. He told me to practice set shots whenever I had the chance.

"Even if you have to hang up a peach basket in your backyard," he said.

That's all I needed to hear. Of course, I put up the peach basket. And I'd practice shots all the time. My mom, meanwhile, had to do her gardening out there, but she got pretty good at dodging my bullets. Eventually, I became very accurate from about twenty feet out with a one-handed jump shot. I even had a hook shot that I could sink from the corner. I was surprised when I found I was able to make the same shots on the court as I made in my backyard. After a while, it seemed that every time I took a shot in a game, I hit it.

Teams started to plan defenses against me, to shove me farther and farther outside. But I once hit for 47 points in a game, another time I scored 46. Nine times I got 30, and I broke the county schoolboy record and averaged 34 points a game. The record lasted for thirty years.

I never expected to become a pro basketball player, but I wanted to be the best at the game. I had to be the best. That's how I came up with that long jump shot. I worked at that as hard as I did at baseball. In the winter, the ground was frozen, but I'd shovel the whole area where I'd be shooting.

I was a great jump shooter from the outside, but I also became very quick. I'd drive, stop, jump shoot. That was almost unstoppable. I could drive, take one step and hang in the air and shoot.

But even after I stopped playing basketball, I never wanted to take the peach basket down. I made a vow to myself that it would stay up as long as we lived in the house. It became a symbol to me of what a guy can accomplish if he works hard.

My mom and dad worked all the time, so when school started I was in charge of taking care of Rich. I'd prepare our breakfasts and then later make lunch for both of us. When I'd come home after school, I would get dinner ready, peeling potatoes, defrosting the meat. Then, when my mom came home, she'd cook it.

In the summertime, we'd work from sunrise to sunset. I'd get that knock on that door at five o'clock in the morning. "Let's go," Dad would say. And we'd be out there, before the days of automation, doing everything by hand—moving the irrigation pipes, sacking, loading the sacks on trucks, then loading more sacks.

The work didn't stop when the harvest ended. During the winter, we'd start cutting the potatoes to plant in the spring. You'd take the seed potatoes, the ones that had started to sprout, and with a sharp knife cut out sections with eyes. Each of those cuttings would form a new potato when you planted them. And we cut potatoes manually, spilling out of hundreds of bags. The place would be filled with a dozen people, bending over those potatoes, cutting out those little eyes.

Years later, when I made it in baseball, people would meet me and expect someone different . . . someone, well, New Yorkish. Instead, they found a guy who was reserved, even shy. If you say you're from New York, everyone thinks of a city guy. But my life, my attitude, was really that of a farm boy's.

We lived on about three acres of land. Behind the house we had a huge garden, maybe an acre and a half. We raised everything, and I mean *everything*—the whole food supply for the year. We had two big freezers filled with string beans, lima beans, corn, beets. That's why, even if the weather was bad or potato prices were down, we always ate well because we grew our own food. We'd even slaughter our own steer, cut our own meat. That was a family affair, too. We had a butcher who'd cut up the meat, and there'd be someone there grinding the meat for hamburger, while someone else would be making sausage. The only things we bought in the store were sugar, salt, pepper, and coffee. We even had our own butter. I pounded that goddam butter churn. We had our own milk. And my mother sewed her own clothes. She never bought a dress in a store in her life. At least, not while I was growing up.

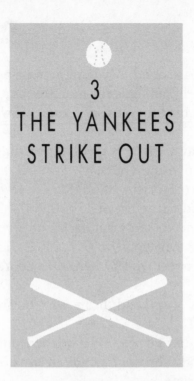

3
THE YANKEES
STRIKE OUT

I came within an inch of signing with the Yankees. But they made a mistake. They got Dad angry.

I was a senior in high school, but they were going to postdate the contract. That's the way they did things in those days. No draft. Different teams would talk to you and try you out. If they liked you, they made the deal, even if they weren't even allowed to be talking to you. They simply changed the date of the contract to make it read as if it was signed after I graduated from high school.

The Yankees had a scout named Ray Garland, and he had been negotiating for some time with my dad after trying me out at Yankee Stadium. Garland had done pretty well signing players from the New York area. He had picked up Whitey Ford and Phil Rizzuto for the Yanks. And Dad was a big, big Yankee fan. So was I, but even more important, from the few tryouts I had at Yankee Stadium, I knew that was the place for me. That short porch in right and the big alleys in left and right center were designed for my hitting style. Nervously, but with great hopes, I sat at the dining room table with Garland and my dad. We—or, I should say, they—started throwing bonus figures around. My dad, being a potato farmer, was coming up with dollar signs for more money than he had ever made or seen in his life. Finally, it came down to serious business.

"Okay," Ray said, "I'll give you my figure on a piece of paper and you give me yours."

Garland wrote down "$60,000." He didn't show it to Dad just yet. Dad wrote down "$100,000." Then they shifted the papers around to see what each one wrote.

"*$100,000?* Are you *crazy?*" said Garland. "No one on the Yankees ever received $100,000. The Yankees will never pay that."

He took his pencil and threw it in the air in exasperation. It hit the ceiling.

Uh-oh. My dad got red. He jumped out of his chair and shouted, "Nobody throws a pencil in my house. Get the hell out and never come back!"

I sat there amazed. I was looking at $60,000 and then it was gone. But after Dad threw Garland out, Dad would never talk to the Yankees again. The head of the farm system, Lee MacPhail, and the owner, Dan Topping, tried to get us to come to New York, but Dad would never speak to them again. They'd call us, but he'd never even talk to them on the phone.

With the Yankees out of the picture, the search for another team was on.

It wasn't as if the Red Sox suddenly discovered me or that I decided to talk to them. They had been following me ever since I was a sophomore in high school. Their area scout was a fellow named Frank Nekola, whose nickname was Bots. He had been telling Johnny Murphy, who ran the Red Sox farm system, about me. In fact, Bots used to tell Murphy about the games I played on Dad's team.

One time Bots was excitedly telling Murphy, "They're some combination. The son's hitting .400 and his old man's hitting .450."

"Are you sure you're watching the right Yastrzemski?"
Murphy said.

The Cincinnati Reds, the Philadelphia Phillies, the Detroit Tigers, and the Yankees had all tried me out, and had all
thrown dollar signs at me . . . or, I should say, at Dad.

But when the Yankee deal died, we started seriously considering college as well. Dad, who never graduated from high
school, always told me that I'd be the first college graduate in
our family. College was fine with me. My average was in the
high eighties at Bridgehampton High, even though I spent so
much time on the teams and practicing on my own. Because
the school was so small, the classes were small, and we all got
individual attention from our teachers. I probably had at least
a hundred scholarship offers from colleges. They included
many basketball scholarships: to Duke, to Florida, to other
Southern schools. Although I also had many offers from
schools up North, the South seemed perfect. It would give me
a chance to play most of the year and to get in some good-
quality competition.

In later years, people would make a big deal of the fact
that I was the senior class president in high school. "Yeah," I
say with a laugh, "president of all eighteen kids in the senior
class."

So it was decided that I might as well go off to college. Of
course, it had to be a college that Dad would pick out for me.
I may have been one of the few kids ever who was reluctant to
go to Notre Dame.

But now, when I look back, I see clearly how that developed. Our parish priest, Father Joe, had a strong hand in it.
He came to Bridgehampton when I was about twelve from a
church in Brooklyn after he had developed cancer. I suppose
they thought this was going to be a simpler, easier parish. In
Brooklyn, Father Joe was friendly with several of the Dodgers, including Gil Hodges, and knew baseball. I remember
the World Series of 1952, when Hodges went 0 for 21 against
the Yankees and one of the priests in Brooklyn asked his pa-

rishioners in a Sunday sermon to "pray for Gil Hodges to start hitting the ball."

Father Joe didn't just wait for things to happen. As a matter of fact, he taught me how to pitch, how to throw a curveball. He also was the guiding hand that my father listened to. So, by the time I was twelve years old, Father Joe was a big influence on my life and on my father's. He was the first one to tell my dad how much bonus money to ask for. He also had another idea. Father Joe told my dad that there was only one owner to play for: Tom Yawkey.

Dad had decided on something else, though. He had a grand idea. We would turn pro if the six-figure bonus was there, along with a guarantee that the team would pay for my college education. That was asking a lot. But by then, my credentials were pretty good. In my next-to-last game in high school, Bridgehampton—remember, a school that didn't even have two dozen seniors—played Bellport. Bellport had a few thousand students, and the baseball team regularly played and beat prep schools, whose kids were generally older. It was a seven-inning game, and I struck out sixteen, allowed only two hits, and scored one of our three runs. Then we played Center Moriches, another big school, for the county championship. It was only three days later, but I struck out eighteen kids and pitched a no-hitter.

The next day the Yankees called. MacPhail, who would one day become president of the American League, asked if I could come in immediately for a tryout.

The dream was becoming a reality.

"Let's sign with them," I told Dad.

"Not until I see Father Joe," he said.

He visited with Father Joe, came back, and said, "We're going to stay with six figures, plus college tuition."

The Yankees of 1957 were en route to winning the pennant by eight games. Bill Skowron was on first, Bobby Richardson at second, Gil McDougald on short, Andy Carey on third. Hank Bauer, Mickey Mantle, and Enos Slaughter were in the outfield. Yogi Berra and Elston Howard shared the catching. The pitchers included Whitey Ford, Don Larsen, Bob Turley, Bobby Shantz. It was a magical team, larger than life to a seventeen-year-old.

Ray Garland greeted us in front of the players entrance when we pulled up in the car. He took me into the locker room. He asked someone to get me a uniform and a place to dress. They wouldn't let me stay in the locker room, though. The club had to hide me because I was only a high school senior and not allowed to talk contract or work out like this. I was so close to Mantle and Ford, and I wished someone had introduced us. I certainly wasn't going to say anything to them on my own. But they never saw me. If they did, they didn't acknowledge me. I wound up dressing in a room with the two bat boys. It was a cold feeling, no one talking to me, no one asking me what I was doing, no one wishing me luck. Officially, I wasn't there. Still, it was my first time in pinstripes, my first time wearing the flannel top with the overlapping NY that was probably the most famous symbol in sports.

Garland led me to the dugout. You're actually below the ground, and you walk into the dugout and up the stairs to get onto the field. Frank Crosetti, who had been a player and a coach for the Yankees forever, it seemed, was waiting to show me to the batting cage. The Yankees would be playing the Indians in a few hours, but it wasn't time for the regulars to bat yet. You never go ahead of a regular and you never cut down on a regular's time in the batting cage. These were the second-stringers, and Crosetti announced, "The kid goes in next."

At times like these, you don't get to see that electric light go off, that *Hey, this is where I've always wanted to be.* It's not happening like a movie, where you'd see the great faces move across the screen at you—Babe, Gehrig, DiMaggio. I was there to do a job. Amazingly, I felt at ease. Naturally, I went through my ritual of thinking and concentrating and talking to myself. But I wasn't nervous.

I never did find out who the batting practice pitcher was. But he threw really nice. He wasn't there to strike me out but to give me good pitches to hit. I lined the first one, a fastball, to center. A few pitches later, I reached the stands. Then the pitcher warned me that he was going to throw a curve. I smacked two of those into the seats, too. In ten pitches, I had hit four home runs. I was just getting warm, figuring I could do this all day, hoping to impress the Yankees even more. Suddenly, Crosetti said, "Enough."

He didn't even ask me to go out to the field, where I figured they'd at least want to see what I could do with a glove. Instead, he told me to go inside and get dressed.

Crosetti had seen enough. But he was afraid the Indians had seen enough, too. He wanted to hustle me out of there before any of their coaches could take a look at me.

Dad and I went up to see MacPhail, a sincere, soft-spoken man. He asked me if I wanted to play for the Yankees. It was the first time they had ever actually asked that question. Was it really necessary for me to answer?

"Sure."

"Okay. We'll give him $40,000," MacPhail said to Dad.

This was more money than we had in the bank, than we could have sold the farm for, than any Yastrzemski had ever seen. So what if it wasn't what Paul Pettit had signed for, or what Father Joe had told Dad I was worth?

"It'll take more than that," Dad said.

"But, Dad, it means I can play for the Yankees," I told him.

"That's an awful lot of money, Mr. Yastrzemski," MacPhail assured him. "It's more money than we've ever offered to a high school kid before." I believed him.

MacPhail could see that Dad's mind wasn't going to change right then. So he continued talking.

"Don't you realize that when you play with the Yankees, you're almost guaranteed a World Series bonus? We've won the pennant the last two years, seven times in the last eight. Every player on our club picks up an extra $5,000 every October."

How could you argue with that? How could Dad argue

with MacPhail when he mentioned the opportunity to play with Mantle and Berra and Ford? Dad didn't argue. He was just polite, and told him, "Let me think about it."

MacPhail said to take a couple of days, and then he'd send Ray Garland over to the house. We all shook hands and I left feeling that, in just a few days, I was going to become a Yankee. But with Dad and his stubborn streak . . .

When we got home, Dad spoke to Father Joe again.

"Don't sign for less than $100,000," Father Joe insisted.

Dad took that advice to heart. And when Ray Garland came over to the house, and lost his cool because of Dad's refusal to budge from that figure, my career as a Yankee was over.

That prompted us, as much as anything else, to consider Notre Dame, even though I wanted to go to a school in the South. Father Joe believed I should get a Catholic school education, and Notre Dame had a baseball team. What was the difference that, in those days, it wasn't very good?

I used to listen to Notre Dame football on the radio. The Johnny Lujacks, the Leon Harts. I followed them and I was a fan. If there was a college team outside of New York we rooted for, it was Notre Dame, which always had a big following in the East. In fact, so many people from the city used to follow the Irish that they were known as the Subway Alumni.

Dad and I drove out to visit Notre Dame. Terry Brennan was the football coach then. Of course, I would have liked to visit some schools in the South, especially Duke. But, as usual, Dad had his mind made up.

"Notre Dame's a great baseball school," he told me. I had never heard anything about Notre Dame having a great baseball team. I could figure out where he heard *that* one. But there was no sense in even saying anything. Once the scholarship came, that was it. In 1957, I entered Notre Dame on a half-basketball and half-baseball scholarship.

4
THE
FIGHTING
IRISH

At ten o'clock at night, they turned the lights out in the dorm. If you tried to turn on the switch in your room, it wouldn't work. They locked the doors, and to make sure no one came in or out, they put a guard by the door. This wasn't West Point. It was stricter. Twice a week they allowed you to stay out until midnight. We went to mass three times a week.

I had a problem. I had been playing, competing, my whole life. But freshmen at Notre Dame were ineligible to play varsity sports. When the fall started and it was basketball time, all we could do was scrimmage with the varsity. We didn't even have a schedule of games against other college freshmen. The routine was getting me down.

I was on the freshman basketball team. We'd work out from three to six in the afternoon, then go to the training table, and I wouldn't get back to my room until seven o'clock. Cripes, you'd have to get all your studying done in three hours. After that, they cut your electricity off. That's right. The room was dark. You couldn't even play a radio.

Of course, you learn the ropes. I was in a room by myself, and I rigged up some all-night lights. I became friendly with an upperclassman who had the room one floor below me. His name was Eddie Wojack, a catcher on the varsity. Eddie had a terrific privilege—all-night lights because he was head of the dorm. So I ran an extension cord outside of his room, up the side of the building, and into my window. I was discovered right away. Father Glenn Boarman, whom I became close to and whose interest in me helped keep me at the school, started sneaking upstairs to check out the room with the light. He took a special interest in me, though, and even though he probably could have nabbed me half a dozen times, he never let on. Maybe it was because he felt sympathy for me over Grandpa Skonieczny, or was friendly with Father Joe, I don't know.

Grandpa Skonieczny was a wonderful part of my life. He was Mom's father, and it seemed as if he was always around when I was a kid to take me places—for ice cream, a walk, crabbing. I still remember sitting alongside him in his tractor. When I was around Grandpa Skonieczny, I never felt any of the tension that I did playing ball. It was just a time for relaxation and fun—and love. He enjoyed doing things with me, seeing my happiness if I caught a crab, or riding the billy goat he had on the farm.

Many years later, when I was trying to help the Red Sox win the pennant in 1967, my motivation at each critical turn was Grandpa Skonieczny. I dedicated myself to him that year. Every time I came to bat when the game was on the line, I said a little prayer to him.

Grandpa had gotten sick before I went off to college. He developed Parkinson's disease, and he decided to risk a brain operation, which could ease the shaking he suffered in his hands. He was such an active man, he had to control his body. The operation appeared to be successful, and I looked forward to going home at Christmas and see him.

But one day just before the holiday break, Father Boarman called me into his office, and I just knew what it was about. Grandpa Skonieczny had died.

Father Boarman kept after me about the lights, though.

The hallway had some loose tiles. When he stepped on one, I could hear him coming. I'd throw the extension cord out the window and crawl under the covers. Wojack finally got nervous about our arrangement and told me that I couldn't use the extension cord anymore after Father Boarman asked him about it. So then I used one of those big flashlights with a wide beam, and studied under the covers.

Finally, I think he had to say, "Enough." He knew I was the one who had rigged up the lights and he was always trying to catch me doing something wrong. He did. I came tiptoeing in at about twelve-thirty one night. I was looking down and I suddenly saw two black shoes in front of me. Then I saw his black cassock.

"Step into my office," Father Boarman said. He was very stern now.

"How would you like me to call your father and tell him you've lost your scholarship?" he asked. You could lose your scholarship for an infraction such as coming in late.

"Oh, don't do that," I pleaded.

"Okay," he replied. "But we've got to come up with a punishment for you. What do you think is a good one?"

"Gee, I don't know," I said, hoping that he couldn't think of one either.

"Well, I think I've got a good one," Father Boarman said after some thought. "I've got to say mass every morning at five o'clock. I'll wake you up at four. You'll serve mass the rest of the semester at five o'clock."

And every day—*boom! boom!*—came the knock on the door. Every day I served mass at five o'clock.

Because I was on a scholarship, Notre Dame provided me with tutors. I used them a lot. I just wanted to have as much time as possible to keep working out, to do the exercises that I was used to doing at home. But when they turned out those lights at ten o'clock, I couldn't do too much studying.

I struggled during my first semester, flunking one subject and barely passing another one. But the experience taught me how to use my time. The next semester I made dean's list.

Notre Dame, I was discovering, was a place that demanded your attention, but the people there cared about you. And the discipline was something I came to accept. After all, I had always been in control of my own body, very disciplined in how I approached sports. I came to see that the rules they insisted upon were good for me, good for the kids, and good for the school.

Luckily, I also had Father Boarman. If he hadn't been around early in my first term, I probably would have left. When he knew I was struggling, we would go out and have a few beers and would talk about my dreams and where I had come from and my family. I had really gotten disenchanted early on. There was no competition, just working out all the time. We scrimmaged with the varsity, once in a while, but that wasn't enough for me.

Even though I never played a game at the school, I have remained close for more than thirty years with Jim Gibbons, who was Notre Dame's freshman baseball and basketball coach. He sensed from the beginning my unhappiness at being unable to play, as well as my difficulty in working out the studies and the practice schedule. Jim had been graduated from Notre Dame only a few years before, and had been a basketball and baseball star. Luckily for me, he could relate to what I was going through.

When I retired from baseball, I designed a ring. I asked the Balfour people, who make all those special sports rings, to have it resemble what I thought a World Series ring should look like, since I never had one of my own. My retirement ring had twenty-three stones for twenty-three years, and it had my stats on one side, the important ones: the 400 homers, the 3,000 hits, the 3,308 games played. I had twenty rings made up and put a different friend's name on each one. I gave them to people who had an effect on me over the years, or to people I admired. So, of course, I gave one to Jim. I gave one to Bob Woolf, who had been my attorney and friend for so long. Another went to Tip O'Neill, who's been a longtime buddy, another to President Ronald Reagan.

Jim had, as much as possible, eased my transition to college. I had come from a background where I adjusted my life to sports. Now it was all turned around. What made it more difficult for me was that I had always regarded Notre Dame as a stepping-stone, not as an end in itself. I wanted to get on with a career in pro ball. And if I couldn't do that right away, I wanted at least to be able to play. But all the freshmen could do was scrimmage. And scrimmage. Life for an athlete—even a nonvarsity athlete—was a continual grind.

In the spring, it was the same routine, only with baseball practice. By then, even though I was adjusting pretty well to Notre Dame, I wanted to play pro ball. General managers were calling me at school. Dad said, "Stick it out."

I used to beg the varsity baseball coach, Jake Kline, to let me work out with them once in a while. I guess I pestered him so much that he finally relented, and let me take some swings against varsity pitching.

The football field was beyond our outfield, close to five hundred feet from home plate. I really clocked one out to right center. It went beyond our field. The ball went over the goalpost and landed right where the football team was in the middle of spring practice.

That really amused Hank Stram. He was one of the assistant football coaches. He didn't like practice being disrupted, but he picked up the ball and said, "I'll bet Yastrzemski hit this."

Another ball I hit, I almost killed the poor pitcher. Jim Gibbons said it was the hardest ball he had ever seen anyone hit, although it didn't go much more than sixty feet. I smacked a liner right back to the pitcher. Luckily, he turned just in time and the ball hit him on the back of the neck. He was knocked out cold. Two weeks later, he still had the stitch marks from the baseball outlined in his skin.

I attended Notre Dame for one more term as a full-time student before packing it in for professional baseball. But even after I went to the minors and made it up to the Red Sox, I continued coming back for several years for the fall semesters. That was becoming very difficult, even though I didn't have to attend classes. Because I was coming in about a month after school started, they figured I'd never catch up. So they provided special tutors for me every day, and gave me only one test—the final exam—which would also be my mark for the term. I treated it seriously, though, and even after I was married and we had our first child, I still went back each fall until 1963. But my days as a full-time student were long gone.

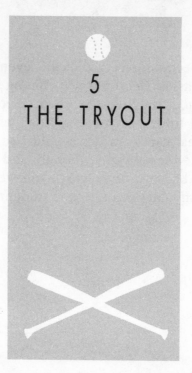

5
THE TRYOUT

Although I had never played a varsity game at Notre Dame, the phone continued to ring when I came back home after my freshman year. If any of the scouts had forgotten me, they quickly remembered my name after a sensational afternoon I had in a showcase game.

With rumors of expansion coming to baseball, it seemed that every player out there had to be scouted. On Long Island, we had a number of outstanding ballplayers. There were so many that we arranged a doubleheader so that all the scouts and front-office officials could see us play.

This was just what I wanted. I loved it when something important was on the line. And it was—my future. In the two games that day, I went to bat eight times and had seven hits. I belted three homers.

By now there were no secret contracts. Everything was out in the open and several teams were after me. For the first time, I had started thinking seriously about the Red Sox. Bots Nekola had gone the extra mile for us. Of all the scouts, he became closest to my father. Eventually, his wife and my mom became good friends. Even when I was away at school, he'd drive all the way out on the Island to have dinner with my folks. He wanted to know how I was doing in school, and Mom and Dad appreciated that.

All the big names in scouting I had ever heard about suddenly appeared at my door or to watch me play at Lake Ronkonkoma.

Al Campanis was the legendary head scout for the Dodgers, the team that had produced all those brilliant young players, such as Sandy Koufax, Don Drysdale, and Frank Howard, who were coming up and were about to replace the old Brooklyn guard. Al and another Dodger official, Tommy Holmes, watched a game and then collared me and Dad.

Campanis, a pleasant man who knew his baseball, said the Dodgers wanted me.

"Any offer you've got, we'll match it. If that's not enough, we'll top it," he said to Dad.

The summer of 1958 was the Dodgers' first in Los Angeles after their move.

"If only," Dad said, "you were still in Brooklyn."

That shut the door on the Dodgers and the West Coast. Dad wanted me close to home, or at least close enough so that he and Mom could see me play.

The Giants wanted me, too, even though they also had left New York. Chick Genovese, who had managed Willie Mays in the minors and was a Giants' troubleshooter, told Dad he wanted me as a catcher. The Giants were having trouble filling the post after Wes Westrum slowed down.

"No West Coast for Carl," Dad told him. "And anyway, he's not going *anywhere* as a catcher."

We heard from Gabe Paul of the Reds, John McHale of the Tigers, Jimmy Gallagher of the Phillies. All fine baseball people, and all of them had teams whose parks would have been perfect for me.

Father Joe said I should go to a team that had an owner who cared. He felt it was important for the owner to know me and to be involved in the negotiations. Father Joe liked the way Tom Yawkey ran the Red Sox. Yawkey had a personal interest in his players. Father Joe also told Dad about the Phillies, whose owner, Bob Carpenter, was a fabulously wealthy man who loved baseball.

We went out to Philadelphia for a tryout. The Phillies were in trouble, about to begin a string of four straight last-place finishes. Jimmy Gallagher was very kind to us. He brought us into the locker room and introduced me to Robin Roberts and Curt Simmons; to Richie Ashburn; to Chico Fernandez, the shortstop; to manager Eddie Sawyer. For a last-place club, the Phillies were pretty loose.

What a difference between this club and the Yankees. I was given a locker right next to the Phillies' players. On the field, Sawyer patted me on the back and Wally Moses, who was the batting coach, took an interest in me while I was in the cage. Even Fernandez, who knew they were thinking about me as a shortstop, told me, "Good luck, even if you think you can take my job."

I almost did right there. With everyone watching, I took about fifty swings, and hit at least a dozen into the stands. Connie Mack Stadium (it was known as Shibe Park when I was growing up) was almost fifty years old. The right field foul line was only 331 feet away, but a few years before, the Phils had bought the Yankees' old scoreboard and placed it in right. The scoreboard was 32 feet high. Center field was almost 450 feet away. But right field moved away gradually as you got toward center. It wasn't a sudden increase.

Moses was impressed. He told me, "Carl, you're the finest young hitter I've ever seen." And Roberts was laughing when he told Fernandez, "Nice knowing you, Chico. This'll be your last year."

As I was getting dressed in the locker room, one of the coaches came over and whispered, "Get all you can." Within a few minutes, that was Dad's idea exactly.

We immediately went into negotiations with the Phillies. Gallagher offered $60,000.

"Everyone knows we're looking for $100,000 and the

rest of his college tuition," Dad replied. He explained that, once I got paid a bonus to sign, I'd lose my scholarship at Notre Dame. I suppose he had a point, since tuition would become an expense we didn't have before.

Gallagher seemed to become desperate. He told Dad he'd sign me immediately to a big league contract, which was the first-year minimum of $7,000. Even though the season was half over, I'd get the full year's pay.

That still wasn't enough.

"Okay," Gallagher said suddenly. "We'll put him in the lineup tonight. He can play against the Chicago Cubs."

In a few hours, I could be a big leaguer at the age of eighteen. Just like that. And have a $60,000 bonus to boot. Gallagher didn't know Dad.

I was at the game that night, but as a spectator. The next day, though, we met with Carpenter. Obviously, we were in a financial area that Gallagher had never visited before. This was up to his boss now.

"We'll up our offer to $80,000," said Carpenter.

Dad shook his head no.

"You know, when you consider the taxes on $100,000, you're better off taking $80,000," said Carpenter.

That line of reasoning didn't move Dad, either.

Almost blurting it out, Carpenter finally said, "Okay, $95,000—plus the $7,000 contract for this season. Since it's almost over, it's like getting $102,000. Can't you see that?"

Finally, Dad could—sort of. There was just one thing more Dad wanted: the guaranteed college tuition. Carpenter had that one figured out, too. He had endowed a scholarship at the University of Delaware. I would go to school in the fall semester, after the baseball season ended, and then play baseball in the spring. Delaware would pay my way.

Even that wasn't quite enough. Dad suddenly hit Carpenter with another demand—$10,000 if I failed to finish college. Dad was figuring that if I quit school after only one semester, Carpenter should turn over the money he would save to us. We hammered that point for two days, but neither side budged. The talks ended with Carpenter doing a funny thing. As we said goodbye, he gave me his telephone credit card number and said to use it as long as I wanted, and to call anyplace I wanted.

Within a week, I was ready to return to Notre Dame to start my sophomore year. My head wasn't in it anymore, though, certainly not after a summer in which I had two offers from the Phillies: to play major league ball right on the spot from Gallagher, and another one worth more than $100,000 from Carpenter. Even the Dodgers and Giants wanted me. And the Yankees kept calling, but Dad still wouldn't even talk to them on the phone.

I was packing for school when the Red Sox called. Bots Nekola wanted us up in Boston for a tryout, but I couldn't leave school. So we made a deal that we'd see him during the Thanksgiving break.

Just before the holiday, the Cincinnati Reds jumped into the picture again. Gabe Paul went all the way out to Bridgehampton to talk to Dad. Paul was offering $100,000 and my tuition. But Dad had changed "our" demand. When he heard how hot Paul was for me to play in Cincinnati, with its comfortable right field, Dad upped the demand to $150,000. Amazingly, Paul offered $125,000.

"What do you think?" Dad asked.

"Let's take a look at the park first," I said.

"Sure," Dad replied. "When you start vacation, I'll pick you up at school, and we'll go to Detroit, Cincinnati, and then Boston. We ought to be able to make up our mind after that."

It was happening! Finally! I knew this was it. I was going to sign a big league contract. I knew I was going to have to promise Dad I'd continue in school, but maybe, I thought, he'd forget about that. Now we were really going to get all that money. *Paul Pettit, move over.*

What I didn't know was how much Father Joe Rapkowski had influenced Dad, who had all but made his mind up where he wanted me to play. I should have seen it. All I could see was Dad rubbing shoulders with the big guys, practically making them beg, raising his demands at each session. And Dad *loved* it.

The Tigers wanted me badly. McHale apologized because they could only offer me $80,000. The Tigers were in the process of being sold to John Fetzer by the Briggs family, which had owned them for decades. McHale, the general manager, couldn't go much higher, even though Dad liked him and was impressed with the fact he was a Notre Dame graduate. "Wait till after the first of the year, when Fetzer takes over, and I'm sure we can increase the $80,000," McHale said.

None of that really mattered. Dad killed the deal when he asked if Fetzer would be the single owner, like the Briggs family had been. The answer was no, and we headed for Cincinnati, even though I would have loved to have hit for seventy-seven games a year in Briggs Stadium. I still enjoyed hitting there when the name was changed to Tiger Stadium. It was only 325 down the line and a gradual lengthening to 370 in right center. The biggest advantage of hitting there, though, was the wind—there wasn't any. Outside of Fenway, I hit more home runs in Detroit than in any other park.

Our next stop was Cincinnati. This wasn't a bad place, but Dad figured it would take the $150,000 to get me to play there. Gabe Paul wouldn't move from his $125,000 offer. That wasn't enough, even though the Reds were going to throw in the college tuition money. So we headed for Boston.

What I remember most was the snow. I had convinced Dad that Notre Dame wasn't the best place for me to play baseball because of the long winter. You could get hurt in the cold weather. Now, here I was in Fenway in the snow. I was in Johnny Murphy's office when Tom Yawkey called. He spent his winters in South Carolina.

"We want you bad," Mr. Yawkey said.

Then, very proudly, Johnny Murphy took me down to show me the field. That's when I got that sinking feeling, especially after Dad said, "Carl, this is a great place for you to hit!"

We talked contract, but as usual, Dad's demands—this time for $125,000—held things up. In the back of my mind, I believed I could get out of playing at Fenway. Murphy knew I wasn't happy about it. The phone rang. It was Mr. Yawkey. Murphy had told him my feelings, and Yawkey said to me, "Look, why don't you go back to the hotel, think about it, talk it over with your dad, and then we'll talk some more in the morning." When we left, though, we were close to an agreement.

That night, in our room at the Kenmore Hotel right near Fenway, I was bitterly disappointed. It didn't matter. I was afraid to say anything. Dad might change his mind on his own, but you could never make him do it. I was lying in bed, thinking, *Jeez, why does he want me to play here?* I tried to sort it all out. If I had my choice—I knew the Yankees were out, he'd never let me sign with them—I probably would have signed with Philadelphia. Every time I thought of a reason to sign with a club, Dad had a good reason why I shouldn't. If I told him I liked Philly, he told me that they already had Fernandez at short, and I'd just be sitting on the bench, withering away. I should have known that Father Joe had been talking to Dad about Boston. One thing I grasped rather quickly, though. I knew that Dad wanted to keep me in the East. He wanted to be able to drive to the games.

"Sign with the Red Sox or go back to school," Dad finally said that night.

The next day Dad came down from his $125,000 demand. The Sox offered us a $108,000 bonus, a two-year deal for the minors at $5,000 a season, and to pay for the rest of my college education.

There was another reason why this offer looked very attractive to us at that moment. We were told that baseball was about to tighten its rules on bonuses again. Some of the owners were becoming nervous about all the money that the richer teams were paying for good prospects. So baseball was considering reverting to its old bonus rule. If anyone got more than $4,000 to sign a contract, he could not be sent to the minors and still be guaranteed club property. He would be subject to a draft by other clubs. That meant a team had to keep its bonus baby on the big club's roster, a move that would slow the player's development. We were afraid of that. The Yankees had a great infield prospect from Queens named Tommy Carroll, but he was forced to sit on the bench when he was only eighteen years old, and never got much playing time in. The Dodgers had a wild left-handed pitcher named Sandy Koufax who was doing the same thing. Just sitting on the bench. I couldn't afford to wait any longer. If I signed right then, I could get the minor league seasoning I needed. We took the offer.

When Joe Cronin, the general manager of the Red Sox, heard the deal finally was finished, he came over to see what he had bought.

Cronin couldn't believe my size—five-eleven, 160 pounds—and the amount of money I was getting. The first thing he said—and I could never forget it—was "We're paying this kind of money for *this* guy?" I guess he expected somebody six-two and 210 pounds to walk in.

My dad had to co-sign the contract because of my age. This was the last time we agreed over the money. In a way, as I look back, it really was funny—how he reacted to it, how I did.

I was a professional ballplayer, or at least about to be. I went back to school to finish the rest of the fall term before heading to spring training. Nothing changed. At Notre Dame, Dad had sent me a weekly envelope that contained $2. I was looking forward to his next envelope, though, when I got back to school a rich man. The next week the envelope came. I opened it—he had put the same $2 inside. I immediately telephoned him.

"I want to go out and celebrate. I want to have a spaghetti dinner on a Friday night if I feel like it," I told him. I was shocked when he said, "Okay, I'll increase it."

I ran down for the mail the next week and I tore the letter open. He had increased it, all right. He sent me $3 instead.

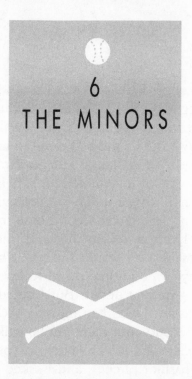

6
THE MINORS

I knew I wasn't going to crack the Red Sox roster in 1959. I was nineteen years old when I went to training camp. And even though the Sox hadn't gotten any higher than third place in the 1950s, the majors still were a big step away.

Technically, I was the property of the Minneapolis Millers, a Triple A farm team in the American Association. And one of their farm teams was in the Carolina League, the Class B Raleigh Caps. They played in Devereux Meadow, an old, run-down park where high school teams also played football and where Roman Gabriel had been a star quarterback. When I joined the Caps in 1959, it was only their second year back in existence. They had folded a few years earlier because they couldn't get a sponsor.

It was a great place for minor league ball once, and now the city fathers were trying to revive it. Because of the huge bonus I received, everyone was looking for me to help turn around the franchise. They gave me a nickname: Yastro. Yaz was still another lifetime away.

Although I had usually played shortstop in semipro ball, the Sox wanted me to learn it their way. I had been self-taught. That gave me some problems. One of the plays you must make from short is the throw to second for the force. It looks like an easy play. But I was used to throwing "over the top." They tried to get me to shorten the throw by doing it sidearm. The way I did it, the ball came in hard. I tried, but I couldn't tone it down. I had a gun for an arm, and I had played the same way for my whole life. When I threw the ball, I just threw the hell out of it. Then they switched me to second base. I had never played second base in my life.

So I not only struggled in the field, making errors, but after a terrific first game I wasn't hitting so hot, either. In my first at-bat for pay, I hit a home run. I followed with a double and a single for a perfect debut. But I tailed off quickly.

After ten games, I was batting only .266. Manager Ken Deal had left me alone until then, but he woke me up one day when he said, "Carl, I'd love to pitch to you."

Deal was a former pitcher, and I asked him what he was talking about.

"You're lunging out in front of the plate to hit the ball. You stand in the middle of the batter's box, and you're off-balance when you lunge that far. *I* could get you out."

I moved up in the box. Suddenly, it was like hitting for the White Eagles again. I hit close to .400 the rest of the season, helped by the fact that they finally put me back at shortstop. By late July, I was hitting .384, but then I hurt my ankle and missed ten games. I think I might have hit .400 if I hadn't been injured.

Did Deal's advice do the trick? I'll never know. Maybe I just needed some minor adjustment, maybe only someone to talk to. And maybe I just needed to become accustomed to pro ball. This was now my living, not something I did on Sunday afternoons, or twice a week at night during the summer. The Caps played six games a week—five at night during the week, and on Sundays. That changed my way of eating and sleeping. Certainly, the farm was never like this new life, where I was sleeping until ten in the morning, having breakfast at eleven, going to bed at one in the morning—if I was lucky. After road games—and we never spent the night away from home, not with the handy bus—I was lucky to make it in by two o'clock.

Something else happened to shake me up. Four of us were living together in a rooming house. We caroused and chugged quite a few beers. We made so much noise that the landlady complained to Deal. Normally, you'd figure a manager would handle it himself. But he called my father. I didn't realize it, but when Dad heard what I was doing, he jumped into his car and drove down to Raleigh nonstop, fuming all the way. He barged into the apartment and scared the hell out of me. He grabbed me by the shirt and started yelling at me.

"Cut out this crap!" Dad screamed. "Straighten out or your career is over and you're coming back home!" And then he suddenly stopped and walked right out the door, got into the car, and drove straight back to Long Island.

That shook me up so much that my attitude changed immediately. I got back my old work habits and made sure I got plenty of rest. There was a career in front of me and I had to learn how to handle it. The Red Sox still wanted a shortstop, so before games I'd go through a double practice, first at second and then at short. The extra work didn't affect me. We started moving out of an early slump that at one point had dropped us into last place. We left the basement with a big victory when I hit two out of the park. That fired us up. Later, we had a fifteen-game winning streak for a league record. My stroke was really in a groove. After some games, though, I'd ask for extra batting practice if I didn't feel right. Almost ten years later, a lot of people made a big deal of the fact that I took batting practice after the opening World Series game in 1967 against Bob Gibson. Heck, I'd been working in the cage after games for as long as I could remember. Whenever things didn't feel right, I just collared someone afterward and got him to throw BP to me.

One of my biggest games at Raleigh came in our fifteenth straight victory, when I got five hits and knocked in the winning run. The rest of the season, I didn't go more than two games without a base hit and we won the pennant and play-offs. I wound up hitting .377, which was fifty-four points higher than anyone else in the league, and third-highest in minor league baseball that year. No one in the Carolina League had hit that high in eleven years. I led the league with 170 hits and in doubles with 34. I also led in errors with 45, but that didn't bother me. I was back at short. It was a shorter season in Class B, and I played in only 120 games, but hit 15 homers and drove in 100 runs. Many of my home runs were to left center, since I was still spraying the ball. It was just as well. You had to hit the ball 386 feet to drive it out of the park in right field. They voted me the Carolina League's Most Valuable Player and the top major league prospect.

When our season ended, Deal had great news for me.

"Gene Mauch wants you playing for him at Minneapolis in the American Association playoffs." There was some question over my eligibility, however, and I couldn't play for them for a few days. Deal added the clincher: "While you're waiting, the Red Sox want to see you. Get up to Boston."

Well, this was it. Or at least a start. I expected that this meant they'd give me a big league contract to stay in Boston. I knew the Sox were in trouble. They had fired Mike Higgins as manager, they were going to wind up under .500 for the first time in years, they were tumbling toward fifth place, nineteen games out of first, and for only the second time since the war attendance had slipped to fewer than a million fans. They couldn't have been much worse off with a twenty-year-old in the lineup.

I had not been at Fenway in almost a year, since signing that contract. I was coming off a great first season in pro ball, but a strange thing happened as I prepared to walk to the park. *I got scared.* I was practically shaking. I could feel the bumping of my heart. I started to sweat. There was no one to talk to about it. I didn't even know any of the players or the coaches. Who could I call? I sucked it all in with a deep breath, packed my stuff and my glove in a bag, and headed for the park.

Well, at least they were expecting me at the gate. Someone pointed the way to the locker room and I walked into Fenway once again. I still remember little things about that moment: the huge board shaped like a baseball. It had holes in it with a player's name over each one, and asked fans to contribute to the Jimmy Fund. Each donation a fan made was in the name of a favorite player. I imagined what it would be like to have my name on that big ball. The Jimmy Fund, for children's cancer research, Mr. Yawkey's baby. Until a new scoreboard was erected in the 1970s—with advertising—the JIMMY FUND sign was the only one that Mr. Yawkey allowed in the park. It was a huge billboard over the right field stands.

Don Fitzpatrick greeted me in the clubhouse. He liked ballplayers. I could tell that. Fitzie was one of the guys who was in charge of the equipment. Eventually, he moved over to the visiting clubhouse. But now he was trying to make me comfortable. I was at ease. The only person I had seen in the clubhouse, I learned later, was Johnny Orlando. He was supposed to be the clubhouse manager. But he was also one of Ted Williams's best friends, his protector. When I came in, Orlando didn't even say hello. He told me to get dressed "somewhere over there." Then he went over to Williams's locker and started puttering around. I didn't know what I was supposed to do, or get. I had my glove, my spikes, and a sweatshirt.

Fitzie took good care of me. He even gave me some extra caps to take home. And a box of balls. He found the right-sized bats; he brought me new shoes. Then he gave me some advice.

"Kid, don't be nervous. They brought you here because they already know what you can do. Just do the same thing you've been doing in the minors." I'll never forget Fitzie for that.

As I was getting dressed, Ted Williams appeared in front of me. I knew he was big, but not this big. He stood six feet three inches, and he weighed more than 200 pounds. Nearing the end of his career, he was getting heavier—no longer the Splinter, but still Splendid and the greatest hitter I ever saw.

As if I didn't know who he was. But he stuck out his hand and said, "Hi, I'm Ted Williams." I don't remember much about what I said, other than my name. But he gave me some advice, in his booming voice, as if he had suddenly discovered something: "Don't let them screw around with your swing. Ever."

And he walked back to his locker. I didn't say another word to him until the following year.

My arrival was a big deal in town. The papers had sent people over to watch me in batting practice. Even Harry Craft, the manager of the Kansas City A's, the team the Sox were playing at the time, took a peek.

I spelled my name for everyone and pronounced it—*Yuh-strem-skee*—and told them about the Skoniecznys, too. At least my name was spelled right in the papers the next day—if not Mom's family. Some of the writers asked me what my chances were to play in the big leagues right then. They told me that Bucky Harris, the new general manager, and Johnny Murphy had hinted that I might be given a chance to stay. The writers pointed out that Robin Roberts came up to the Phillies after pitching only eleven games in the minors, and that Dick Groat moved from the campus at Duke to the Pirates, and that Frankie Frisch went straight from Fordham University to the Giants.

What was I supposed to say? No one had prepared me to talk about my future to the press. But I just sensed I had to be diplomatic, even though I was scared to answer the wrong way. I said something like "I don't have any expectations. All I want to do is hit as well as I can wherever they send me." *Was that good enough?* I wondered. *Did it sound too cocky? Too humble?*

The Sox worked me at shortstop and I know I impressed people with my throwing. Then in batting practice, I hit three into the bullpen—the one 380 feet away, the place I had

looked at with dismay last Thanksgiving. I could see it now—
and I could reach it, too.

The press and the public wanted me to stay, but the Sox
didn't see it that way. Manager Billy Jurges had to explain to
the public that the pitchers in the American League were in
their best shape of the season, that they were getting ready for
the stretch run. Here I was, a kid who had turned twenty only
two weeks before, and had faced only Class B pitching. Why
screw around with my confidence with only two dozen games
left in a meaningless season? Jurges, meanwhile, was trying to
put the icing on the cake of his own season. His good friend
Bucky Harris had been named the team's general manager
after Cronin left to become president of the American
League. At midseason, with the club nearing last place, Harris
replaced Higgins with Jurges, who got the club playing better
than .500. Mr. Yawkey liked Higgins, and gave him a front-
office job. The turnaround shocked everyone. Maybe they
didn't want to monkey around with their newfound success.

Before they sent me down, I met Tom Yawkey for the
first time. He and I had spoken only on the phone when I was
signing my contract. I liked him immediately.

"I know you'll be back in a year or two, Carl. I'm looking
forward to having you around," he said.

Mr. Yawkey put me at ease, a quality that was to cement a
friendship that lasted until his death. We were to become bud-
dies, our lockers adjoining, talking baseball. He may have
been worth hundreds of millions of dollars, but he also knew
the game. How he loved talking about it, dissecting what happened the game before, thinking about what we were going
to do next.

As much as he might have wanted me to stay, the front-
office people had other plans for me. It was down to the Minneapolis Millers, where Mauch was managing. They were in
the American Association playoffs, and had lost one of their
key players to the draft. They needed me, Mauch said.

They really must have. I arrived in Minneapolis around
four o'clock and was met at the airport by someone from the

team, who drove me straight to the game. I went right into Mauch's office. We finally got together. In spring training he had told me he wanted me to play for his club, but Murphy had ended that possibility. "He needs seasoning, Gene," Murphy had told him. I was impressed with Mauch, a former major league infielder. I knew he had been with the Red Sox only two years before. Still, it was strange seeing a thirty-three-year-old as your manager. But he had a lot of confidence and he was very decisive. He knew exactly what he wanted.

"Can you play tonight?" he asked. Of course I could. He was concerned about the eligibility problem, though, because in theory I wasn't allowed to play until September 20, a few days away. He figured that since I was replacing a player who was going into the military, it would be okay. Just before game time, he heard from the league office that I could suit up.

The Millers were tied with Omaha at two games apiece in the best-of-seven series. We had another close game and went into the tenth inning tied at 2–2. I got on with a single and then I scored the winning run. As soon as I did, Omaha's general manager, Bill Bergesch, who went on to a long major league front-office career, protested. Ed Doherty, the president of the American Association, upheld the protest. We had to replay the entire game. But it was now getting into late September in Minnesota. It was *cold*.

The next day, with me ineligible, sitting on the bench, we beat Omaha in a doubleheader to take our round of playoffs and head for Fort Worth and the American Association championship.

I sat out the first game and finally got my chance in Game 2. I didn't waste it—3 for 4, three runs scored, two RBIs—and we won. We went on to take care of Fort Worth in six games. In my first exposure to Triple A pitching, I went 7 for 18 in the series. We qualified for the Junior World Series against the International League champions, who happened to be the Havana Sugar Kings.

The weather got so bad in Minneapolis that we didn't

♦ *I'm five—and intense.*
(COURTESY CARL YASTRZEMSKI)

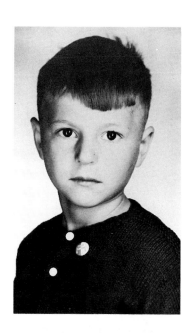

♦ *Dad, flanked by me, right, and my brother
Rich, left.*
(COURTESY CARL YASTRZEMSKI)

♦ *Even then, I* knew.
(COURTESY CARL YASTRZEMSKI)

• *The legendary—for the Yastrzemskis—Bridgehampton White Eagles baseball team. That's my dad, kneeling, second from the left. And that's me in front. We're surrounded by uncles and cousins.*
(COURTESY CARL YASTRZEMSKI)

• *I was twelve years old on the Little League Bridgehampton Lions team. That's me under the flagpole, fifth from the left in the second row.*
(COURTESY CARL YASTRZEMSKI)

• *Jumping for the bag on my Little League team.*

(COURTESY CARL YASTRZEMSKI)

• *I loved basketball, and practiced my jump shot as hard as I did my hitting, but there was never any doubt about which sport was my true passion.*

(COURTESY CARL YASTRZEMSKI)

♦ *Jim Gibbons, Notre Dame's baseball coach, took me in hand when I was a freshman. We remained wonderfully close.*
(COURTESY UNIVERSITY OF NOTRE DAME)

• *Our Impossible Dream team of 1967, taken during spring training. I'm the first on the left, sitting in the front row.*

(COURTESY BOSTON RED SOX)

• *This was my dear friend Tom Yawkey in
1966, smiling, even though we were a year away
from the Impossible Dream. He owned the Red Sox
for forty-four years.*
(COURTESY BOSTON RED SOX)

• *Ted Williams and I never played on the Red Sox together, but we shared our love of the team.
I always thought they gave me number 8 to keep the connection with Ted's number 9.*
(COURTESY BOSTON RED SOX)

even stay to finish the first three games, as the rules called for. Instead, the leagues decided after the first two games (in thirty-degree weather) that we'd finish the series in Cuba. The Sugar Kings were thankful. Eight of the players on the team were Cuban natives and they had never experienced anything as bad as that Minnesota cold. It was so cold that they built a fire in a trash can in the dugout and huddled around it.

We were the last American professional team to play in Havana, but we went out in style. Our five games there attracted over a hundred thousand fans and produced what probably was the strangest and most exciting Junior World Series ever played. For, earlier that year, Castro had taken over the government of Cuba. Not long after we got there, the United States cut off diplomatic relations. But we were greeted at the airport with bands and a parade that took us to city hall. More speeches, and two thousand people cheered us as bands played both national anthems. Still, I was not very happy.

You had to be there to understand what it was like. Sheer chaos and anarchy. People marched in the streets, parading with guns and signs. Worse for us, they did the same thing at the ballpark.

Havana was really Cincinnati's farm team. But the fans didn't treat them as if they were Americans—*we* were the foreigners. In the hotel, I sat around with some American businessmen. They were scared and wanted to get out, but there *was* no way out. People in the lobby would tell me they had been sitting around for two weeks, waiting for a flight. Some of them had tried to take their money out of Cuba and discovered that they couldn't.

Maybe it will be different at the ballpark. I hoped. I knew the Cubans were great baseball fans.

The first game was scheduled to start at 8 P.M. The stadium was packed. I had never seen more than twenty thousand people before. But this was what it was like: soldiers were lined up on the foul lines. You couldn't even see the lines—it was as if they were the lines and if you hit a soldier it was a fair ball. That's not where the craziness stopped. People stood on the sidelines, right next to the soldiers. And we were supposed to take batting practice.

We came out for our workouts. The place was crawling with kids. They couldn't have been more than fifteen or sixteen years old—walking around with guns and rifles and bayonets. They took everything we had, or at least everything they could see. First, they grabbed all the balls. When they started going through the bat bags, Mauch shouted at us, "Everybody back in the clubhouse!"

We sat there, figuring we'd get a call when the game was supposed to start. But it was almost eight o'clock and no call. Finally, someone came in and said, "The game will not start until Castro arrives." Where was he? We didn't know. No one told us a thing.

We couldn't sit in the dugout because it wasn't safe. So we just sat in the clubhouse. We sat for about an hour and Mauch was getting angry. Finally, he jumped up and said, "Screw it, we're going to get in some damn practice." He found a sergeant or someone in charge of the troops and explained that we had to get out and warm up—but that no one could touch our equipment. "Okay," the soldier said. We were able to get through a light drill, then we went back to the dugout. Still no Castro.

Around ten o'clock, we heard this buzzing and all of a sudden the crowd went wild. Some of the kids even fired their guns into the air. Castro was arriving.

"Fidel! Fidel!" they shouted and we saw this helicopter coming right onto the field out of the sky. It hovered over the pitcher's mound, and then landed just in front of second base. And out came Castro. More cheering. He was wearing those fatigues that were the symbol of the revolution. He had a beard, wore a soldier's cap, and smoked a cigar. He took off his cap and waved it. People waved sugarcane, yelled, and screamed. It was not an anti-American demonstration so much as a pro-Castro one. Then Castro walked to the pitcher's mound to throw out the first ball. It was some performance. We started the game close to 11 P.M.

The next night Castro drove onto the field in a Jeep. He walked to the mound, and again threw out the first ball. Then he went to sit with the people in the bleachers. The first night he sat behind home plate. Another night he sat in the dugout. Before Game 7, one of our guys asked, "Where's he gonna be tonight—pitching?" The fans really loved having Castro sit among them. They took out signs that said VIVA CASTRO, they yelled, they showed their guns, blew their trumpets.

We played five games in Havana because of the snow in Minneapolis, and every game was held up until he showed. After a while, we got smart. We started scheduling the buses to the park later and later.

Castro didn't come into the clubhouse or say hello to us during the first few games. But Havana took a 3–1 lead in games and he said he wanted to meet us. He had been sitting in the stands near where I ripped a homer that must have traveled 450 feet. An interpreter said he wanted to meet me. Castro knew the game. He had pitched semipro. He seemed to be interested in how young I was, much younger than the other guys. This was Triple A ball, and many of the players were major league veterans. His interpreter also said to me: "He wants to know how a man your size could hit the ball so far." We didn't say much else. Castro always stayed right up to the end—except the game when we tied the series at 3–3. He left in the eighth inning that night.

We had been warned not to leave the hotel between games. It was like a revolution in the streets, even though it wasn't violent. But with the guns and the noise it was just scary. In the daytime, though, we'd go shopping, making sure at least six of us went together. Lu Clinton was my roomie, and he liked to razz me about the bonus. One day when I was getting dressed, he started asking me about my clothes. I never liked to take along a lot. My theory always was to avoid changing jackets and pants and pack light.

"With all the money you got?" said Clinton. With that,

he took my suitcase with all my clothes and threw it out the window.

"Now," he said very proudly, "you've got to buy yourself new clothes."

Castro made his presence felt before Game 7. Our pitcher, Lefty Locklin, was warming up in the bullpen. Somehow, Castro showed up there. With his interpreter by his side, Castro patted the gun on his hip and said in Spanish, "Tonight we win."

I saw Castro one last time. We lost Game 7, even though we took a 2–0 lead into the eighth. They got two in the eighth and then won it in the bottom of the ninth. He was happy and shook everybody's hand.

"If there's anything I can do," Castro told Mauch through the interpreter, "give me a call." I enjoyed the party that night, even though we had lost. In my first crack at Triple A ball, I had batted .353 in eleven playoff and Junior World Series games. Against the Cubans, I hit .312.

We were so overjoyed at going home that we went crazy that night at the team party in the hotel. One of the players threw a chair into the pool; someone else threw in a table. The fun was broken up when what looked like a platoon of soldiers suddenly appeared. They wanted to arrest all of us.

"Wait a minute!" shouted Mauch. "I'm going to call Castro." The soldiers may not have understood what he said, but they understood "Castro." So Mauch, accompanied by a sergeant, called Castro on the phone. He was staying at the same hotel, but it took forever to get through. The next thing we knew, there was Castro. He was shouting orders to the soldiers. The only command we were interested in, though, was to let us go.

He wanted to make sure we got onto the plane and out of Cuba, and he provided an escort for us—an armed one, at that. We got to the airport around 9 A.M., and sat for almost five hours. It still was a little hairy. They searched every piece of our luggage. A lot of the guys were smuggling jewelry out, or had a lot of cash. They stuffed it in their shoes, or in their underwear. When that plane—a two-engine job—finally took off, we cheered as if we had won the Junior World Series.

Mauch did one last nice thing for me. I had played in only seven games, but he insisted that the players vote me a full series share. It was less than $1,000, but it meant a lot knowing he was behind me. When we said goodbye at the airport back home, he said, "I'll see you in spring training, kid. Make sure you take care of yourself and show them you're ready for the big leagues."

Between seasons, I got married.

7
FAMILY

There were times over the dinner table that I didn't see my wife, Carol, or any of our four children. Oh, I'd be sitting with them all right. Somewhere in the background I'd hear them talking. My mind was on the next game much too often. Or, if I had a bad day, I'd be replaying how I screwed up. I didn't pay the attention I should have. But I just couldn't lose my focus on baseball.

It is not an easy life and it is not the ideal situation for a marriage. We had our ups and downs. A baseball player's wife raises the children and is a mother and father to them. Even when I was home, with all the night games going on in modern baseball, you'd hardly see me around the house.

Sure, the night games were over by ten-thirty, but I'd stay in the clubhouse until twelve-thirty, one o'clock in the morning, just mentally replaying the game. The last one out— that was me. I'd go over every pitch in my mind. I never got ticked off at myself if the pitcher got me out. But I'd get angry if I swung at a bad pitch, or I didn't look for the right pitch that the count called for. That's the only time I'd be mad at myself—if I made a mistake in my thinking.

When I finally did get home, I'd have a big meal, and it would already be two in the morning. Then I'd get up around eleven, eat, and head to the ballpark again. I needed to be there early to start concentrating on the game. So I was never really around the house, even when I was there.

I wish I could have been, but there was something I just couldn't do. I could never leave the game at the ballpark. I had to take it home with me. Even when I was eating with my family, even though I was talking to them, I wasn't really talking to them. I was thinking—about the game coming up: *Who's pitching? How did he pitch me two years ago? What would Palmer throw me?* The family—my wife and kids—they'd be talking to me, but I'd be thinking of something else.

I started mellowing out, started to leave the game at the ballpark, after Mr. Yawkey and my mother died. But that wasn't until the late-1970s. That's finally when I started thinking, *It's a game.* I finally told myself, *Okay, replay your at-bats in the clubhouse, and then leave them there.* But before then, jeez, I was so intense.

That's why I never enjoyed it. That's right, never truly enjoyed something after the moment had passed. I was so intense about the game. I never even relaxed on a good day after the game ended. If I was 3 for 4 and won the game with a home run, I'd say to myself, *That's it, it's over,* as soon as I stepped into that clubhouse. I'd replay it just a little. *Okay, you did everything right today. Now who's pitching tomorrow?* And fifteen minutes after the game was over, I'd start worrying about tomorrow. *Who's pitching? How are they going to pitch me?*

Worse, if I went 0 for 4, my stomach would be knotted up, especially if I could have done something to help the club win. I'd sit back in my chair, put my feet up against the locker, and sit there for twenty minutes—not moving, just thinking. All of a sudden, I'd kick the locker. I'd be sick inside. There were times after a bad game that I'd sit in front of my locker with such dark thoughts that I'd think about jumping off the Mystic River Bridge.

Soon after I had signed my Red Sox contract, and was

back at school, a friend invited me to come home with him to Pittsburgh for the weekend. The $3 Dad was sending every week couldn't pay my way, but Father Boarman loaned me some money. My friend got a blind date for me. Her name was Carol Casper, and by the end of the evening we had a special feeling for each other. Her girlfriend even took her aside and said, "This is the guy you're going to marry." Carol was an outgoing, attractive young woman. With many other girls I had dated before, I was self-conscious about my background. Maybe "embarrassed" is a better word, especially when I'd go to college dances and meet girls whose fathers were professionals. Carol came from a working-class background, and was employed as a secretary for an oil company. Before long we made it official, but we decided to wait until after my first year of pro ball.

After the Junior World Series, I returned to Notre Dame for the fall semester under a special deal. Because I was coming in about a month after classes started, I was allowed to take the final exam, which would be my grade for the term. It was a routine I followed for three straight fall semesters until it just got too tough, especially after Carol and I married and had children. I was able to get by at Notre Dame, though, because of special tutoring. When the term ended, Carol and I went down to Raleigh in January 1960 and got married. We had wanted to be married before training camp started and after the term ended. We were faced with a time problem. In Pittsburgh and Long Island, it would take almost a month to get married after the banns were posted. We were able to get married almost immediately in Raleigh.

The Yastrzemski family caravan was on its way.

The Sox trained in Scottsdale, Arizona, where we headed after our honeymoon. The Minneapolis Millers trained in Deland, Florida. I didn't know anyone on the Sox, so we were a couple of twenty-year-old kids, just in from our honeymoon, in a strange setting with no friends. I was hoping to make it to the big club, even though the track I was on called for me to

play my second year with Minneapolis. But they had me up
with the Sox, and maybe, just maybe . . .

They put my locker next to Ted Williams's. That first day
he was nice to me. But in general he was moody. Sometimes
he'd go for three days without saying a word. And then when
Williams would talk about hitting, I didn't know what the hell
he was talking about. Ted had some of these advanced ideas
and I was twenty years old and I'd listen and not say a word,
hoping he'd get finished soon. My theory of hitting was simple. Look for the ball, get a pitch in the strike zone, and hit it.
But he started talking about some stuff, about hips and rotation and getting in front. I'd try to stay with him on it. Then
he'd ask me questions. It was like I was being tested, but I
didn't have a clue as to what the questions or answers were. I
didn't say a word, not only because I couldn't understand him
but because I didn't want to give the wrong answer. I tried to
stay away from him, even though we had adjoining lockers.

Writers would ask me about what Williams was telling
me and I'd say, "Yeah, I'm learning a lot from him." What
else could I say? Everyone thought I was his protégé. I figured
they put us next to each other for a purpose. But what I did
learn from Ted that last spring training was how hard he prepared himself. He must have weighed 240 by then, but he did
all those situps in the outfield, trying to get into shape. I
couldn't believe how quick and how good a hitter he was at
that age. He was going on forty-two. I liked to watch Williams
take batting practice. It looked as if he wasn't even swinging
and the ball would fly out of the park. When I was up, I'd go
through all these mental and physical gyrations, gearing up to
try to hit the ball, and he wasn't even trying and it was going
out. So easy, so quick. That's what I'll always remember about
him—and how far the ball went. He'd go at his own pace.
First game of spring training, he'd take one at-bat and he'd
quit. He'd leave the field, go through the clubhouse, and he
was gone. I thought, *How's he's going to be ready to play?* I guess
that's what amazed me about that guy—how well he knew
himself.

But I was trying to duck him. Then one time Ted grabbed me while I was walking away from the batting cage, and he started talking about all that stuff of his, and he just wouldn't stop. He started to question me about unlocking my hips, showing my back to the pitcher, asking where I placed my weight. It embarrassed the hell out of me because I couldn't answer him. So for the rest of spring training I tried to duck him. I didn't want to get into another conversation with Williams about hitting. Every day, though, there were the stories: WILLIAMS HELPS YASTRZEMSKI. YASTRZEMSKI CREDITS WILLIAMS.

Williams? I was just as concerned about the average ballplayers. One of the things that continued to bother me was my size. I was five-eleven, but only weighed 160 pounds. I looked at all those other young guys and they all looked to me as if they were six-one, 210 pounds—all from big cities. What was I doing here? I saw myself as a small guy from a small town.

Meanwhile, Carol and I were miserable. The Red Sox were a team with little success and players who were nervous about their jobs. I think they saw me as a threat. Worse, I was richer than any of them, at least with the bonus. Word of that bonus preceded me faster than my stats. It wasn't "Here's Carl Yastrzemski, Carolina League batting champion." I was "Carl Yastrzemski, $100,000 bonus baby." Except for Frank Malzone and his wife, Amy, none of the married players had anything to do with us. I was bitter, and I became a loner in the clubhouse.

Still, I had a great spring. Dad and Mom were along and, as usual, he was trying to give me advice. He was around so often that one day Billy Jurges, the manager, told him, "Get off the field when Carl's batting." That didn't stop dad from giving out interviews and proudly telling everybody how we had played together on the White Eagles and how we once hit back-to-back home runs.

I thought the Sox would keep me. This was not an outstanding club. I was playing second base and doing pretty well. I also was hitting about .360 playing the first ten exhibition games. I hit some home runs—including one off Juan Marichal, who would be pitching for the Giants at the end of the season. I drove in some runs and I felt as if I was on my way. Then they stopped playing me. All I did was sit there.

I went to Jurges and asked him what was going on. He put his arms around me and said, "Son, you're going to be a great ballplayer."

"Don't give me any of that crap," I told him. "When am I going to play?"

"Son, we're sending you down."

I was astonished. "Bull, absolute bull!" I shouted. Of course, they had Pete Runnels playing second at the time, and he was coming off a .314 season and about to win the league batting title, but I thought I was good enough to make him move to another position. And anyway, Pete could play someplace else. I guess going down to the minors wouldn't have been so bad if I wasn't leading the club in hitting.

There was nothing I could do. I sent Carol back to live with her folks in Pittsburgh, Mom and Dad went home, and I flew to the Minneapolis camp in Deland.

I quickly learned what this was all about and what the Red Sox had in mind all along. Mauch himself picked me up at the airport. It was about 6 P.M.

"Feel like going for a workout?"

"What workout?" I asked. "It's almost nighttime. Who's working out?"

"You and me," he replied.

"What for?"

"We're switching you to left field."

Left field. That's Williams's position, I thought. But why was I being switched there? I was playing pretty well at second base. And Williams was coming back for another season.

"Williams is going to retire after this season and they want you for left field," Mauch said.

We got into the clubhouse and while we dressed I asked him how he wanted me to play left. I had never played the outfield before to any extent. "Should I charge grounders one-handed or two-handed?"

"Play it any way you want," said Gene, which made me feel better about things. At least he wasn't going to be rigid. I was still thinking I'd be happier at second. I covered a lot of ground there, got a good jump on the ball. I wasn't the greatest at pivoting—turning to make the throw to first—but I got the job done because of my strong arm.

Pivoting meant nothing now. I was going to be a left fielder. Mauch called over Chuck Tanner, who was a player-coach, and told him to get a fungo bat. Chuck hit some balls to me and I shagged them. I was comfortable doing that because I had shagged balls as a kid. What I had to learn now was throwing the ball to the right base, or to the right cutoff man, and throwing the ball in to get the maximum effect. I'd grab a ball and throw it to second or to home, making sure it was shoulder-high. I charged balls on the ground with one hand, but Mauch shouted, "That's fine! That's what I want you to do, whatever's natural!"

I have always believed that the big mistake the Red Sox made was never making Mauch manager. He was a remarkable baseball man and could get more out of his players than they knew they had. He also was quite a teacher. The first few days he didn't even want me swinging a bat. He just wanted the fundamentals, as if it was a school.

• • •

That night I was talking to Mauch. He knew I was ticked off about being sent down. He tried to assure me that it would all work out for the best. He was a great theoretician, and he wanted my ideas about hitting. I didn't know much about it then, but I told him that, to me, it was "feel." Sometimes I closed my eyes and put my hands on my head and pictured myself gliding into the ball. I didn't know that much, I explained, just get a good pitch and swing hard. Mauch nodded.

After I left Mauch's room, I ran into some of the older players. We went out and I didn't get back until five-thirty in

the morning—and we had an eight o'clock bus. I knocked on
my door so my roomie, Chuck Schilling, would let me in. But
my pounding woke up Mauch, who was only a few doors
away. He opened the door, looked at me, didn't say a word,
then closed the door. I didn't think much of it because at the
workout the day before Gene told me I wouldn't be playing
in the next game. I went into the room and told Chuck to
wake me just before it was time to get on the bus. Chuck and I
were old friends. He was raised in New Hyde Park on the
Island and we used to play ball together as teenagers. Then I
put the uniform on and went to sleep.

When we got to the park, I sat around, ready to relax.
Someone came over to me and asked why I wasn't getting in
any hitting.

"What for? I'm not playing today," I said.

"Guess again. Don't you ever look at the lineup? You're
batting third."

I think I struck out three or four times. Mauch never said
a word to me. When the bus took us back to the hotel, Mauch
walked over. I knew he was mad at me.

"I want to see you," he growled.

Gene had a heck of a temper. He took a bat and slammed
it down on his desk.

"What time did you come in?" he asked.

"A little after midnight," I said.

"You're lying!" he screamed. "You came in at five-
thirty."

"Well, yeah, but I was with some of the older guys
and . . ."

"Goddam it, stay away from them. I want you hanging
out with Schilling. And that's it."

That was the end of the lecture, I figured. But Mauch was
a pretty cagey guy. Then he said to me, "When you got up
this morning after two hours' sleep, and then found I put you
in the lineup—did you go home and put your hand on your
head and concentrate?" He had on a big grin.

I loved him and he loved me. But a few days later, Gene

called me into his office and said he was leaving. The Phillies had just hired him as manager.

"We'd love to have you in a Phillies uniform. Mr. Carpenter says he's sorry he let you get away last year. If we could work it, would you like to play for us?"

"Go to Philadelphia? Sure," I answered. I was still teed off about being sent to the minors and I wasn't crazy about the way some vets had treated Carol and me. But the trade never came off.

I didn't have time to worry if I could hit Triple A pitching. I had to learn how to play the left field Wall in Fenway Park while I was in the minors. The Millers assigned Eddie Popowski to teach me. Eddie became one of my best friends, a guy who never seemed fazed, who smiled all the time and was the perfect kind of fellow you want around a ball club.

First, he had to find a wall that simulated Fenway's. There's no such thing. But there were two high walls in left in the American Association, in Fort Worth and Houston. They were about twenty feet high. Popowski used to take me out there whenever we'd be in those cities. Because of the Texas heat, they'd play night games. So he scheduled 10 A.M. workouts. He'd hit the ball off the wall, and make me turn and face the wall. I practiced catching it off the wall with my back to the infield, then wheel, and turn, and throw. Because of my pitching, I always had a long extension in my arm. That's a good trait for an outfielder, because you're making long throws. So playing the outfield seemed natural. No one ever really showed me how to do it.

Take charging the ball hit on a bounce, which became a trademark of mine. I was probably the first—at least in my league, I don't know if Mays did it—to charge the ball one-handed. The way they taught in the minors was that you two-handed everything in the outfield. Of course, today outfielders one-hand fly balls. But when I charged those balls with one hand, I found I had more mobility and could run more naturally. I didn't have to slow down to position my body.

Because of the big bonus and the fact that everyone saw

me as Williams's heir in left, my arrival in Minneapolis was a
big deal. I told one interviewer, "I won't be satisfied unless
I'm a star. I won't settle for just being an average player."

But I was below average soon after the season started. I
asked Popowski—Pop—if he minded if I called in my dad for
advice. I was so young, I didn't think there was anything
wrong with that. Popowski didn't think so, either. When Dad
came—after driving from New York with Mom—he took one
look at me and told me I was crouching too low. He also
didn't like the way I was holding the bat. I changed the angle,
got a couple of hits that night, and everything was fine the rest
of the season.

In 148 games, I led the league in base hits with 193,
while batting .339. In August, I began a hitting streak that
reached 30 games (batting .432 during the stretch) and enabled me to pass Larry Osborne of Denver. But he came back
to take the batting title with a .342 average, beating me in the
final week of the season. I didn't hit with much power, even
though it was only 365 feet to right center. In fact, I had more
triples (8) than home runs (7). But I also had 18 assists in the
outfield and a .981 fielding percentage.

Because I was in such a groove, I figured that if the Sox
had an emergency and needed anyone, I'd get first call. But at
midseason, I was shocked when I heard that Gary Geiger, a
young outfielder with the Sox who was hitting .300, was going to miss the rest of the season—and they sent for Lu Clinton. I was hitting about fifty points higher than Lu. I was so
miffed that I told Pop I was going back home.

"I'll get them to trade me," I insisted.

It wasn't easy to make demands then. In fact, you didn't
have any bargaining chips at all. Popowski patiently explained
that if they didn't want to trade me, I wouldn't be playing for
anyone else. My career would be over.

It was the Millers' last season in Metropolitan Stadium.
You were always aware of their great history, of the fact that
Ted Williams and Willie Mays and Orlando Cepeda and Van
Lingle Mungo had played for them. The next year, 1961, the

American League expanded, ending the sixteen-team major league setup that had been in effect since 1901. In the big shake-up, the Senators left Washington and came to Minneapolis, changing their name to the Twins. The Millers disappeared. But my big league career was about to begin.

8
THREE
PRESENCES

In my rookie year I became intimately acquainted with three formidable presences, each of them shaping my career, each a factor in my development as a player and man, and to each of whom I will always be grateful: Tip O'Neill, Tom Yawkey, and the Wall.

There is a sense of intimacy about Boston, and I got to know the city quickly. It's the type of city where sports stars and politicians are never far apart. In fact, that was how I made one of my best friends, Thomas P. (Tip) O'Neill, Jr.

Even though it was my first year, before long I was a regular at a Boston restaurant where the staff put up with my finicky eating habits. Remember, as a kid I used to prepare many of my own meals. I got to know the people at the restaurant, and they would let me go in the back and fix a special sauce for my steak. I didn't realize that Pier 4 was one of O'Neill's favorite places. He was a congressman in those days, and when he came back to Boston, he enjoyed stopping by.

One time the owner told O'Neill that I was in the kitchen. That's all Tip had to hear. He was a heck of a Red

Sox fan. He came into the kitchen, introduced himself, and asked, "What are you doing back here?"

"Cooking some wine gravy for my steak," I said.

"Look, I've got to get back to Washington, but I'll be back in a few days. Come over for a sandwich on Friday."

And that started our friendship, which has lasted for all of my twenty-three Red Sox seasons and beyond. During the off-season, I'd come in to see Tip and we'd talk. I was more conservative than he was, and I was fascinated by aspects of the military—weapons and costs and troops. Of course, Tip was a liberal, but he never tried to change my mind and I never tried to change his. Despite our political differences, we loved to talk. Tip O'Neill is one of the great people of our time.

Tip never missed a Red Sox game when we came into Washington to play the new expansion team that replaced the old Senators. Whenever we got to town, Tip and I would have lunch together. How Tip loved those hours. He would invite all the officials from Massachusetts, so I'd see Edward (Ted) Kennedy, and Sil Conte from Pittsfield. Sil loved to fish in Alaska, and he'd bring back salmon. Since he prided himself on being a great salmon chef, he would put on his chef's hat and fix it in the dining room Tip had next to his office. Sil was the only Republican there. Everyone wanted to talk about baseball, all these fellows who were making decisions to run the country. But for one hour all they wanted to talk about was the Red Sox and Sil and the others were united in a way. Talking about the Sox was an obsession with them. They just couldn't hear enough stories; there weren't enough answers for all of their questions.

When the expansion Senators left for Texas after 1971, I didn't visit him as often in Washington, but Tip couldn't wait until the Red Sox came to Baltimore. Then he'd bring in a busload of people, and even keep a scorecard of every game.

Later, I'd visit him in Washington when he was Speaker of the House. We don't talk as much baseball these days, but we still visit each other.

Another venerable institution I visit sometimes is the Green Monster. Whenever I'm out at Fenway, someone asks me about it and somehow I wind up walking back there, explaining what life in left field was like under that thing. It's sort of like seeing an old friend—or maybe like seeing an old enemy that you've come to have a civilized relationship with.

There is nothing like it in baseball. The Wall is thirty-seven feet high, with a twenty-three-foot screen over it. Nowadays, the Wall is covered with fiberglass. It's practically playable.

When I came in, I saw the Wall as another obstacle. That first day in the outfield, shagging flies in practice, I had a lump in my throat. Williams never told me much about the Wall, and even if he had, it wouldn't have helped. Those walls in the American Association didn't prepare me for this baby.

The first twenty-five feet or so was concrete. It got interesting from there. Then you came up to the tin part. Then it had steel girders behind it, rivets that were holding the tin in, two-by-fours. This was crazy. If someone was trying to drive a left fielder nuts, this was just the way to do it. You had to make a decision as soon as that ball hit in the rivet area if you were going to move to your right or your left, but you had to take into account if the batter who hit it was right-handed or left-handed. Whichever batter hit the Wall, it would bounce differently off the rivets—sharply—one way or the other. Then you also had to make a decision as soon as the ball was hit whether it would hit the cement or go above it to the tin. If it hit the cement, you had to back up from the Wall because it would come back hard. If you thought it was going to hit the tin, you had to come in close, maybe up to the dirt track, because it would come straight down. Also, you had to wonder whether it was going to hit a two-by-four, or a steel girder behind the tin. If it did, it would carom over your head. So you'd run back to the warning track, then follow the flight of the ball again to determine whether it was going to hit the two-by-fours or just the tin and drop.

Playing the Wall changed tremendously when they went

to fiberglass. It got easier. I hated that, because so much of the Red Sox tradition involves the Wall. Instead, the fiberglass gave everything a truer bounce. With the tin, nobody could figure it out. You could hit a million fungoes and it wouldn't help. It was all instinct.

Until 1976, the left field scoreboard was directly behind me. Now—get this—it had a ladder hanging over the side. So there were metal rungs sticking out as well. The scoreboard was not like today's electronic screen. This was operated by hand. It had slots for each inning. A guy behind the scoreboard would slip in a 1 or a 2 or whatever in the slot for the runs scored that inning. If the ball hit those slots, there were other nutty ways it could bounce.

I vowed to learn how to play this thing better than anyone ever had. More than that, it was going to be mine and I would be in control, not only of the Wall but the entire left field area.

This Wall could make you feel as if you never had played baseball before. But by trial and error I used everything out there—the stands to my right, the grass field. Take the Wall under the stands to my right, the extension of the left field stands. It was only three feet from the foul line to the stands. If I ran toward the line and caught a ball, my momentum could send me crashing into the stands. But I used that Wall as a push off to make my throws after a ball went into the corner, or if I had caught a fly ball. I'd run into that Wall and plant my right foot on it, push off, and get momentum.

The Wall—rightly so—is what everyone talks about and it's what I spent so much time figuring out. But playing that corner became an art in itself, requiring tremendous concentration. Because it was only a few feet from the foul line to the people, I'd be camping under a fly ball while the fans would be leaning out of the stands for that same ball. They'd be shouting down at me, or sticking their hands in the air, or their gloves, or even their caps, trying to catch the ball. And I'd have to concentrate just to see that ordinary fly ball come down, not lose it in the nest of flailing arms, screeching kids, guys yelling, "Ya got it, Yaz!" And in a day game, it was even worse. Then you had the sun out there staring you right in the face.

That corner produced weird events. We were playing the Indians in 1963 and our big home run hitter was Dick Stuart. He became known as Dr. Strangeglove because he had a heavy hand with the mitt. He was a big, lumbering guy, six-four, 212 pounds. Anyway, he was batting against the Indians' Pedro Ramos. Stuart hit a high fly to left. It was so high that by the time it came down he was midway to second. But a strange combination of circumstances led to an inside-the-park home run.

The left fielder was Johnny Romano, who was actually one of the Indians' catchers. He played a couple of games in the outfield that year. They never prepared him for Fenway, though. The ball finally came straight down and hit the ledge on top of the scoreboard. Instead of bouncing straight out, it caromed to the left, to the corner. Vic Davalillo, the center fielder, was helpless because the ball was a hundred feet away from him. So Romano had to chase it. He tried to control it as it kicked around the corner and we were all standing and cheering on top of the dugout steps as Stuart churned around the bases.

Romano finally got a handle on it, threw the ball in, and Stuart exploded in a mighty slide home, like a runaway truck. He slid under the high tag. We were hysterical. Stuart, out of breath and almost collapsing, couldn't figure out what was so funny. The next day we read that it was the first inside-the-park homer to left field anyone could remember seeing in Fenway.

Another ball hit there seemed to gobble up Don Baylor when he played for the Orioles. He went chasing a ball in the corner. But because of the way the stands in left jut out, you can't actually see that corner from the visitors' dugout along-side the third base line. Manager Earl Weaver and the other Orioles stuck their heads out of the dugout, looking for either the ball or Baylor. They found neither. Weaver said later he thought Baylor had been swallowed up.

Still, I became so aggressive out there because of the grass and the field. The way it was kept—I've always thought it's the best field in baseball—made me confident. I didn't have to worry about a bad hop, so I could charge balls and take chances, knowing I'd always get a true bounce. If there was a spot out in the field that wasn't quite right, especially in the dirt part past the foul line, I'd ask Joe Mooney to come out and he'd pound it down by hand. Joe was in charge of the park's maintenance, and he took exquisite care. What an advantage that was, knowing you could play your game on the field. The Wall? Well, that was something else. But that became part of my game, too.

There were the "dekes." I had a decoy move for every situation. If I knew, for example, that the runner on base was slow, and the ball was going to hit off the Wall, I'd set up as if I was going to catch the ball. That would freeze the runner off the bag with a short lead. Then suddenly I'd turn around, grab the rebound off the Wall, and throw to the next base, or home. The trick was, I had to catch the rebound clean off the Wall. All the deking in the world wouldn't help if the ball got past me, or if I bobbled it, or if it came to me on a bounce.

The Wall got to be a game with me. I had to develop new tricks to be more effective. I could deke a guy who hit the ball so that he thought it would be a home run. I'd look down as if I was teed off. He'd start in his home run trot, and all of a sudden the ball would be off the Wall and I'd turn and fire it to second. Sometimes I caught the guy or held him to a single. You couldn't do that too often with the same team, or else they wouldn't fall for it. Word got around the league about what I was doing. So I decided I'd deke a guy only if the game was on the line. There were a lot of late-inning situations when the other team would start a rally. They'd get a runner on second and the batter would hit a drive toward me. I'd stand there as if I knew I was going to catch it. Was I faking? They couldn't be sure. *Bang*—the ball would hit the Wall and the runner, who had held up, could only go to third. The batter would be on second with a double and the run wouldn't score. Yet, I knew from the moment the ball was hit if it would hit the Wall.

Too bad I couldn't steal many signals. But I did have something going for a while when Ralph Houk was managing the Tigers in the mid-1970s.

He was an outstanding manager, and he was the best I ever played for. He used to stand on the left side of the dug-out, leaning forward on the top step. He gave very basic signs to his third base coach. In Detroit, the home dugout is on the third base side, which is where the visiting dugout is in Fenway. So I was able to watch him quite a bit. He was always playing with his hands, picking up pebbles. He'd shake his hands and put the pebbles down. After a while that pebble business intrigued me. I noticed that he'd always give his third base coach signals with the hand that had the pebbles in it. When Ron LeFlore was with the Tigers, he was an outstand-ing base stealer. After a while I figured out when Houk was giving him the steal sign or the hit-and-run. Houk would grab a fistful of pebbles, drop them, and flatten his hand over them when LeFlore got on base. Sure enough, LeFlore went. Now, I was ready. The next time LeFlore got up, he walked. Sure enough, there was Houk's hand going down. I was positive I had the steal sign figured out. Then I learned their hit-and-run sign because Houk would drop the pebbles and shake his hand by the side of his leg.

I told our catchers, Carlton Fisk and Bob Montgomery, what was going on. We arranged signals between ourselves. If I was playing left field, I'd have to give them a sign they could pick up pretty easily. I'd rub my glove across my chest twice if I picked it up. When I was playing first base, I didn't need to give such a detailed signal. I might just put my open hand behind my back.

If I caught the sign from Houk, I'd let our catchers know what was happening. Monty never had a great arm, but he was throwing those Tiger runners out. This went on for about a year. We tried to prevent the Tigers from catching on, and sometimes, when we were ahead in the count, we'd pitch out even when we knew there was no steal on. We just wanted Houk to believe we were guessing. But Houk was smart enough to figure it out. One day he peered at the outfield after he had just signaled for a steal—and he caught me giving the sign home, rubbing my glove across my chest, signaling for a pitchout. I was doing it a little more vigorously than usual because I was trying to get Fisk's attention. We threw the guy out. The next day LeFlore was on first and Houk gave the same steal sign, and I signaled the catcher. But LeFlore didn't go. Houk turned to me and stuck his thumb on his nose and waggled his hand at me: *Gotcha.* I had to laugh.

More often than not, though, I was the one doing the trickery—or trying to. One of my dreams was to throw a guy out at first on a ball hit to left field. I had seen Carl Furillo do it from right field in Brooklyn. There was the short right field wall there, and he used to play in for the weak hitters. But a right fielder like Furillo had a good shot at it. From left it was almost impossible.

Still, I tried. There were two guys in particular I thought I could catch: Harmon Killebrew and Frank Howard. Both were big, slow, right-handed home run hitters. When the wind was blowing out, I'd give them all of left field. I figured if they got it up at all, it was off the Wall anyway. So I'd come in like a linebacker and play almost right behind shortstop. *This way,* I figured, *I'll take away their line drives. And maybe even take away a base hit if I can catch them at first.* I almost nipped Howard twice on balls he hit on a bounce to the outfield. Both times I threw the ball wide of first.

Of course, hitting was what I loved. I couldn't wait to get to the batter's box. But you know what? After a while, I couldn't wait to get to left field, either. I loved it out there at Fenway. When I went into big ballparks like Yankee Stadium or Cleveland's Municipal Stadium, with their big left fields, they showed more of my talents as an outfielder. I could roam in those places and make great catches and great throws. At

Fenway, players just wouldn't run on me. Sometimes I had to laugh to myself when there was a guy on second and the batter hit the ball over the screen onto Lansdowne Street. I mean a rocket. But I was making believe I was camping under it, and the third base coach would hold up the runner at second. The batter practically bumped into him.

Although I led the league in assists seven times, and was a Gold Glove winner seven times, I rarely got an assist at Fenway in my later years in the outfield. The other teams wouldn't run on me there unless the game was on the line and they *had* to try to score. And if a batter hit the ball real well, it would have to be a sure double before the first base coach sent him to second base. If there was any doubt, they'd hold him up at first. But the other teams liked to challenge me in the bigger ballparks.

How could I get guys to run on me in Fenway? Even if there was a hit to the alley in left center, the batter would be held at first. This was not good. I had to try to get that sucker to run on me. I devised a routine to make it look as if I had dropped a ball after running it down. But I kept my back to them so they couldn't see that I had really come up with the ball. Then I'd wheel and throw to second and chalk up another assist.

The record book says it's 315 feet to left. I think it's shorter. From the corner it was no effort at all to throw the ball low—I'm talking neck-level, and hard—all the way into second and get the guy out.

Of course, my throws were usually from closer range after I made my charge. Forget about the people I threw out at Fenway. A stat that doesn't show is: How many people did I stop from taking an extra base?

I always felt that when you analyzed Fenway, you had to look at it as a two-way street. Over the years, a lot of people have knocked the Wall, talking about a cheap double a banjo hitter might get off it. But how many other shots that hit high off the wall and bounced back onto the field for singles would have been home runs in other parks? That Wall did a lot of things, affected a lot of games, played tricks with people's minds.

In 1976, they changed it completely. They made the Wall one smooth fiberglass construction. They moved the light tower and scoreboard more to left center. They put padding on the Wall. There'd be no more of those nails that Joe Mooney put in every spring—the ones I'd have to flatten by throwing balls at them.

Luckily for me, learning the Wall was like learning to ride a bike. It was a good thing I never forgot how. In 1975, I had played first base for 140 games, and only 8 in the outfield. Then Jim Rice broke his hand and the manager, Darrell Johnson, asked me, going into the playoffs, "Yaz, do you think you can go back and play left field?"

"In my sleep," I told him.

I wasn't kidding.

• • •

Well, I certainly loved the old park. But that wasn't the reason I spent more time there than anyone else. The reason was Mr. Yawkey.

Tom Yawkey owned the Red Sox for forty-four seasons, longer than any other owner in the history of baseball. And he never won a World Series. From my rookie season in 1961 until he died in 1976, his visits with me were a ritual. I used to get to the park early because I needed to concentrate, true. But I also was there because Mr. Yawkey had a million questions for me. God, did that man love to talk baseball. And very often when a game was over, and I couldn't take my mind off the game the next day, he would sit down next to me and we would talk again, or sometimes just sit and have a drink—me with my beer, Mr. Yawkey with his Canadian rye.

Until he died, I was next to the only open locker in the Red Sox clubhouse. It belonged to Mr. Yawkey. All he ever hung in it was his sweater, a beige sleeveless sweater that was as plain as he was. No player ever took that locker. He wanted it open so he could sit next to me and talk. When things were going well, no one made an issue of that. But when the club did poorly, then people speculated that I told him to change managers, or that I would tell him which players the club should bring up, or who was dogging it. None of that was true. Mr. Yawkey never discussed a managerial change with me.

What a fabulous person. He was probably the most affluent man I've ever known, and also the simplest and most direct. "Don't you have anything else except those old brown pants?" I would tease him. He'd get insulted and when I saw him the next day he'd bring in pictures from his days at Yale, showing me what a fancy dresser he had been. For many people, he was the reason the Red Sox were known as the Fenway Millionaires. He had a reputation for spending and spoiling players, and had the rap that we weren't serious about winning, just having fun. But that wasn't how it was and it isn't how I remember Tom Yawkey.

I remember him in his sixties, taking batting practice in Fenway when it was deserted. He hit right-handed and his dream—after winning a World Series, which we never did— was to hit a ball off the Wall. He never could do that, either. He was a line drive hitter.

He enjoyed playing the game so much that if he rented Fenway to some group, say the Jehovah's Witnesses, he made sure the contract read that he was allowed to play pepper and have batting practice in the morning.

When the team was on the road, he'd always come in and work out. He didn't want any outsiders watching him play, though, so he'd be in early and then—get this—he'd lock the ballpark up so no one could get in. His wife, Jean, would sit in the stands and watch him hit. He'd play pepper with Vince Orlando, the clubhouse kids, and Don Fitzpatrick, and would drive Fitzie nuts. In pepper you batted the ball to a fielder fifteen feet away. You did it quickly, keeping the other guy on his toes. Mr. Yawkey's rules were that he had to catch twenty in a row. What the heck, it was his bat, his ball, his glove, his park. His rules. Fitzie would hit him eighteen, and he could field them flawlessly, but if he dropped the nineteenth—watch out. He'd throw his glove on the ground and shout, "God-dam it!" Fitz would have to start all over again.

Although Mr. Yawkey never hit the ball off the Wall, he enjoyed hitting it into the stands. But what he did was to bring the batter's box right next to the seats. He'd take the batting cage to the outfield. Vince Orlando, who had taken over the clubhouse from his brother Johnny, would throw to Mr. Yawkey and he'd have a hell of a time enjoying it when he hit one into the stands.

But he never hit that Wall. He used to promise Vince's brother, "If I hit that Wall, Johnny, you're getting a brand-new Cadillac!" He would have bought John one, too.

Mr. Yawkey always enjoyed coming to the clubhouse very early before a game. That's one of the reasons why I eventually spent so much time there. But he would only ask me to play pepper with him on off-days. He'd walk in briskly, see me sitting at my locker contemplating last night's game, and he'd say, "Come on, Yaz, let's get out there. I wanna see if you can play this game." Mr. Yawkey didn't fool around at all when he played pepper. He could tell if I was jaking it, so I had to look as if I was really trying to get the ball past him—or when he hit it to me, as if I was trying to catch those sharp little one-hoppers.

Besides the team and the ballpark, he also owned lumber and iron mining interests out West, paper mills in Canada, and more than forty thousand acres in South Carolina, most of which he used for conservation in his later years. That was sort of strange, because in his younger days he was a big-game hunter and he loved fishing. Yet, he donated thousands of acres to government agencies working with ecology. There were lots of things about him that were unusual, though. When he died in 1976 at the age of seventy-three, the stories I read estimated his worth at more than $200 million.

He hardly ever spoke about his own money to any of us on the club, but he once told Vince that his grandmother had left him $25 million. It was as if his business life was separate from his baseball life. Business was in New York, where he kept an apartment. He did business out of the Graybar Building there.

I know that he bought the Red Sox in 1933 when he was only thirty years old, and that Yawkey wasn't his real name. That was his uncle's. Tom's last name was Austin. His father died when he was very young and he went to live in Detroit with his mother's brother, William Yawkey, who owned the Tigers.

Tom loved hanging around with ballplayers and he used to tell me about Ty Cobb and all the other great ones. He was able to deal with problem players, like Jimmie Foxx. That helped promote Mr. Yawkey's image as a guy who pampered his players. His adoptive father had a reputation for carousing with the Tigers. After one especially bad loss, which extended a losing streak, Bill Yawkey loaded the whole team into a bus and took them to the nearest saloon. On his orders, the players lined up at the bar and knocked one back. Then another, and another. Then he took them to a Turkish bath, where they all got massages and a steam bath and spent the night. The next day at noon the Tigers returned to the park. They won five straight.

So being close to his players was something that Tom Yawkey did naturally. He was loyal to us and a man of his word. He was furious if someone crossed him. He used to tell us about a falling-out he had with Ty Cobb. Cobb and Mr. Yawkey and some of his friends enjoyed hunting in the Rockies for mountain goats. One of the men was sick with cancer. It was probably going to be his last hunt, and everyone agreed they'd let him get the first shot at a ram.

The next day, as they were climbing, they spotted a big ram. I had always heard that Cobb was a heck of a competitor and would do anything to win. It's true. Cobb wouldn't let the guy take the ram. Cobb got off the shot and killed it. Mr. Yawkey got so mad that he jumped all over Cobb and they wrestled right there on the side of the mountain. Mr. Yawkey said he never spoke to Cobb again.

"How did you do against Cobb in the fight?" I asked
him.

"Cobb kicked the crap out of me," he said.

He had a plainspoken way about him, even though he
went to a boarding school outside of New York City and then
to Yale University. When his mother died, his uncle adopted
him. He had gone to a private school with Eddie Collins, who
became a Hall of Fame second baseman. When Mr. Yawkey
bought the Red Sox, he gave Collins a small percentage of the
team and made him the general manager.

Mr. Yawkey estimated that he spent $10 million trying to
make the Red Sox a winner. It took him over a decade to win
his first pennant. His Red Sox teams were only in three World
Series. That is one of my biggest regrets. After twenty-three
seasons, sure, I wanted a Series ring for me. But I wanted one
for Mr. Yawkey more.

A misconception grew about him and the club. Because
he liked ballplayers and was in the clubhouse, some people
thought he spoiled us, that he wasn't demanding. Nothing
could be farther from the way it really was. He was a baseball
fan who knew the game. Yet, some people in the press
thought, *Here's a guy who's down in the clubhouse every day. He
can't make intelligent decisions about the players. He's too close to
them.* One thing they forgot was that no one wanted to win
more than he did. Mr. Yawkey controlled that anxiety,
though. He hated losing, but he rarely got on a player. I was
one of the exceptions. Maybe Ted was, too.

Who knows why? Maybe it was because I was so honest
with him. I never misled him when he asked a question. And
since he never second-guessed his managers, at least to their
face, I was the guy he could air his frustrations to. There were
only a few players in the twenty-eight years before I got there
that he would get on. The thing is, he'd never bother you if
you were going bad. That's when he'd pat you on the back.
He waited until you were going well, and then he'd jump
down your throat and rake you over the coals pretty good.

Certainly, he had good reason to be frustrated, but that

showed only in flashes. In those twenty-eight years he had owned the club before I made the team, his Red Sox had brought him only one pennant in 1946. In 1948 they lost the first playoff in the history of the American League when the Cleveland Indians started a rookie southpaw, Gene Bearden, in Fenway, while the Red Sox countered with Denny Galehouse.

When it was over, Fitzpatrick was crying, but Mr. Yawkey went over to him and said, "Now, Donald, hang in there."

The next year the Sox were down, then put on a spurt in the second half. Going into the last two days of the season, they had a one-game lead with two to play against the Yankees. The Yanks won both and the Red Sox finished second. Since that 1949 season, more than a decade before I arrived, the Sox had done no better than third.

Talk about frustration! In all, Mr. Yawkey lived to see only two more Series appearances—in 1967 and 1975. He had come close to another pennant in 1972 when we went into Detroit with a half-game lead over the Tigers and three to play. We were knocked out. When that one ended, I was crying, just like Fitzie had been twenty-four years before, and Mr. Yawkey put his hand on my shoulder, and said, "Don't worry, we'll get them next year."

He could have become a bitter man about how close he came. Frustration is part of loving the Red Sox, but he was more upbeat than their greatest fans. Through tragedy and bad luck, he lost great players in their prime: Harry Agganis, who died in his second season; Jackie Jensen, who quit over his fear of flying, then briefly returned; Tony Conigliaro, one of the finest young home run hitters in baseball, who was never the same after a beaning; Jimmy Piersall, who suffered a nervous breakdown. Whenever anyone tried to pick Mr. Yawkey up, he'd turn it all around and tell you how things were going to get better.

That didn't mean that he accepted defeat. During my first four or five years, Mr. Yawkey only talked a little with me about the games. After a while, he'd call down to Vince or Fitz and tell them, "Ask Yaz to stay after the game. I want to talk to him." He would bring over a few beers. Finally, he'd tell me, "Dammit, I'm tired of this, finishing thirty games out." Then he got warmed up: "I'm going to fire everyone in here. I'm going to trade the whole goddam ball club." That was a lot of crap about him being calm and promoting a country club atmosphere and how losing didn't matter. Mr. Yawkey said to me once, "I'm going to trade everyone in here, including you."

I was aware of another rap that the ball club had—a bad rap. It was that the Red Sox—and Mr. Yawkey in particular—were anti-black. We talked about that a lot. All I know was that I was on one side of his locker and that Joe Foy and then Reggie Smith, who were both black, had seats on the other side of him. He spent more time talking with us than with any of the other players. Newspaper reports bothered him. Whenever he read a story that claimed we didn't have enough black ballplayers, he'd come to me and say, "Yaz, don't you think I'd rather have signed a Willie Mays instead of a Gary Geiger?"

Tom Yawkey was obsessed with questions. He understood the fine points of the game, but he didn't want anyone to think he was second-guessing his manager. So the next day he'd sit down, pat me on the shoulder, and start firing away: "Dammit, where was that pitch to Mantle? How could they pitch him away when he's batting right-handed?" I was in left field. I didn't know. He *had* to know. "Jeez, you guys have a pregame meeting with the pitcher. What's the sense of it if he doesn't throw the ball where he's supposed to?"

Sometimes he'd invite the rival manager up to his office for a drink after the game, and the next day he'd come in smiling and tell me, "I pumped him for some information. Now, here's how I think they're going to try to pitch you." Mr. Yawkey liked having an edge—or *thinking* he had one. Because his mind was always on the Red Sox, he expected everyone else in the organization to be the same way. He would not tolerate a guy who did not put out. He understood if you didn't have talent, but if you had it, you had damn well better use it.

If a player was injured and couldn't suit up, Mr. Yawkey might invite the guy to sit in his private box. My mom and dad became regulars there after she developed cancer. Both she and Mr. Yawkey were sick at about the same time, although she lived three years longer. She and Mrs. Yawkey grew to be good friends, and Mr. Yawkey and my dad loved talking baseball. When Mom was ill during the 1975 playoffs against Oakland, Mr. Yawkey made sure Mom could accompany us in style. He had someone get her a place on our charter, meet her at the gate to the park, and see that her wheelchair could be moved to her seat.

Ironically, Mr. Yawkey, who had raised millions for the Jimmy Fund, was dying of leukemia himself. I visited him in the hospital less than a year after his last World Series. He had this habit of never saying goodbye. It was always: "See ya." He told me, "See you soon."

When I got to the park one day, I heard the news that he had died. I left the clubhouse and went out to the parking lot and started to cry. Darrell Johnson, who was our manager at the time, came out and said, "Yaz, you better not play tonight." I told him, "No, Mr. Yawkey would want me to." I hit a home run that night. Out of the 452 I hit, it's one I remember the most.

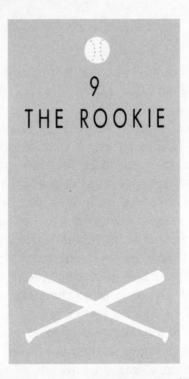

9
THE ROOKIE

I went back to Notre Dame again in the fall, only this time with Carol. Before the term was half over, guess what? We had our first baby, Maryann. We lived off-campus and I had to pay for housing. With our additional expenses, our budget was a little tight. Well, that's what you've got money in the bank for, right? Uh-uh. Not with Dad. We fought about that money all the time. In a way, it was almost funny.

Take the car. I wanted one. We needed one. So I called Mom and Dad and said, "Take out some money for me."

"That money stays in the bank," Dad said.

"Not even the interest?" I asked.

So there I was, with more than $100,000 in the bank, and I couldn't afford to buy a car. I took a loan from the Red Sox to buy the one I wanted: a white Chevrolet Impala with a red interior.

When the term ended, we wanted to go home first before going to spring training. I didn't have the money for the trip and I asked Dad to send it to me. He refused again. "Not even the interest?" I asked. Finally, I had to call Johnny Murphy and tell him to wire me money. But that's the way my dad was. "Keep it in the bank until you want to buy a house. Spend your salary, not the bonus money," he'd tell me.

Eventually, part of that bonus money went to buy our first house in Lynnfield, Massachusetts. To tell the truth, I'm a little bit like my folks myself. I didn't want to take out a lot of that money. I only used some of it to buy our house. That was after my first year with the Red Sox and my salary was the major league minimum, which had increased slightly to $7,500. But I borrowed a few thousand on my second year's salary.

Am I conservative still? Even today? Oh yeah. Some people don't understand that sort of mentality. But when I grew up, it was hammered into me that unless you pay cash for something you don't buy it. Even when I bought that first house, I had to leave that cushion in the bank.

With all the success I've had on the field and in business, I don't believe I have ever gone out and bought myself a present. When I've bought big cars and big houses, it was always for their usefulness or as an investment.

When I joined the Sox in spring training, I found myself with the locker next to Ted's. And they had given me a new number: 8. When I had come up in 1960, they gave me a 44, which should have been the tip-off that I was being sent down. But now, I had number 8 and the locker next to Williams. You could tell it was all set—the 8 next to the 9.

Ted was now a batting instructor, and he seemed to have changed. He wasn't as moody and he enjoyed coming over and chatting. He also suddenly made more sense to me. He was not quite as intimidating, and the conversations were a little lighter, about things that I could understand. Actually, I came to like him. More importantly, I could trust what Ted said. That was to become very important in just a few months.

In 1961, if you came up as a rookie, you never spoke to anyone unless spoken to. And the only players who ever spoke to me were Frank Malzone and Pete Runnels. If it hadn't been for my good friend Chuck Schilling, I would have been even more lonely than I was. Once in a while, the

Malzones would invite Carol and me out to dinner, but that was about it.

My big start in training camp didn't change things. I ripped seven hits in my first sixteen appearances, including a shot that hit the 430-foot sign in straightaway center in Scottsdale. But most of the players still thought of me as "the rookie with the big bonus."

The pressure to do well started from the very first day of camp. I felt as if I couldn't be myself. Instead, I was always on guard to say the right thing. I never really expressed my own feelings, but said what I thought would look right in the newspapers. I think that's why, for a long time, I was very guarded against the press. It was because I could never be myself. I don't think I ever really relaxed with the press until my last year. I'd always give the writers time, but only under my conditions: "You want to see me at two o'clock, fine. I'll be there, but not once batting practice starts." I had to prepare myself mentally for the game. And after the game I needed some time to get my head together, just to sit back and think about it and my own performance at the plate. Yeah, I was always on guard. But I loved it when Ken (Hawk) Harrelson was with the club and then when Bill (Spaceman) Lee was with the Sox. Instead of coming over to me, the writers would seek out Harrelson and he'd give them some crap to print. And you could always count on Lee to say something outrageous. I enjoyed having those guys around.

Usually, baseball's Opening Day grips America. But the day before the 1961 season opened, the Russians put a man, Yuri Gagarin, in orbit for the first time, and that was grabbing all the headlines. *Great,* I thought. *Just leave me alone and stop comparing me to Williams.* I didn't even want to read that I was being picked by the Associated Press and *The Sporting News* to be the American League Rookie of the Year. Just another added expectation that everyone else had for me.

It was cold and windy as hell in my first game as a Red Sox player in Boston. The first thing I saw was the Wall. I had never seen anything quite like it. It seemed to hover over everything. When I went out for the pregame practice, I felt as if it was looking over my shoulder. As if there wasn't enough for me, a twenty-one-year-old, to be thinking about.

I faced Ray Herbert of the Kansas City A's, a right-hander, in my debut. And I lined a single off him to left center. When I got to first and stopped, I let out a "Whew!" That first one was out of the way. It was another eighteen years, going for number 3,000, before I felt that edgy thinking about an at-bat. I made out in my final four at-bats that first day, though, striking out twice. We lost, 5–2.

But what I remember about that day, as much as the hit, was the standing ovation the fans gave me for a fielding play. Here I was, a scared kid, but my instincts were still there.

In the second inning, Leo Posada was on second. Haywood Sullivan—who was later to become the Red Sox general manager and then an owner—hit a grounder through Runnels at third. I charged the ball one-handed and Posada took off for the plate. I really got off a good throw and beat him there. The crowd, especially the ones in the left field stands along the foul line, shouted and stomped their feet. On the very next pitch, the batter hit a bloop to left center. It fell in, but I snared the ball while running to my left, and saw Sullivan trying for third. I had to turn to my right to make the right-handed throw to the bag and just missed him.

The pressure didn't let up after the game was over. The next day's *Globe* ran a box headlined YAZ VS. TED. It described what Williams did in his first game twenty-two years before (doubling at Yankee Stadium against Red Ruffing). *Yaz vs. Ted?* Was I going to have to live with this?

The answer was immediate: yes. Every new park I went into for the first couple of months, there were the questions and comparison with Williams. If a Whitey Ford struck me out, I'd cry. There were some great pitchers around in my rookie year, guys like Ford and Early Wynn, who were legends even before they made the Hall of Fame. Then there were guys like Jim Bunning, Frank Lary, Steve Barber, and Jim (Mudcat) Grant.

I didn't get my first homer for almost a month. It came against the Angels' Jerry Casale in Los Angeles, but people were more interested in the fact that Jackie Jensen had returned. The *Globe* had stopped running that box YAZ VS. TED. Jensen was one of the great all-around players, but he hated to be away from his family and he was afraid to fly. So he quit after the 1959 season and sat out all of 1960. Then he came back in 1961, but all of a sudden left the team after twelve games. His first game back, he hit a homer and single against the Angels.

Because he had taken off for almost two weeks, Jensen had time to make it to California by train. If not, he wouldn't have played on the West Coast. He missed a series in Kansas City because he couldn't get there by train.

As a kid, I was so worried about where I was headed that the craziness going on around me sometimes went over my head. We had some characters on that club. The Sox always seem to—more, I think, than anyone else. Maybe it was because Mr. Yawkey could tolerate a guy as long as he put out. Or maybe it was simply that in Boston, with all the nutty events the Sox have been involved in, a spotlight has shined on some of our weirder happenings. Boston's small enough so that everyone finds out when something unusual happens on the team, yet it's a big enough city to get the word out when it does.

Jensen seemed like a nice enough guy, but he was one of those veterans who didn't say a heck of a lot to me. He was a slugger with so much speed that he could lead the league in stolen bases one year and in RBIs the next. And while the team was shocked when he quit, I was struggling. He was the least of my worries.

I knew another interesting character, Gene Conley, a little better. Free spirit? That's an understatement. He was six-eight and also played basketball for the Boston Celtics. He had tremendous athletic skills. He just couldn't stay in one place. So he used to take off.

We'd get on the bus and someone would ask, "Where's

Gene?" Now, you might wonder how it is possible to misplace a six-foot eight-inch right-hander. Well, Gene could figure it out.

His legend was made one day after he had gotten bombed by the Yankees. Blame me. We were tied and the bases were loaded and he got a guy to hit a fly to left. Because I was new to the Stadium, I had trouble with the sun there. Left field in Yankee Stadium is one of the worst places during a day game because of the angle of the sun. I misplayed the ball and three runs scored. Then Conley gave up a homer and Higgins yanked him out. You'd think that after he showered, after getting dressed, he'd be over it. But he got on the bus at the Stadium for the ride to Newark Airport, and you could see that Gene was going nuts with frustration. He was talking to himself, then he'd look out the window and mutter. Going to the George Washington Bridge, we got stuck in rush hour traffic. That was it. Gene had had enough.

"C'mon, Pumpsie," he said to Elijah (Pumpsie) Green, a skinny infielder who followed him around. "Let's get off. I can't stand this." He pushed the door open and shot out of the bus with Green. You can get away with a lot of strange and bad things in baseball—you can break a water cooler, you can throw your bat against the dugout wall—but you never got off a bus, for God's sake. All of us had seen players do unusual things. But this . . . this violated some rule that just couldn't be violated. It couldn't be happening. But it was.

When we finally arrived in Washington, we figured they'd be right behind us. Even if they rented a car, it was only a four-and-a-half-hour drive. But one day passed, then two. Both of them had vanished.

Green was the first to return.

"Pumpsie, what the heck happened?" someone asked him.

"We were trying to go to Israel."

"What? What are you talking about?"

"Gene had to get away. So we went to dinner and then a nightclub. Then we spent the night at a fancy hotel. Gene decided we should go to Israel. So we went to the airport, but they wouldn't sell him a ticket. He didn't have his passport."

Conley showed up a day later.

That was neither the first nor the last time Conley disappeared. He once failed to show up on the plane, and Higgins was beside himself. He camped out in the lobby of the hotel, waiting to nab Gene when he arrived.

I was walking through the lobby on my way outside when I saw Higgins pacing, eyes fixed on the revolving door at the entrance. After a few minutes he sat down. Just then Gene walked in, and Higgins jumped out of his chair.

"Where the hell have you been!" Higgins shouted, while everyone in the lobby began to stare.

"Oh, Mike, there was some sickness in the family," Conley said.

With that, Mike backed down and he started to look around, embarrassed.

"Gee, I'm sorry, Gene. Who was it?"

"Me," said Conley, and walked away.

I can enjoy those stories now. Back then, when I was a young kid, I was fighting the comparisons to Williams. I thought that fans expected me to hit .350 and hit 40 home runs. The first two and a half months, I just played completely under my ability. I was trying to hit a home run every time up. A base hit didn't mean anything. It tore me up inside, tore me up to the point that I almost threw away my career. I was damn close to it.

We were in Detroit and I had to face Frank Lary and Jim Bunning in consecutive games. I couldn't even get a loud foul. I was breaking my bats—not by banging them in anger, but by having them sawed off by the pitchers. They'd throw inside and I'd swing at a bad pitch. The ball would hit the trademark and—*bing*—split in half. That's how the pitchers sawed you off. I sat there at my locker on Saturday after facing Lary. No one else was around except for Chuck Schilling. I started to cry. Goddam, I felt as if everything I had ever worked for was gone. I doubted myself. I told Chuck I didn't think I could play in the big leagues. My average was down to about .220. Just then Higgins came by.

Higgins was the manager again. In 1960, while I was in Minneapolis, he replaced Jurges midway through the season when Jurges's magic seemed to stop. Ironically, Higgins's record as a manager was practically the same in 1959 when he was fired—31–41—as it was in 1960 after he was rehired—31–42.

Mike was a conservative guy. He had never said much to me from spring training on. The thing is, he didn't say much to anyone or really do much with the club overall. Maybe he should have. It needed something, but he was such a quiet guy. You had a better chance talking to him in a restaurant than at the park. In a restaurant Mike would have a couple of drinks, then he'd come over and sit down to have a few words with you. But it was strictly baseball in the clubhouse. That made for a pretty quiet, businesslike clubhouse.

Mike might have been a good manager on an established team where all he had to do was push some buttons. But I'll always remember that he came over to my locker after that bad game against Lary and said, "Don't worry about it. Don't worry about being Ted Williams or anyone else. Even if you hit .200, you're my left fielder every day." But even though I was his left fielder, he never learned how to spell my name. He'd start to write it down in the lineup card: "Yastr . . ." and then let it tail off into a scrawl, figuring the umpires knew what he meant.

I felt better about his vote of confidence and it helped for a while. But I couldn't shake my slump. Here I was, a guy who had hit almost .380 and .340 in the minors, and I was down to .220. I was being platooned against left handers or benched entirely. It was something I couldn't handle. I really began to think: *I can't play in the big leagues.*

Where could I go for advice? I had built up a rapport with Mr. Yawkey, so I went to him. I told him, "I feel guilty about not giving you your money's worth. Could Ted come in for a day or two and take a look at me?"

"Goddam, I don't know where he is," Mr. Yawkey said in that gruff way of his. "He's out fishing somewhere—New Brunswick or Florida—I don't know. Jeez, when that guy takes off, how the hell are you supposed to find him? But we'll get him."

It took them three days to find Ted. Whenever he went out on one of his fishing expeditions, Ted went far away from civilization.

When Ted arrived, he surprised me. He didn't say anything technical about hitting, but he pumped me up mentally. "You look good swinging," he said. "Think of the count. Be aggressive." Not really advice, and none of his theory. For the first time, I understood him. Twenty-two years later, in my last spring training, we sat down before a game and reminisced about that day. We were very honest with each other. I told him how I had resented him and his advice when I first met him, how he had told the press that I was going to hit .320, but that I finally needed his help to straighten me out.

"I could see there were some things you were doing wrong, the way you were bringing your bat down, but I didn't want to tell you too much," Ted recalled. "I didn't want you thinking about too many things. So I just tried to give you confidence."

Something worked. I went on a July tear, hitting at a .478 clip with 22 hits in 46 at-bats. My average went from .236 to .269. It was similar to what I had done the second half of the season at Minneapolis. Now I was getting to see the pitchers for a second and third time. Even though they were in a mid-season groove, I was adjusting to the speed of a major league fastball, and I wasn't getting fooled by the pitchers' breaking stuff.

My summer exploits were recorded in *Goniec Polski,* a Polish publication with a feature that followed athletes. I saw a copy of the paper with a note about me under the title OTHER POLES ON WAY UP. Proudly, it also spoke about Bill Mazeroski of the Pirates, who had a 16-game hitting streak.

So now I was expected to uphold my heritage as well. After some of the early problems I had, that was easy.

My first season ended in Yankee Stadium. The Yankees had won the pennant again, of course, but this game was special. Roger Maris was still trying to break Babe Ruth's record of 60 homers in a season. Roger needed one more and this was his last shot. Before the game, we had a team meeting about it, and Higgins told the pitchers, "We're going to give him his chance. I don't want anyone walking him on purpose. If he hits it, he'll earn it."

I went out for batting practice and was standing around the cage. I had gotten friendly with Moose Skowron, probably because he was also Polish. But now I was talking to Maris. I wished him luck on breaking the Babe's record.

"Are you guys going to try to pitch around me?" Maris suddenly asked. He was concerned that he wouldn't get a good pitch to hit. No one, after all, wanted to be the guy who served up the record number 61. I wasn't that surprised he asked me about it. As hitters, we had a certain feeling for each other. I could imagine what he was going through.

"No," I told him. "We're going to go at you. We had a team meeting about it. You're going to get your chance. Tracy Stallard's a competitor. He'll go at you with his best stuff. It'll be him against you."

Maris wanted to know what kind of competitor Stallard was. Roger was afraid of someone pitching around him, not giving him a chance, which is what Pete Rose claimed when he was going for Joe DiMaggio's 56-game hitting streak.

I knew Tracy from playing with him at Minneapolis. I knew the kind of guy he was. He'd bring it to Roger with his best stuff.

In the first inning, Tracy fooled him on an outside pitch. Roger was usually a pull hitter. But all he could do was stroke it to left field—right to me. In the fourth, though, Roger got around on a fastball—waist-high, down the middle. He hit it ten rows back in the right field stands. That record shot was the only run of the game. But I had told Roger the truth.

Tracy wouldn't pitch around him. It ended our season thirty-three games behind the Yankees, in sixth place.

If you looked at the next day's stats, you would have found Al Kaline led the American League in doubles, Whitey Ford in wins and winning percentage, Hank Aaron on top of the National League in doubles, and Sandy Koufax the strike-out leader. All of these fine players made the Hall of Fame while I was still playing.

My first season ended with me batting .266, although I was hitting .300 the last two months. I finished second on the team in RBIs with 80, and led in doubles (31), tied in triples (6), and led in total bases (231) and extra-base hits (48). I hit only 11 homers, but I was glad to get out of the season in one piece. And not bad for a rookie.

Within twenty-four hours, I was back in school. I drove to Pittsburgh to pick up Carol, who was staying with her folks because she had recently given birth to our second child, Carl Jr., whom we called Mike. We all piled into the white Impala with the red interior and headed for Notre Dame.

As I write this, our family has grown to four children and now a grandchild. At one time, I fantasized that Mike and I would become the first father-son combination to play in the big leagues at the same time. We came close, but it didn't quite happen. That honor went to Ken Griffey and his son, Ken Jr., in 1989.

With three girls and one boy, you might think I was a father who paid all the attention to the son, especially since I was a ballplayer, but that isn't what happened. I rarely imposed my beliefs on him and never "forced" him into baseball. Carl Michael Yastrzemski, Jr., has always liked to be called Mike. He wanted an identity other than Carl Jr. He's the only "junior" in the family, since my dad and I have different middle names.

Our oldest, Maryann, lives in Southboro, Massachusetts, and married a fellow named Kevin McCarthy. We had our first grandchild in 1988, Kevin Charles McCarthy. I call him

K.C. Mike married Anne-Marie Wesson, who was from Andover, Massachusetts. They live in Pompano, Florida. Our third child, Suzanne, lives in Boston. She's working on major accounts for Chesapeake Packing and Display, a company that creates packaging. The youngest, our baby, is in college— Carolyn. She attends Boston University. Before going there, she had attended Florida Atlantic University, right near our place, which is in Boca Raton, Florida. She particularly liked that because it was right on the ocean.

Mike is settled into the produce business now after a distinguished but brief career in the minors. He was a talented player whose speed, hitting, and fielding might have taken him farther if he hadn't suffered injuries. He didn't give up playing ball until August of 1988. He had made it as far as Triple A ball in Hawaii, where he nearly batted .300. But in a game late in 1987 he tore ligaments in his ankle. They wanted him to play winter ball, but the ligaments weren't healed. So he went back to the minors, and he injured his shoulder and the leg still bothered him. It was tough to play the outfield with bad wheels and a bad throwing arm. Then he got the chance to become a produce broker.

"I think you ought to give baseball up and go into business full-time," I told him. It was a tough thing for me to say and tougher for him to accept. If he had been a shortstop or second baseman, I think he would have made the big leagues. But as an outfielder, he just didn't have enough power. He'd hit 6 or 7 home runs as a switch-hitter, although he led the league in outfield assists in 1987. I explained to him the only chance he had was as a fourth or fifth outfielder, but when you're second-string like that, you spend years just going back and forth to the minors.

"You're better off making a move now, Mike," I said.

When he was growing up, I never imposed myself on him. Actually, I sort of left him to develop on his own. Unlike my own formative years, when my father was always around to practice with me and give me instruction, I was away when it was time to play ball. But when Mike was a senior in high school he told me he wanted a shot at being a professional ballplayer.

You want to hear something wonderful? Bots Nekola scouted him in school. It had to be twenty years after Bots had scouted me, but he was still working for the Red Sox. He came down on a day Mike went 3 for 4—home run, triple, double. He threw a guy out at the plate, too.

"Kid, you just might make it someday," said Bots, which picked Mike up wonderfully.

I really started working hard with him. We had our place in Boca Raton by then and we worked out together in the winter. When he came up to Boston in the summer, along with the whole family, I'd take him out to the ballpark early, work out with him, and let him hit.

Mike went to Florida State for four years before signing a contract. He just lacked a little something extra to make it to the majors. Like me, he suffered when things didn't go well. Playing for Atlanta's farm team in North Carolina, he got so frustrated one time that he punched a washing machine. He worked hard at the game. I don't know whether he'd ever say it, but I've always believed there was just too much pressure on him. That's a difficult obstacle. Also, he was limited in his power because of his weight. Even though he's my height, he never got his weight above 170. Still, if he had been more aggressive at the plate in making contact . . . well, who knows? I thought he could have hit 20 home runs a year. Maybe because of the pressure, he was determined not to strike out. It prevented him from taking a really full cut. I watched him in a lot of games in college and in the minors. Once his name was announced, you'd hear people yelling at him. When he was with Birmingham, a Double A club, they'd play in Orlando, and I'd make sure to drive up from the Sox camp and see him. The fans were on him pretty good. I never said anything to him. I think he was afraid to strike out, afraid to be aggressive, because every time he'd make an out you'd hear someone say, "You're not like your old man."

That's why he always wanted to be called Mike, not Carl.

Even at Florida State, when he came to the plate they announced his name as Mike Yastrzemski.

I could never figure out, though, why the back of his college uniform at Florida State read: YAZ.

10
THE LONG,
SLOW CLIMB

The Red Sox of my first six seasons finished sixth, eighth, seventh, eighth, ninth, ninth. That's pressure. The playoffs? The great run for the pennant in 1967? The Series? Hell, that's not pressure—that's a pleasure. Pressure is coming to the park thirty games out of first place and trying to make some meaning out of your day.

God, was I frustrated the first six years. You're always optimistic in spring training, but that optimism's gone after the first two months of the season when you're twenty-five games out of first place and looking at two thousand people in the stands in springtime. Even Opening Day was tough playing under those conditions, knowing these happy fans would turn surly after a few weeks.

That's why in our miracle month of our Impossible Dream season of 1967, I always surprised television interviewers. Every time I turned around there was a microphone in front of me asking about the pressure of a pennant race.

"What pressure?" I'd say with a smile and notice a dumbfounded look in return. They couldn't understand. This was great. I'd never been in anything like this. A pennant race, for crying out loud! Pressure was going 0 for 4 in an empty ballpark and you're in last place and they boo the hell out of you. You had to get a hit to get them off your case.

More than Ted did, I came to understand and feel for the Sox fans. You have to understand a couple of things about being in love with the Boston Red Sox. First, you're right next to them when you go to the park, especially in left. Then, there's the other part—that the team has been so close so often but didn't win that final game since 1918, their last Series. They have been hounded since then by the fact they sold Babe Ruth to the Yankees, or lost the 1946 World Series to the Cardinals, or lost the 1948 playoff to the Indians, or blew their one-game lead over the Yankees with two to play in 1949, or in 1972, or in 1978 . . . The Sox fan remembers these seasons.

And yet for me, out in left, where they were so close, when they cheered it sounded fifty times louder. And when they got on you, it was so magnified that you thought the whole city of Boston was after you.

When I first came up, the Sox were losers but the fans saw themselves as something special. It was like: "I'm a Red Sox fan, dammit. I'm different." Even when I was at Notre Dame and had just signed with the Sox, people I had never met would seek me out and say: "Hey, Carl, my grandfather saw Cy Young pitch." Or "When I was a kid, I saw the Babe when he played for Boston." Or they had an uncle who had seen Tris Speaker. It was a tradition—no, it was a *calling.* I couldn't believe the types of people who approached me: professors, priests, kitchen workers, the gardener. And they all had a story why they were Red Sox fans. And that's in South Bend, Indiana. Imagine getting them all in one place in Boston.

No matter how crummy the team was, if you had only two thousand people in Fenway, that corner in left field would always be filled. It stuck out like a ship's prow along the foul line. They were alongside you and right above you, so they could always shout down to you. Hide? It was the worst thing you could think of doing. Because you couldn't hide, no matter how badly you had messed up a play in the field or how terrible you had looked at the plate. Actually, I liked to listen to them. Some guy would get on me, and another fan would yell, "Don't listen to him, Yaz. He's a jerk!" The next thing you knew, a fight would break out. My protectors against my detractors.

From the beginning, they got on me pretty good. If we won, they'd leave me alone. But those first six seasons, they didn't have many excuses to let me be. We lost 101 more games than we won. So they were accustomed to getting on me. I couldn't blame them. Baseball is one game where you can't blame your teammates if you screw up. Oh, maybe there's a blown hit-and-run sign, but when you mess up, you do it in front of everyone and there's no excuses.

One day, after four or five years in Boston, when we were playing typical ball, I said to myself, *Screw it. I'm going to have some fun with the fans.* I was having a miserable day, struck out a couple of times, and when I got out to the field they were yelling and screaming. I was laughing to myself at some of the stuff they were coming up with: "Yaz, you can't even spell your name!" "Yaz, bring back Williams to left!" This was going to be it. When I went to the dugout in the seventh inning, I stuck these two big pieces of cotton in my ears. When I went back on the field, I couldn't hear them but their mouths were moving and I saw their expressions, and I was smiling at them, which got them going even more. These fans always believed you've got to take them seriously. But I riled them some more when I tipped my hat at them.

All of a sudden, I took the cap and put it between my legs. I put my hands to my ears and pulled out two big pieces of cotton. Wow! They started yelling and screaming, "We love ya, Yaz!" They even gave me a standing ovation. And from that time on, the fans left me alone.

I came to realize that they never really disliked me. When things go bad, they single out a person. In recent years, it was Bob Stanley. They stay on that one guy. Then they do a

180-degree turn. If a guy struck out four times, they would cheer him hoping he breaks his slump. But you can be hitting .300 and they boo you. So what the hell do you know about them? I do know this. Their expectations are high.

That's what's so great about being in a pennant race. You didn't have to get a hit. You get a walk. You make a play, you throw somebody out, or go from first to third. You could help in half a dozen ways. So the pennant races were fun, easy.

I won my first batting title in 1963 when I was only twenty-four years old, but it didn't mean that much to me. We finished seventh, twenty-eight games back.

That season Johnny Pesky replaced Higgins, who moved to the front office. For a while, I thought Pesky would be the man to get us on track. He was a peppery guy and seemed to be the one to shake us up. Mike, meanwhile, had given me some off-season advice on batting, and I had taken it and was having a good spring. For most of my career I had kept my bat high, like one of my heroes, Stan Musial. I probably started doing that when I was a kid and copying Stan the Man. After a while it just became my natural stance. But it had its draw-backs. I held the bat so high that my hands were next to my left ear. Higgins showed me that, as a result, I wasn't getting the bat around quickly enough. That wouldn't have been so bad if I had not been trying to hit the ball out of the park so often. So now I lowered the bat, and didn't swing as hard. All of a sudden that spring, I found I was hitting the ball for base hits all over the field. I held the bat at chest level and became a .300 hitter. *Maybe,* I hoped, *with me more consistent at the plate and with the new attitude that Pesky has brought, we can shake this Sox thing of losing.*

Not quite. It was great early in the season, but at the first signs of collapse after a good start, the whole thing unraveled. Players quickly fell back to their old cliques and there was finger-pointing. It was no secret in Boston that we didn't get along. That was our "rep" for years. I remember Eddie Andelman of "Sports Huddle," a radio talk show that is the favorite of all the second-guessers and Hot Stove Leaguers in Boston, once called a restaurant while he was live on the air.

"Hello, are you open for dinner tonight?" he asked.

The listeners heard the maître d' on the other end say, "Certainly."

"Okay, this is the Boston Red Sox calling. We'd like twenty-five tables for one."

After a while, the locker room just seemed out of control. The thing is, if you live with it from the beginning, it doesn't seem that unusual to you.

But it was brought home to me one day before a game. Dick Williams, not yet known as a genius manager, was a well-traveled infielder-outfielder who joined us in 1963. He was a heck of a cardplayer. He beat one of the guys for a few hundred bucks, but he said something that made me realize things weren't quite right around here: "Nobody should be allowed to win or lose this much money on a ball club. You guys shouldn't be playing for these kinds of stakes."

Well, that was only part of it. Pesky had trouble maintaining discipline of some players, especially our newest slugger, Dick Stuart. He was a heavy-handed first baseman who earned the nickname of Dr. Strangeglove for his erratic fielding at first. He was a massive player and a big home run hitter, but he had two bad faults: he struck out a lot and he used to argue with Pesky in front of us.

In his two seasons with us, Stuart struck out 274 times. He explained that away by saying, "I'm valuable to the team because I strike out a lot. This way I don't ground into a lot of double plays." You had to like a guy who had that attitude, and cracks like that kept us loose.

The strikeouts weren't as bad for the club as the effect his constant bickering with Pesky had. It was oil and water. Pesky was from the old school: "Do anything you can to get on. And don't boast about it." Stuart swung away. But he bragged. He once tagged one deep in Yankee Stadium and he shouted out to the front of the bus, "How far was that, Mr. Manager?"

Pesky took the bait. He should have kept his mouth shut,

but he started talking about the pitchers from his time, how Stuart wouldn't have gotten around on a Bob Feller fastball. That started it. Stuart shot back: "And you could, huh?" Pesky told him he was a guy who got 200 hits a year for three straight years and Stuart replied, "Yeah, a singles hitter." The thing was, they weren't kidding each other anymore.

Because Stuart could get away with that needling, he would confront Johnny over other things as well. One time Stuart was benched against a righty, and in front of everyone he blurted out, "What right do you have to bench a guy earning more than you do?"

Pesky started defending his right to bench Stuart, instead of just telling the big guy to shut up. Incidents like that one escalate when a club is losing, and you make more of them in your mind than you should. That's typical of what happens to a losing team.

In 1970 I had a real good year—as good as 1967—and almost won the Triple Crown again. But when you're not in a pennant race, nobody notices. In a pennant race, you're at a different level, and so are the fans and the news media. When I got a hit at Fenway during my first six years, all it did was get the fans off my case. That's what it came down to anyway.

I started taking tranquilizers late in my second season when I went into a slump and couldn't drag my butt out of bed. The doc thought it was nerves—I always had those—and he figured the tranquilizers would calm me down and stop me from wasting so much nervous energy. I was tense and tired. It turned out that what I really had was jaundice and hadn't realized it. So there I was, battling fatigue and taking tranquilizers. But I insisted on playing, even though it was another lost season for us, because I was hitting near .300 and wanted like heck to see if I could finish at that level.

With only a few days left in the season, they finally figured out what was wrong with me.

"Is it okay if I play?" I asked. "I'd like to get to .300." I was hitting in the high .290s and they said, "What the heck, you can't do anything more to yourself."

I went into the final day of the season, a doubleheader
against the Senators, batting .295. This was not as dramatic as
Ted's final day of 1941, when he insisted on playing even
when he already had reached .400. It was a big deal to me,
though. I knew the odds were stacked against me. I had the
third-most at-bats in the American League, more than 640,
and in order to pick up points I needed a big afternoon. Even
though we were playing the Senators—the worst team in the
league—they weren't about to do me any favors. When a club
is that low (they had already lost 100 games), it doesn't want
anyone fattening up on it. It's like an insult.

It was a chore for me to get to the park. I felt miserable.
We faced Tom Cheney in the opener and I managed to get
two hits in four at-bats. That brought my average up to .297. I
could get to .300 with a 3 for 3 performance against a nineteen-year-old kid named Jack Jenkins, making his first major
league start.

The kid was good. We beat him by only 3–1 and he gave
up just seven hits—none by me. I went 0 for 2 before Higgins
replaced me in left. My final average was .296, which actually
didn't put me too far down from the league leaders, since
Runnels won the batting title with .326. He sat out the final
day with the flu, and kept his lead by five points over Mickey
Mantle.

If I hadn't been trying to turn into a home run hitter, I
could have been at the .320 level that year. I must have given
away fifty at-bats because I was swinging so hard. I hit 19 out
of the park, but my average suffered. But I was still learning
about myself and about baseball. Look at what I did in the
field. I was learning to master the Wall. I led the league in
assists with 15—and I also led the outfielders with 11 errors.
Many of them came because I was overthrowing. I was so
intent on trying to get people out at home that I'd throw the
relay over the cutoff man and over the catcher's head, or I'd
throw it wildly to a base when I should have conceded it to
the runner.

Finishing the way we did made me feel so miserable,

combined with the jaundice, that I just couldn't go back to school again. The docs agreed. "Forget this term," they told me. I didn't realize it then, but that long grind of playing a full season, then going out to school in Indiana in the fall, was going to end. I never did return to Notre Dame. But I made a promise to my folks that I would graduate from college. So the following fall I enrolled at Merrimack College, just outside of Boston. I went back the next few off-seasons, but to night school. We played more day games then, and whenever I finished playing I'd head right for school after showering. The priests at Merrimack were helpful—they also had been at Notre Dame, but at Merrimack everyone was a Red Sox fan. They understood my situation and, just as they did at Notre Dame, gave me one test, the final, which served as my grade. Some of the priests burned the midnight oil with me to try to help me get through. Finally, my higher education, which began in 1957, ended when I got my degree in 1966, majoring in business with a minor in finance. There's not many college graduates who have their wife and children and family see them wearing the cap and gown, but I did. The proudest people were Mom and Dad.

Funny to think that a college graduation was one of the highlights from the first six seasons in a major league career. But the early 1960s weren't fun for Red Sox players or fans. The 1960s started with our attendance at Fenway at more than a million. It fell below that for six straight seasons, though. In 1965, when we lost 100 games, our average attendance was eight thousand. I had a personal highlight that year. It was the first and only time I hit for the cycle.

The Tigers were starting a twenty-one-year-old right-hander named Denny McLain in mid-May. Good fastball. Good control. In the late sixties he became the ace of their staff, winning 31 games in 1968, the last pitcher to do so. But this time I belted him for homers the first two times I faced him. I crushed a 1–0 pitch—I knew he'd have to come in with a fastball—beyond the bullpen in the first inning with a man on. The next inning I came up with two on. This time, on an

0–1 pitch, I reached across the plate and hit it into the left field net for a three-run shot. We led by 5–0. But it was typical of the Red Sox of those days. We lost by 12–8 in ten innings. I had a five-hit night, though, by adding a single, double, and triple.

That week meant something else to me. It was to prove I could be tough as well. For me, the combination was critical—hitting and toughness, being as hard as I could be. It's no surprise that I was worried about my size and how I would react to pain and injury. I was concerned that I didn't have enough in reserve to overcome an injury, or the strength to compensate for one. I had learned two years before I had the mental toughness to battle despondency and still play pretty good ball, good enough to win a batting title on a seventh-place club. But now, for my first time in the big leagues, I was faced with a serious physical challenge.

The day after I hit for the cycle, I went hard into second base. Not only did my spikes catch, but I crashed into the Tigers' Jake Wood. In the collision, he drove his knee into my ribs. We didn't have portable X-ray equipment in 1965. They helped me off the field, examined me in the locker room, and sent me home. "Give us a call if you've got any more pain," they said. More pain? I had actually broken two ribs and damaged a kidney that started to bleed. I was in the hospital the next night.

Tom Yawkey visited me the nine days I was in the hospital. That time together cemented our friendship. For the first time he disclosed to me how he had suffered those years of coming close.

"All I want is one pennant," he said. He reminisced about blowing it in 1948 and 1949, and told me he thought I would be the key to the turnaround when it came. I wanted right then, more than anything else, to help him with his dream.

I missed a total of 29 games that season. Yet, I still played in 133, proving to me that I could will myself into the lineup. I suffered a knee injury, too, that season and my average, which had been in the .340s, dropped. I finished at .312, second to Tony Oliva's .321. But I had finished. That desire, that will, was part legacy of my early years, when I would practice for hours on end by myself, no matter what the weather. But it also was pride and it also was an insistence that, dammit, I would help Mr. Yawkey get that pennant. In my twenty-three seasons, I was on the disabled list only once, for a month in 1972 with a torn knee. At the age of forty-one in 1980, I broke a rib by crashing into the Wall—now what the heck was a guy my age doing out there anyway?—and missed 32 of the last 35 games. I still played for three more years.

Overall, I was able to accomplish what I was driven to—overcoming the injuries, not letting them cut me down. I set an American League record of twenty straight years of playing at least 100 games. And after Hank Aaron, I become the second player ever to perform in at least 100 games for twenty-two seasons.

Even if I had played a full season in 1965, it wouldn't have had much of an impact on our club. Something had to be done in 1966. The trouble was, no one really had any answers.

You look back at the players we had during those dismal years and wonder why the team wasn't better: Dick Radatz, a terrific reliever, one of the best in the majors; Tony Conigliaro, easily the top young right-handed slugger; Jim Lonborg, a heady young right-handed pitcher; Rico Petrocelli; Earl Wilson; Bill Monbouquette. We changed managers—from Pesky to Billy Herman. But nothing seem to work.

Herman was fifty-five years old when he took over, and maybe that's why he seemed as interested in golf as in baseball. Instead of talking baseball around the clubhouse, he was always talking golf—how he did on this course, what club he used on a certain hole. Maybe I was the wrong guy to bounce all that golf talk off because once I got to the park, baseball was the only thing on my mind, so maybe I resented his golf conversations more than the other guys. It just seemed to me that if you're trying to turn around a team, the team should be thinking about baseball. So should the manager.

I don't know what effect the talks we had in the hospital had on Mr. Yawkey's thinking, but he was more determined than ever to change this thing around. He got more involved in the front office. First, he fired Mike Higgins as general manager and put Dick O'Connell there. O'Connell then named Haywood Sullivan as director of player personnel. His job was to make the deals to bring us the right combination of players.

Herman, though, was given another chance in 1966. There was a feeling of a new beginning with the new people in the front office. We also had moved our training camp from the Cactus League in Arizona to the Grapefruit League in Winter Haven, Florida. On our first day of camp, Dick Radatz decided we'd have a closed-door team meeting.

Everyone has team meetings these days. You keep the manager out and you clear the air. But you just didn't do that in the 1960s. A meeting without the manager? It was like you were plotting mutiny.

"Are they nuts?" I asked Chuck Schilling when I found out. "How can you have a meeting without the manager?"

"Beats me," he said. "I just found out about it myself, and I'm the union player rep."

Actually, Herman was there, but only at the beginning, sort of like an official greeter. He told us he thought it was a great thing to meet like this. Then he left and we closed the door.

I didn't agree with any of this, and I told the players. They had been jumping up and speaking like it was some revival meeting: we were going to obey the rules, we were going to go to bed early, we were going to have a balanced breakfast. The point was, none of that was our business or our job. The man in charge, the manager, is the one who sets the rules and we're supposed to follow them. It's hard enough, I explained, getting ready for a season and to maintain that level. But maybe I spent more energy on playing than some other guys. Maybe I spent too much. In any event, I said I wasn't going to follow anyone's rules but the manager's. Old-fashioned? Sure.

It didn't take long for the rules thing to fall apart. Pretty soon, the old ways returned. Guys who wanted to sneak out were doing it again. If we would not have bothered with the meeting in the first place, then breaking the rules wouldn't have made the whole thing seem so useless and divide us.

My reservations about Herman increased after he dumped Chuck Schilling. This wasn't the first time I griped about how a manager treated my old friend. Pesky didn't have a world of confidence in him, either. I'll admit that where Chuck was concerned, I was not being totally objective. Loyalty was important to me, though, and I simply felt that neither manager was playing fair with Chuck. As a twenty-three-year-old rookie with me in 1961, he played more games, 158, than anyone else on the Sox. He was the second baseman and he drove in 62 runs. For five weeks he played without an error. But the next year Chuck broke his wrist and he eventually became a benchwarmer. After he left us, Chuck never played again. I missed him because he was my only big league link to the old days back on Long Island. I guess another way of saying it is that Chuck was a link to my childhood and some really good times.

Well, maybe with the 1966 season ready to begin, we could put the sputtering of spring training behind us. I desperately wanted just to go out and play ball and see how good we could be. The last thing I wanted was another distraction. That's what I got the day before the season started. Someone came up with the idea we should vote ourselves a captain.

"Hey, wait a minute," I said. "The manager picks the captain. It's his guy. He needs someone he can talk to in private, someone he feels comfortable with."

Nobody listened. Despite my objections, they voted me in for the job.

The worst part of it wasn't dealing with the gripes—a guy

not being used properly, an unfair fine, a late payment on meal money—it was having to put the touch on Mr. Yawkey.

The man loved his players. And they all knew that. Everyone knew I had a wonderful relationship with the man. They saw his daily visits to my locker. These also were misinterpreted. There were suspicions that I was somehow running the club on an underground basis, calling the shots on trades, telling him what I thought about the manager. None of that ever was true. But I did know him better than anyone else and I loved him. Some of the guys started to ask me to put in a word with him on an advance, or a loan, or a problem with moving his family. All of a sudden, I found that I was constantly asking Mr. Yawkey to bail out some player for one reason or another.

I don't know how or why this business with the money started. It was bad enough relaying gripes to Herman. Then someone came up with the idea that I should have a daily meeting with Herman and I would relay his thoughts to the club. All that did was put more distance between a manager who wasn't in tune with his players to start with. But picture the situation developing with Tom Yawkey. I had to wait for him to be in the right mood before I could ask him for money for other players. I did it at first for one guy, and the word got around. Others waited to tap me on the shoulder: "Hey, Yaz, I need this, I need that." How much money was the average player making—$15,000, $20,000? If a player could get a loan of a few thousand dollars, that was a lot. But it put me in a very bad position. I grew more uncomfortable with my role. I knew some of the situations where they needed money was legitimate, but I knew some of the others were just con jobs. That's why I gave up the captaincy.

The strange thing about that was it looked as if Dick Williams was asserting his authority when he became the new manager in 1967 and said, "There's only one captain around here, and that's me." But even before he became manager— before I knew who the manager was going to be—I told O'Connell after the 1966 season that I wasn't going to be the captain anymore. I explained my reasons. I also told him, "Look, Dick, I don't care how you release it to the press. Just don't make anyone look bad." So when Williams took over as manager, he announced it as if he had made the decision.

Of course, if we had played as we were capable of in 1966, these events would have seemed less significant. We had more bickering once the blush of spring training came to an end. Herman in particular used to get on Petrocelli. The kid's locker was near mine, and we would have long talks about what he needed to do. The conversations were as much about emotion as playing. Rico had a dark side, and it would take over if he screwed up a play or if Herman ragged him.

Herman was gone before the end of the season. That ended the longtime Yawkey-Higgins-Herman connection, and indicated that the Red Sox were on a different course. Higgins was an old-time Yawkey man, and it was Higgins who had hired Herman. Runnels replaced him for the final sixteen games. We played .500 for Pete, and that enabled us to climb up to ninth—and finish ahead of the Yankees for the first time since 1948. They finished last and we finished . . . well, at least playing .500. Winning eight and losing eight is hardly a pennant-winning pace. But strange as it seems, it allowed us to end the season on the upbeat. And the day after the season ended, the Sox introduced our new manager, Dick Williams.

This guy was obviously what we needed. He was all baseball, no distractions. I had played with Dick for two years and appreciated his attitude toward the game. He had a good track record as manager, although it was short—a pair of International League championships with the farm team in Toronto.

Will I be a part of this new order? I wondered. I was coming off an okay year. For the third time I was the league leader in doubles, drove in 80 runs, scored 81. But my average fell to .278, my worst since my rookie season. Herman had told me before he was canned that I would be gone in 1967. He complained that I wasn't hustling. I knew I was, but had to think about why he believed that. It could be because my whole being was wrapped up in hitting, and when I wasn't doing

well, it affected the way I ran or fielded. Or at least seemed to.
I already had won two Golden Glove awards. I had more
stolen bases (8) than any regular on the team in 1966. In
1965, playing for Herman, I won a Gold Glove and stole 7
bases, which was only one behind the club leaders. So in my
mind I had put out for the guy and the team.

Yet, what Herman had told me stayed on my mind even
after he was gone. If you're a ballplayer—even the highest-
paid on the team—at a time like that you try to put into perspective what you've done, where you are, how you helped
the team. Even though Mr. Yawkey assured me I wouldn't be
traded, I continued to wonder. Herman had planted the idea,
and then I started to read about the possibility.

What had I done, really, my first six seasons? The club
had a combined won-lost record of 434–535. Six straight seasons with attendance under a million. Four managers. And a
bunch of second-division finishes. As for myself, there was
only one year when I hit 20 home runs, although I had one
batting title and a pair of .300 seasons behind me.

Well, hell. I wasn't going to be traded. And I was going
to turn myself and the team into a new direction. That's all
there was to it. If I could will myself into becoming a better
ballplayer by spending hour after hour, day after day, year
after year, in the garage back home, then I could do it up here
as well. *Yes,* I vowed, *1967 is going to be different.*

11
THE
IMPOSSIBLE
DREAM

I look back at 1967 and see a time when we were balanced on change—not just the Boston Red Sox but all of sports. The first Super Bowl had just been played, but the Green Bay Packers, the NFL Establishment team under Vince Lombardi, took care of the AFL. The Yankees were in decline, but Willie Mays still was hitting homers. Sandy Koufax had retired, but Tom Seaver was the top rookie. Muhammad Ali had refused to go into the Army, and was fighting exhibitions. The Boston Bruins were last again, but they had an incredible rookie in Bobby Orr. The Celtics' string of championships ended, but Wilt Chamberlain was still playing basketball. We were approaching a time in which you could break the mold as a ballplayer, do the unexpected. Ken Harrelson of the A's even called the team owner, Charles O. Finley, "a menace." Of course, you would be singled out if you were different, but more and more, people and teams and ideas broke with the old tried-and-true ways. It was all around you—on the campuses, in politics. And, as usual, last on the playing field. Americans also were starting to question what was going on in

Vietnam. It was a time of change, although it hadn't started the avalanche that would affect us all.

In baseball, we still were dependent on the manager's whims. We weren't free agents, hadn't even heard of the term. Strike? Picket? I was never in favor of those tactics, and I did what I was told, just as we all did. We griped, but we showed up for work. In 1967, a Dick Williams could still run your life.

The Red Sox training camp of 1967 was the most rigorous—and most instructive—in all the years I had been with the club. Williams was everywhere, poking into everything. It didn't matter if you were the oldest veteran, or had won a batting title, or were a rookie. He watched you slide, or make the cutoff throw, or bat. In one intrasquad game, Williams even put on an umpire's home plate gear to work a game behind the plate. And then he called a balk on one of the rookie pitchers.

"What the hell did you expect?" shouted Williams. "You wouldn't be able to get away with that in a real game."

He had strict rules that he expected everyone to follow— I had to move into the single-guys' hotel after Carol left, and he once chewed out Ted Williams for telling stories to the pitchers while they were supposed to be running in the outfield. Dick also had the pitchers playing volleyball to stay in shape when they weren't throwing. But Dick also knew how to work on each guy. Take Petrocelli. From Dick's first stint with the club as a player he remembered the kind of person Rico was and what he needed—confidence and someone who showed he cared. Rico had been fined $1,000 by Herman the year before for bugging out on us during a game when he was concerned about his wife, who had been sick. Dick didn't have time to mother everyone who needed it. That's one of the big reasons he brought up Popowski as third base coach and second-in-command. Rico would listen to Pop, who had a way with kids and wouldn't scare them. Their lockers were near each other and it was apparent that Rico's confidence was growing.

Yet, there were some players Dick worked on through the media. George Scott was one. George was a power-hitting first baseman who struck out a lot. For some reason Dick thought the way to get through to him was to make fun of his "smarts." So he'd tell writers that Scott wasn't thinking on a play, or that it was difficult to tell Scott what to do.

We were getting stronger, though. That was apparent. Reggie Smith and Mike Andrews joined us as rookies. Andrews took over second immediately and Reggie was the new center fielder. When I looked around the field at the start of camp, I was impressed that not one player was thirty years old, and only a few pitchers had reached that age.

Instead, we had a really special blend of guys in their early to mid-twenties, along with a few players such as myself who had five or six years of experience. For several years we had been adding one or two rookies at a time: Lonborg, Petrocelli, Scott, Joe Foy, Tony C., Dalton Jones. We all took instruction and listened. No one on this team thought he knew it all. How could he? We hadn't won anything. But we knew this: we were better than the ninth-place team of 1966. Who cared that in Las Vegas, an oddsmaker named Jimmy (the Greek) Snyder had us at 100–1 to finish first?

Not many people thought of us as being much better. You stay on the bottom for so long, it becomes an accepted way of life—not only for you but for those who watch you. Our fans had come to accept the inevitability of defeat. I think they were like a lover who has been jilted so often that he finally says, "It's not in the cards for me." Look at how poorly the team had done in every one of my six years here, those second-division finishes and the succession of ridiculous events that symbolized the kind of team we were: the game we hit into six double plays, or one in which we struck out seventeen times, five seasons without a 20-game winner, a crowd of 461 for a Fenway home game, a season's record of 1–17 against the Twins, the 1961 Rookie of the Year fiasco (when everyone predicted that I would win it), Don Schwall, who hurt his arm the next year and was traded. And these followed close-but-no-cigar finishes when the team really was good, when it had Ted Williams and Bobby Doerr and Johnny Pesky and Mel Parnell and Ellis Kinder. Good teams, bad teams—it never seemed to matter up in Boston. The Sox always found a way to blow it.

But you couldn't tell that to Dick Williams. He had precise schedules and you had better adhere to them. A couple of guys were late because they didn't get a wake-up call. He hauled them into his office and grabbed the telephone, called the hotel, and started to scream at the manager. The operators never missed making a call again, and no one came late, either. If you weren't hustling, Williams said, "I don't care who you are, you're gonna be sent down."

The tough exhibition season finally ended and we moved up North, back to Fenway, for Opening Day. Opening Day is such a national holiday that it doesn't even need Congress to make it official. It's already capitalized.

As far as I was concerned, I always wanted Opening Day to be someplace else. The first thing I would do when the new baseball schedules came out in the winter was to look at where we were going to be playing in April and May. I estimate I lost 5 or 6 homers every year in Fenway because of the wind that blows in from right during those months. The wind played havoc with my mind.

I guess I never stopped being psyched in this ballpark. The first thing thing I'd do in the morning—and it became an obsession with me—was to listen to every goddam weather report there was. I'd tune in to every TV station, listening to what the wind currents were. If there was a chill in the air, I knew the wind was blowing in. And when I got to the park, the first thing I did when I got out of the car—before I even went into the clubhouse—was to go right into the stands and see which way the wind was blowing. That used to set my mood. If the damn flag was blowing in from right field, I'd get ticked off. I'd sit in front of my locker and think, *I'll have to change my style a little bit.* The northeast wind would come in off right in April and May, and forget it. No chance to hit it out.

I'd just as soon play our April and May games on the road. In September, there'd be days when you could get a break. The rest of the time, that wind would sour me and I had to adjust. Maybe it was just me, as it was with so many other little things that didn't seem to upset other ballplayers. Ted Williams never changed his style when that wind came in. But me, I'd start thinking, *Damn, I'll just try to hit ground balls up the middle.*

I never came to understand it or accept it. I just knew I had to change, hated to see the ball die like that. It was tough enough trying to drive it 380 feet. The worst thing was to get that long homestand in April or May.

I knew before the season that I needed to be stronger. No one on the club had driven in 100 runs since Stuart left. I wanted to be that man, to become a slugger, to hit more than 20 homers. We didn't have enough home run hitters and the club needed one.

Now that I had graduated from college, I was free in the off-season. It was the first time I was able to put in an all-out effort working out once the season ended. At Notre Dame I didn't have the equipment to prepare for the baseball season and there certainly wasn't much I could do at Merrimack except study.

For some time I had been friendly with the people at the Colonial Country Club in Wakefield, not far from our home in Lynnfield. Over dinner one night I mentioned that I wanted to begin a program of light exercise, something to get me ready for the season.

"Have you ever met Gene Berde?" one of my friends asked. "He runs our health club."

Gene Berde (he pronounced it *bird-ee)* was a fabulous little guy from Hungary, where he had been an Olympic coach. He was intent on proving that European athletes were superior to Americans, and I was going to prove him right.

"Big shot, huh?" were his first words to me. Here was this five-foot six-inch pipsqueak and he started off by jabbing me in the stomach and saying, "Okay, it will be hard, but we'll get you in shape."

His first workout nearly killed me.

He kept saying, "Big league ballplayer, huh? Sure. You're not in shape. You've got a lot of work to do to get in shape. In Hungary, you a big joke."

It didn't take me long to see how he operated. His emphasis was on speed and endurance. And motivation. Get you angry. He started me off with calisthenics, and then switched to other exercises—sit-ups, push-ups, a sprint. Berde wouldn't let me take a break. I don't know how long that first workout lasted—maybe fifteen minutes—but I was bent over, gasping and sweating.

"Okay for today," he said. "You coming back tomorrow?"

"Sure sure," I answered. Neither one of us believed it.

But when I got home I started to feel really good about what I had done. And I wondered, *Just how far can I go?* As a kid, hadn't I been obsessed with just this sort of thing, only on a different level? I was back the next day.

I quickly discovered that the first workout was only the beginning. Berde was a fanatic about using the same training techniques that boxers employed. I believe he was a European boxing champion. He'd have me on the speed bag, then jumping rope, then lifting weights. After all that, he'd hand me a bat and tell me to swing it repeatedly. I never had a break. It was a constant tearing down and building up. Ninety minutes, two hours, two and a half hours a day, six days a week.

I'd be doing some exercises, and all of a sudden Berde would shout, "Stop! Climb the rope!" Up and down that rope, and then it would be "Okay, chin yourself." I'd hang in the air and he'd make me swing backward. I thought my arms would tear out of their sockets. He wasn't through. "Jump rope!" And I'd skip rope for three minutes.

We didn't have a running track and it was getting cold. No matter. I did sprints down the hallway on the first floor of the Colonial. There I was, dashing through the halls, past the hotel rooms. If someone opened a door, I'd have to pull up short to avoid hitting him. Sometimes people would open their doors, see me coming, and they'd be so scared that they'd run back into their rooms. It didn't matter that it was wintertime—"Okay, outside!" There was snow on the ground and there I was, sprinting outside the building, going around it a few times. Then back inside, swinging a lead bat. A lot of the exercises ended with me hoisting that bat, thinking, *This is what it's all about. This bat is why I just busted my butt for two hours. To pick up this thing.* Boy, that Berde was something.

One day I suddenly realized that it was all paying off. I felt stronger. I had endurance. I moved smartly through his routine. At our last session Berde slapped me in the stomach and said, "Yaz, you're going to have your best year ever."

When I got to spring training, I could feel the difference. In 1966, I hit only .198 against lefties. But in an exhibition game I hit two homers off a Cardinals' southpaw, Al Jackson. I said to myself, *I'm going to change my whole batting style. I'm stronger. I'm going to become a pull hitter.* I stayed with it in spring training and I was successful, and I thought, *No matter what kind of start I have, I'll stick with it in the season.*

• • •

Opening Day. I got up feeling the chill in the air. Wind blowing in—no doubt about it. Thank God the game was called because of those winds, which hit forty miles an hour. We opened a day later in the cold and wind, of course, and beat the White Sox. We beat them with some scratching and clawing, which felt good. To be successful over the course of a year, you've got to win games in which you get lucky or take advantage of odd things that happen. We got the winning run in the sixth. Jose Tartabull was on second, which he reached after getting an infield hit and then stealing. I hit a grounder to Ron Hansen at short, but he threw it away and Tartabull scored. We kept the lead in the ninth, with Conigliaro and Scott making outstanding fielding plays.

Two days later we opened a weekend series against the Yankees in New York. Maybe that first game in New York was the one that made us start to think we could really do it: win something that was important to us and win it for one of us. That helps make a team, too.

We had a rookie southpaw named Bill Rohr who had looked good in spring training, so Dick put him into the starting rotation. Some of us were laughing before the game at the kid's nervousness. He was so edgy the night before that he switched roommates, from Bob Tillman to Lonborg. Rohr figured that Lonborg knew the Yankees better, so he kept asking him questions about how to pitch to Tom Tresh or Mickey Mantle or Elston Howard.

The Yankees' dynasty may have been over, but they still could put out a lineup that impressed you: Whitey Ford was starting; Mantle, who had pulled a thigh muscle, could pinch-hit; Howard was catching; Joe Pepitone was at first; Tresh was in left. It was still a time when Mrs. Babe Ruth and Mrs. Lou Gehrig were on hand for home opener ceremonies, with Major John Lindsay throwing out the first ball. Jackie Kennedy was there with her son, John-John. Two old friends also were there: Lee MacPhail, who tried to sign me for the Yankees, was now their vice president, and Joe Cronin, who did sign me, was the president of the American League.

For us, Reggie Smith was now playing second base. Andrews had been bothered by a bad back in spring training but hadn't told Williams about it. The story was that Mike either was weight lifting or hoisting heavy crates onto trucks in an off-season job in a warehouse. Williams discovered the injury during an exhibition game when Mike couldn't bend down for a grounder. That teed off Williams, who sent Andrews to the bench and moved Reggie in from center. I was in left, Foy at third, Conigliaro in right, Scott at first, George Thomas in center, Petrocelli at short, and Russ Gibson was catching.

Of course, I wasn't aware at the time how one game symbolizes an era—or the end of one. But that was to be the last Yankee Stadium opener for Whitey Ford, who retired during the 1967 season. And it was the last one in a Yankee uniform for Elston Howard, who joined the Red Sox late in the season.

What happened that day nearly made the record books. Rohr, in his very first game, had a no-hitter until two outs, two strikes in the ninth. Pitchers had hurled no-hitters in their first start, but no one in his first appearance on the mound. From about the sixth inning on, all of us were pulling for the kid and it's exactly that sort of situation that whips a team together.

Smith led off the game with a homer, and then Ford was tough. Meanwhile, Rohr retired the first ten batters. He was working under pressure most of the way, with that 1–10 lead. In the sixth, Horace Clarke hit a sinking liner to left that I caught running in. Then Bill Robinson smashed the ball off Rohr's foot, but it caromed to Foy at third and Joe threw to first in time.

Then came the ninth. There wasn't much of a crowd—about fourteen thousand—but they gave Rohr a standing ovation when he took the mound. People in left were encouraging me to help the kid out if I could. Tom Tresh led off and worked the count to 3–2. He tagged Rohr's next pitch. He drove it deep to left, way over my head. As soon as he hit it, I was glad I was in a big park. I knew that the ball was going to stay in. Now, if I could just reach the damn thing. I chased it at full speed, running with my back to the plate. I turned to take another look as it was coming down and I knew I might not be able to outrun it. *What the hell.* I dived for it. And caught it with my glove, then somersaulted forward. The New York fans whooped and hollered. Later, the kid said to me, "Yaz, after you did that, I wanted to pitch a no-hitter for you. It was the greatest catch I ever saw in my life." It was a pretty good catch, I'll say, but circumstances tend to make good plays seem even better.

The kid hung tough. Pepitone hit a high fly to Conigliaro in short right. That brought up Howard. In his three at-bats, he had grounded out, flied out on a hard shot to center, and fouled out. Never saw a curveball. All fastballs. Williams went to the mound to remind Rohr that Howard, a right-handed hitter, liked to swing at the first pitch.

"Throw it outside into the dirt," Williams told him. "He's a dangerous first-ball hitter." Then he patted Rohr on the fanny and walked off the mound. Rohr got Howard to swing and miss on the first pitch—outside and into the dirt. Howard then took a ball and a strike. Now, for the first time all day, Rohr threw Howard a curve. It was low and away. Rohr tried again, this time on the corner. You could tell Gibson behind the plate thought it was strike three. But Cal Drummond, the home plate umpire, hesitated for a second and then said no.

Rohr told me later, "I thought I'd throw him another curve. I didn't think he'd expect three straight."

But the curve didn't curve. It stayed flat. Howard drilled it over the second baseman's head into right center. A base hit. And for the first time in his career at Yankee Stadium, the crowd booed Howard like crazy. Mrs. Kennedy, though, hugged John-John with delight. I guess she was a Yankee fan, even with her Boston connections.

"Hay, I've got three kids to feed," Ellie said later. Imagine, he had to be defensive about getting a hit in front of his own fans. Ellie was such a good guy, though, he really might have felt a little funny about it.

After the hit, Charley Smith flied out to right and it was over. We mobbed the kid and we were all genuinely happy for him. Mrs. Kennedy was even among the well-wishers. Williams surprised me when he second-guessed himself somewhat. "Maybe I shouldn't have come out before he pitched to Howard," Dick said. Well, in one-hitters there are lots of "maybes." Still, because he had come so close to making history in New York, Billy became an instant celebrity. When our series ended on Sunday, we all went home, but he stayed. That night he officially became famous. Billy was on "The Ed Sullivan Show."

His one-hitter kicked off a wild weekend, a wild season. How could you ever figure that, before the year was out,

Howard would wind up playing for us, and that Rohr would be down in the minors?

We were exhausted after that opening weekend. Mel Stottlemyre shut us out the next day and then on Sunday we played the longest game ever so early in the season. It lasted eighteen innings, took almost six hours, and the temperature was in the forties most of the time. Reading about the stats the next day, I shook my head: almost six hundred pitches, thirty-five hits, twelve pitchers. They won it on a hit by Pepitone. I had a big game, 5 for 8, and tripled my first two times up. When you play that many innings, you have a lot of chances to win. Dick Williams, though, seemed to save all his anger for Scott.

George went 1 for 8, but worse, he struck out his last three at-bats and left seven runners in scoring position. Then Dick issued his famous blast: "Talking to Scott is like talking to a cement wall."

That bothered me. The next day I showed up at the park, even though Dick had given me the day off. I had to talk to him about what he had said. We didn't have many conflicts in his three years with us, but the ones we had were beauts. He usually let me do whatever I wanted. Most of my complaints with him, though, were about how he treated other players. I didn't like it. He had a habit of going to the press. So when he knocked Boomer with his "cement" comment, I got angry.

"Why don't you bring him into your office and talk to him in private?" I asked Dick. But he was stubborn. I know this: if I had read in the papers that talking to Yaz was like talking to cement, I wouldn't have played for the guy. Dick also was hard on the guys who were trying to hang on, the twenty-third, twenty-fourth, twenty-fifth guys. It really got much worse in 1968, though. In 1967, he was trying to get something out of them. Still, you had to give Dick credit for a new attitude. Strictly baseball. The clubhouse no longer was lax. The manager wasn't talking before a game about what he had shot on the golf course. So I guess Dick was a necessity. He loved being right. Over the season, Scott was caught twice tagging off third too early, and each time you could see Dick shaking his head, like *I knew it.* I ran into problems with him in 1968. The guys who helped him win the pennant in 1967 —Jerry Adair, Scott, Jose Tartabull—I stuck up for them in 1968. That's where we had some friction.

Rohr wasn't in Dick's doghouse at the time. A week after the one-hitter, the kid beat the Yankees again. He lost a shutout in the eighth, when Howard singled in a run. Who knew it was the last victory Rohr would ever have for us, that he would win only one more game in his big league career?

As April drew to a close, we were keeping our heads above water, winning more than we were losing. That was a change in itself. Then we had another game for our memory bank. We blew an early lead against Kansas City, and struggled into the fifteenth. They took a 1–9 lead. But in the bottom of the inning Tartabull hit a two-run single and guess what? We were tied for first. I got so excited in the locker room, I shouted, "We can do it!"

I really started to get a little worried about myself, though. I had only 2 homers when May began. My hitting had been tailing off. Finally, Williams benched me after we went through a four-game losing streak. What the heck, he had done it to everyone else, or had lifted other guys for pinch-hitters. Williams, though, had to defend it, and he told a newspaper reporter, "I don't care how much they're making. I'm trying to win ball games." There really wasn't very much I could say. When the newspeople talked to me about it, I sidestepped the question.

Williams would try to make an example of anyone, at any time. It was as if he looked for situations to make his point. In early May, Lonborg lost a no-hitter against the Angels in the seventh, then lost a shutout and the whole game in the ninth by 2–1. The winning run scored on a wild pitch. When it was over, Rico ran over to Jim as they headed for the dugout and said, "Good game, Jim. Tough luck."

"Tough luck? My ass!" shouted Williams. Lonborg started jawing with him, but what was the use?

What the heck is going on here? I wondered. *A kid almost pitches a no-hitter, we almost win, and the manager gets angry.* If you think about it, that was Williams's way of insisting that mediocrity wasn't good enough, that coming close wouldn't count with him. He had lost eight games at that point, and five had been by one run. Coincidence? Maybe. But Lonborg's attitude on the mound changed after that. He was meaner and I had the feeling that he would never throw a wild pitch again to lose a game.

Even though it was only mid-May, I was struggling and needed help. I had the same 2 homers I had started the month with—the only 2 homers in the twenty-four games I played. The power I had expected from my off-season conditioning was there, but I wasn't using it properly because my swing was off. We got bombed on a Saturday when the Tigers got six runs in the ninth, all against John Wyatt. Williams—stubborn, or maybe trying to make some kind of point with his pitcher—refused to lift Wyatt, who had done an outstanding job in every relief appearance until then.

After the game I told Bobby Doerr I needed help. Bobby was our batting and first base coach, but Sox fans knew him better as their great second baseman of the 1940s. He was going to make the Hall of Fame. He could hit, field, and drive in runs. I told him I needed him immediately. The next morning, at nine o'clock, before facing the Tigers in a doubleheader, Bobby watched me hit. I was popping some of the pitches up, not hitting them solidly, and after they took off, they'd die.

"I think you ought to try holding your bat higher," Bobby said, "maybe as high as your left ear." I raised my arms to Stan the Man level once again. The next pitch came in and I whacked it on a line over the pitcher's net. Then another pitch, another liner. I was getting my arms around quicker by holding them higher, and striking the ball level. I not only was driving it, I was pulling it. It felt good. Real good. So good that I stayed with it for eight years. I only dropped my hands once again, after I had reached the age of thirty-five, because of a shoulder injury that made it too painful to keep them high.

In my first at-bat with the new stance, I faced McLain. I had started off my big cycle game against him two years earlier. This time I homered into the center field bleachers. *Now, this is more like it,* I thought. *This is why I spent all those hours with that crazy Hungarian.* In the second game I hit another one out. In one afternoon I had equaled my output for the season. We won both games as I broke out with a 3 for 8 afternoon, 3 RBIs and 4 runs scored. More importantly, we won. Williams should have been happy, right?

He always got defensive when he was second-guessed about a move. The morning papers ripped him over leaving Wyatt in for so long. Some of the other pitchers even griped (anonymously, of course) to the writers, claiming that a manager should never embarrass a guy by doing that. So after we beat the Tigers, Williams flipped the writers the bird, so to speak. He refused to talk to them after the games.

We moved out of our slump, which had dropped us below .500. Chicago and Detroit had jumped out to the best records in the league, and a bunch of teams were trying to chase them. Some good things began to develop for the Sox: after his benching, Scott returned and started to hit. He wasn't swinging from the heels as ferociously, which pleased Williams. Our pitching was a problem, with only Lonborg pitching consistently well. No question, he was our stopper. Jim showed guts and was willing to knock down one of another team's players if one of their pitchers knocked one of us down. There was a classic game in late May, a workingman's performance, when he bore down in the clutch against the Tigers and McLain. The only run was Dalton Jones's homer in the second. Jones didn't start many games at third, but Williams knew that he could hit at Tiger Stadium. So Jones, a left-handed hitter, played instead of Foy, a righty batter. Lonborg pitched out of a first-and-third situation in the second, a bases-loaded jam in the seventh, and a man-on-third situation in the eighth. Scott, whom Williams believed was as fine a fielder as

Dick's old Dodger teammate, Gil Hodges, made another great play to preserve the shutout in the seventh. With the bases filled, Scott charged a slow grounder by Dick McAuliffe and zipped the ball home to get Norm Cash on the force. Lonborg went on to strike out eleven batters. He was our guy. We called him Gentleman Jim, but that was *off* the field.

Brief visions flash back of the pennant run that people still feel compelled to talk to me about. It's as if they're spilling out their childhood, or their fondest memories, and I was a part of it. They recall a hit there, a strikeout here, a catch by one of their heroes. They remember cutting school on a certain day when we did this, or being at the park when something special happened. The thing is, I remember them, too. Maybe not all 162 games, and maybe the things I remember aren't always what most fans remember. But we both share the sense that this season was "impossible," or "a miracle," or "magical." The truth is, it *was.* And it was also very funny at times.

We finished the month of May with a four-game winning streak and we were ecstatic. I hit a pair out against the Angels and we were 22–20 after Memorial Day. For the first time, you could see my name among the leaders in batting (I was up to .299, still forty-eight points behind Kaline), in homers (at 10, I trailed Frank Robinson of the Orioles by 4), and in RBIs (Robinson led with 37, while I had 30). Robinson seemed on his way to another Triple Crown title, since he also was batting .333. The year before he had been the first Triple Crown winner in baseball in a decade. I had some vague awareness of this fact, but what seemed most important was that my slugging was helping us win—finally.

Then we got support from the front office. It wasn't business as usual and when a player knows that, it's a tremendous help. The O'Connell-Sullivan front-office team made two big moves in early June. In Fenway, you've got to have a good right-handed pitcher to stop those right-handed batters from reaching the Wall. But except for Lonborg (who was 7–1), our righty starters couldn't win. They had a total of 4 victories for the first two months. So we made a deal to get Gary Bell from the Indians, where he was only 1–5. He became a 12–8 pitcher for us. We also acquired Jerry Adair, one of our biggest moves of the season. He was hitting only .204 for the White Sox, but he wound up playing second, third, and short for us, while batting .291.

Now I was really grooving. I had a four-hit game against the White Sox in Bell's debut. In a six-game road trip I was 11 for 22. Even more, I was fielding so easily, making the plays. I was even stealing bases. Baseball was fun again, the kind of fun I missed since playing with all the Yastrzemskis and Skoniecznys.

When you're having fun, you laugh. That's what I did one morning in the middle of June when we were about to play the White Sox. I was reading the paper about our game coming up and the Chicago manager, Eddie Stanky, was being quoted. All of a sudden this quote of Stanky's hit me: "Yastrzemski is an All-Star from the neck down." Now what the heck was he trying to do? Of course, he was giving me the needle, trying to upset me. But more than that, it meant that he was worried about us. The White Sox were in first, and he obviously was taking us seriously. It was one of the first indications I had that someone other than the Red Sox players and their fans were serious about us. He was always a loudmouth. As a player, wasn't he known as the Brat? And as a manager, he tried some tricky maneuvers. After Adair was traded to the Red Sox, he accused Stanky of using a damp, musty storage room for baseballs so that they would lose their pop and get heavy. Stank had a weak-hitting team with slow infielders. A heavy ball could help his guys.

"I'm surprised their pitchers don't get sore arms throwing those balls," Adair told us. He also warned us that the way the White Sox watered their field so heavily and kept the grass so high, Hansen had time to get to the grounders at short. I knew all this about Stanky, and I knew that some guys could be hurt by his needling. I was going to handle it, take it better than he could dish it out.

That afternoon, in the second game of a doubleheader, I was up for my final at-bat. I hit the ball out of the park. As I trotted toward third, I tipped my cap at Stanky. Not a bad day. I was 6 for 9.

We gave Stanky something more to worry about the next day. How about a scoreless game through ten innings? That is a rarity and another significant event in the making of a pennant-winner. Gary Waslewski came as close as he would to pitching a complete game (he never did that season) by keeping the White Sox off the boards for nine innings before he suffered back spasms and was relieved in the tenth by Wyatt. Meanwhile, Bruce Howard of Chicago stopped us for seven, then Hoyt Wilhelm, who was forty-three years old and still a damn good pitcher, kept us checked for two more innings. John Buzhardt relieved him in the tenth. When was the last time you saw a scoreless game go into extra innings? In the top of the eleventh, Scott saved us. Walt (No Neck) Williams led off with a double and we all expected Don Buford to bunt him to third. So Scott charged in from first when Buford crossed him up and swung away. He drilled a liner down the first base line, but Scott dived for it and snared it. Williams scored anyway on Ken Berry's single. I led off the bottom of the inning on a pop-up and then Scott made the second out. Foy kept us breathing, though, with a single. "We're alive!" we shouted in the dugout. "Keep it going!"

Conigliaro stepped up. He'd been having some trouble lately, following his annual two-week summer tour of duty in the Army Reserves. Tony missed the first two pitches, both curves. But Buzhardt missed with his next three pitches. You can't get it any better, or more nerve-racking, than 3–2, bottom of the eleventh, man on, down by a run. The next pitch was gone. Tony whacked it high into the net and it was the Fourth of July in the dugout. Tony had this funny style of running around the bases after he hit a homer. His head was down, almost as if he was ashamed. Or maybe he didn't want to show up the pitcher. Anyway, when he got to third he looked up and—surprise!—we were all standing around home plate. That set him off. He started hopping up and down, and for the final ninety feet between third and home Tony C. was jumping and jogging until he touched the plate and we mobbed him.

There are some victories you can say you won because the other side blew it. Or you know you simply had luck on your side. But this was one we earned, that we scratched and fought for, and dammit, it was ours. The dramatics of that victory served as another signal to us that we could overcome almost anything because we had this crazy idea that we could. It didn't matter that Stanky accused Wyatt of throwing a Vaseline ball, his version of the spitter. Scott confused the issue by admitting that Wyatt really did. But Wyatt used to laugh and say, "It's all an act." The thing is, whether it was or wasn't, Wyatt had the other guys thinking he was loading up the ball. Nothing like needling Stanky, I always said.

When you think about what makes a winning team, you have to start with talent. But how many clubs have even half a dozen dominant players? Over the course of 162 games, a lot of victories come down to this: how much are you still in the game when others might have already given up? For us, for that season, we never were out of a game again. And that desire—that idea that no matter what, we could come back—was always there. We never quit. That means we won some games we would have lost if didn't have that confidence. You give up, not consciously, but somehow that spark would have been missing. That couldn't happen to us again, at least not that season.

In late June we went into Yankee Stadium. Our record was at .500, and the Yankees . . . well, their dynasty was over. But the won-lost records of the teams never really told you anything about the Yankees-Red Sox. It was a rivalry almost of cultures—the New Englanders against the New Yorkers—as it was anything else. And for us and our fans, it was one of frustration that made hating the Yankees so easy.

You can't be on the Red Sox for very long before the sad history is brought up to you. Sure, the Sox have had great teams over the years, and great players. But the Yankees were the ones who took what could have been our greatest years away from us.

Every Sox fan knows how we lost Babe Ruth to the Yankees, after Ruth not only was established as the best home run hitter in baseball but also was Boston's greatest pitcher since the days of Cy Young. When I broke in, Babe Ruth's American League record for southpaws of 9 shutouts in a season still stood. But after the 1919 season, the Red Sox owner, Harry Frazee, needed money. So he not only sold Ruth to the Yankees for $125,000, Frazee also mortgaged Fenway to them. The Yankees had the mortgage on Fenway Park! If he defaulted, the Yankees could be our landlords. With this sort of insider dealings, the Yankees picked us clean over the next ten years. Frazee was long gone by then—he went to Broadway and produced *No, No, Nanette!*—but the Yankees still got healthy by raiding us of stars: Waite Hoyt, Herb Pennock, Carl Mays, Ernie Shore, Joe Dugan. Every time a Sox fan looked at a Yankee pennant, he had to be bitter over what those guys were doing in New York uniforms, and what it could have been like having them in Boston.

Who knows where it would have led? The Babe had the best won-lost record against the Yankees of any pitcher who won at least 15 games against them. By Ruth's last year with the Sox, the manager, Ed Barrow, had come to realize that Ruth was going to be the slugger, not the pitcher. He hit more home runs (29) than the first-place White Sox did as a team. He led the majors in runs scored with 103 and runs batted in with 114 and slugging percentage with .657. He was also only twenty-four years old.

You know this when you're on Boston. Somehow I don't think the Yankee players were as aware of this anger that people had who follow Boston. Yankee fans always assumed their team attracted great players because it was a Yankee birthright. Who else should the Babe or Gehrig or Mantle play for? Over the years the two teams had historical connections: the Babe hit his first homer against the Yankees, Ted

Williams his first hit, my three thousandth. The Yankees in 1949 also stopped Dom DiMaggio's thirty-four-game hitting streak—the longest in the American League since brother Joe's 56-game record of 1941. Joe had broken Willie Keeler's record of 44 against Boston. Lou Gehrig's first homer came against the Sox. And then there were the Williams-DiMaggio stories: how Joe beat out Ted for the MVP Award in 1941, even though Ted batted .406. Or how, in 1947, Tom Yawkey agreed to trade Williams to the Yankees for DiMaggio. It happened at Toots Shor's one late night. It could have resolved a controversy that had been going on for almost ten years: How would Ted have done in the Stadium, with its short porch in right, and how would Joe have made out in Fenway, with the short Wall. In the morning though, Tom changed his mind and called the Yankees' owner, Dan Topping. He told Topping that the people in Boston wouldn't stand for such a deal, as great as DiMaggio was. Williams been sensational in 1946, and was four years younger than Joe.

"Throw in your little left fielder, Berra," Yawkey said. Yogi wasn't established as a catcher yet, but Topping nixed the deal and that was that.

Although it had been almost twenty years since we were battling each other for a pennant, both of us still got excited about meeting. We grabbed a 4–0 lead in the first against Thad Tillotson. He was ticked, naturally. It really wasn't surprising that when Foy got up in the second inning, Tillotson sent him down in a heap by zinging him with a fastball to the helmet. Foy had hit a grand slam the night before. Foy was able to get up, but didn't retaliate. Joe just stared at Tillotson and ran to first. Foy came home and we had a 5–0 lead. Lonborg, though, was growling about the beaning. Lonborg had become a mean pitcher in 1967. In the other years on the mound, he was just like he was off it—a nice guy, just what you'd expect from a Stanford graduate who listened to classical music. In the off-season he dropped fifteen pounds and had become leaner, as well as meaner. Sal Maglie, our pitching coach, was known as the Barber in his great days with the Giants. He got the nickname because he shaved batters very close. In 1967, Maglie gave this advice to the staff: "Keep the ball low, and throw it as hard as you can as long as you can. We'll get you a bullpen to bail you out." He also expected his pitchers to knock guys down if the situation called for it.

So Lonborg, who always had a big fastball, with which he could intimidate batters, finally learned to use it that way. He came into New York leading the league in strikeouts and hit batsmen. Jim wasn't about to send any "messages" by coming close to just any batter. He went right at Tillotson himself. When Tillotson got up in the second, Lonborg immediately hit him on the shoulder with a fastball.

Tillotson started to run to first, and then shouted at Lonborg, "You're gonna be up again!" Foy, still mad at being beaned himself, started walking toward the mound and screamed at Tillotson, "If you've got any ideas, you'll have to get past me first." Suddenly, Scott moved toward Tillotson and both benches spilled onto the field. It was sort of funny, as these baseball brawls usually are. How it got nasty I don't know. Maybe it was because Pepitone, who was being wrestled to the ground, picked up a handful of dirt and tossed it toward Petrocelli. The two were old friends from Brooklyn, and always kidded each other. But someone, I think it was Scott, grabbed Joe for throwing the dirt. Pepitone had a thing about his hair. He was the first ballplayer to bring along a blow-dryer on road trips. He started screaming because his hair was messed up. Now it was really a pile of bodies. We all wore spikes then—no cleats yet—and when you were tussling with somebody who went down, you made sure his spikes didn't get you. I stuck my hands in the pile and bear hugged someone. It turned out to be Ralph Houk, the old war hero. I let go of *him* in a hurry.

Pretty soon the Stadium police came in and one of them started pulling some of the Yankees off Petrocelli. *What the heck is this?* I wondered. It turned out it was Rico's brother. He was a Stadium cop. Through all this, nobody was ejected.

We got back to playing, but the beanball war didn't stop. In the third, Tillotson served some chin music to Smith, knocking him down. Two innings later, Lonborg hit Dick Howser on the helmet. Jim won the game, bringing his record to 9–2 (we were 24–29 when he wasn't involved in the decision). We were tied for third with Cleveland, six games behind the league-leading White Sox, and two and a half behind the Tigers.

We were not a consistent team yet, but I thought it was coming, that we were on the verge of putting together a streak. Then we suffered the first major injury of the season against the Indians. Rico was hit on the left wrist. It concerned me because the team's chemistry could be badly messed up. But Adair went right to short and started producing immediately in the clutch as well. We all felt bad when Rohr was sent down the end of June, but Adair's play picked us up. He was in for Rico for one month, and we broke out. He played errorless ball in twenty-eight games, and we won nineteen. Jerry was a quiet guy who stayed by himself in the locker room and after games. We found out later that he had a son who was dying of cancer. But when it came to performing on the field, Jerry never showed the effects of worrying. Even when Rico returned, Williams made sure that Adair was somewhere in the lineup.

Sparky Lyle, who was going to become another outstanding player that we would deal away to the Yankees, joined us as a rookie in early July. He coolly pitched the last two innings in a loss to the Angels and impressed everyone on the team with his attitude. But that started a losing streak that we brought into Detroit on the weekend before the All-Star Game. That's the annual midseason point, supposedly a predictor of where you're going to finish. It has symbolic importance for everyone in the game. But we lost our first three games in Detroit, including the opener of the Sunday doubleheader. Five straight losses. Suddenly, we had a must game. No way we were going to go into the All-Star break with a six-game losing streak. And if we lost, we'd have gone back to .500. It was appropriate that Lonborg was the guy who was going to try to give us some momentum going into the second half.

It was a an awful day to play ball—*any* sort of ball. It was so hot and muggy that Jim could last only seven innings, even though he was shutting out the Tigers. We could tell something strange was happening to him as the result of dehydration. In the sixth inning on the bench, he was talking about how he had just struck out a guy with a curveball—except that had happened three innings before. Jim was disoriented, yet he continued to blow down the Tigers. He wouldn't give in to them or the heat. But Williams lifted him after seven shutout innings—and after dropping twelve pounds. We scored our runs on a two-run shot by Smith and my solo homer. With a five-hit afternoon, I had broken out of small slump. A victory like this, with a couple of homers and a big pitching performance, is just how you want to establish the tempo for the rest of the year. It was a great way to go into the break. In half a season, I already had 19 homers, just one under my season's high for the last six years. We were fifth at the turn, with a 41–39 record, six games behind the White Sox, with Detroit second, Minnesota—playing 20–11 under their new manager, Cal Ermer—in third, and California fourth.

How tickled I was for this game, more than most of the fourteen I was to play in. Here we were, four Red Sox players going to an All-Star Game: Rico, Tony C., and me starting, and Lonborg selected as a pitcher. None of us even was twenty-eight years old, and it told me that this Sox team of ours had a bright future. Tony actually wasn't voted in as a first-stringer, but earlier that week, Kaline and Robinson both had gotten injured. Al fractured a thumb when he got angry after striking out and broke his bat when he jammed it into the rack, while Frank was having double vision following a base-running collision. Both of them were ahead of me in the batting race. I looked forward to the All-Star Game in

Anaheim, which also was a symbol of the new wave in baseball. It was on prime-time TV back East for the first time.

I got on base five times, with three hits and two walks,
and guess who greeted me like a long-lost brother each time?
The first base coach—Stanky. "Good eye, Yaz," he said to me
when I got on with my first walk, and he put his arms on my
shoulders. When I got on with a hit, he congratulated me,
"Way to swing the bat, Yaz." He was friendly and we chatted.

It would have been a great time for an American League
victory, especially for Boston, with so many guys in the
lineup. But neither team did much scoring. In fact, it was the
longest All-Star Game ever played, not over until the Reds'
Tony Perez hit a homer in the fifteenth to give the National
League a 2–1 victory. In the bottom of the fifteenth, the National League manager, Walt Alston of the Dodgers, showed
some guts when he put in a rookie pitcher from the Mets
named Tom Seaver to preserve the lead. He got the first two
outs and then I faced him. He was a big, confident kid with a
humming fastball. But I could tell he was being careful with
me. I walked. I didn't get past first, though, as Seaver got the
third out.

This was only the second All-Star Game I played in, although I had been voted onto it for the third time. My first
was in 1963. In 1966, I couldn't make it because of an injury.
The 1967 game was important because it showed what I could
do with big things at stake under a spotlight. It was to help me
for the rest of the season and set a pattern for me in the annual
summer game. In 1970, I was 4 for 6 in the game and voted
MVP, tying a record by getting three singles. In 1975, I became one of the few players in an All-Star Game to hit a
homer as a pinch-hitter. In 1979, I was 2 for 3 at the age of
thirty-nine. Overall, I batted higher in the All-Star Games
than I did for my career. I hit .294 with 10 hits in 34 at-bats
with 1 homer, 2 doubles, 5 RBIs, and 2 runs scored. Look at
the biggest games the Sox played in my twenty-three seasons:
I seemed to be able to raise my level of play a notch or two
when it mattered the most.

That's how the second half of 1967 became my crusade.
There finally was a reason to go all-out all the time. We split
the first two games after the break. And then we went to town
—more accurately, out of town—to extend a winning streak
to ten games, our longest since 1951.

In the second game of the streak, Russ Gibson didn't like
the way Gary Waslewski was warming up before starting
against the Orioles. Gibby went to Williams and told him that
Waslewski's stuff was hanging. Williams immediately told Santiago to warm up. A good thing, too. Waslewski walked Luis
Aparicio and Russ Snyder and then got to 2–1 on Paul Blair.
The game was ready to get out of hand before our first at-bat.
Williams, though, heaved Gary out and brought in Santiago,
who already was warm. He went to 3–2 on Blair. Hank
Bauer, the Orioles' manager, called for a hit-and-run. So everybody was off and running and Blair hit a liner to Foy's left
at third. It was a perfect triple-play ball. Foy caught it, tossed
to Andrews at second to catch Aparicio, and Andrews relayed
the ball to Scott at first. We got out of a big jam. The next day
we moved into a third-place tie with the slumping Tigers by
trouncing them. Tony C. hit one out, and I got number 21—
tops in my career. I started to wonder how high was up. Ted
Williams had once hit 43 homers for the Sox, the most by a
left-handed batter in the club's history. Until now, that record
had seemed safe from everyone. A day later, we hit the road
after beating Detroit again, this time taking over third place
all by ourselves with a four-game winning streak. With Win
number seven against Cleveland, we moved into second
place, only a game and a half out.

Detroit was fading fast. I was sure that Kaline's injury
played a factor. That angry moment when he broke his thumb
was to cost him twenty-six games. But I learned that in 1967
you couldn't count anyone out. Today's dog was tomorrow's
hero. Today's fading team could be baseball's hottest in a matter of days.

This was our turn. Now we were getting the attention
that had eluded Red Sox teams for . . . how many years was

it? We were getting attention and respect. Now, you could be a so-called Fenway Millionaire—a spoiled Red Sox player—and not be ashamed of it. We were winning, dammit. With win number eight we moved to within half a game of the White Sox. And then, with a doubleheader at Cleveland that closed the road show, we were the winners of ten straight. Lonborg captured his fifth in a row in the opener, in which Conigliaro, at the age of twenty-two and a half, became the youngest player to hit 100 career homers. Foy hit his second grand slam of the year and I socked my home run number 24. Nine in a row—and counting. After this, we'd be going back to Boston.

"Come on, guys," I said as I greeted each of them as they went through the clubhouse door. "We wanna go back with ten. Don't let up now." If being captain would have consisted of just this sort of thing, I never would have given it up. I enjoyed helping to get the guys up for the games.

We took the nightcap as Tony belted another one. We had our streak. And we were headed back to Boston.

Boston was waiting for us.

What the heck had we done, really? Yes, a great ten-game streak. But we still were in second. No matter. We had given some hope to the folks back home. For a week news bulletins had interrupted radio broadcasts with the latest about how we were doing. By keeping the streak alive, we had kept—or maybe rekindled—Boston's hopes. Not only Boston, but all of New England and all those professors and gardeners from South Bend and everyplace else who told me they had seen Babe Ruth play or their grandfathers had seen Cy Young pitch.

There was an unusual announcement on our plane ride back to Boston. The pilot got on the speaker to tell us, "Strange things are happening at Logan." I half-listened to it. For years my time on the planes was taken with playing bridge, which I had learned at Notre Dame. After I joined the Red Sox, I got nervous about flying, I think because Jensen's fears had heightened mine. So playing bridge kept me occupied. From the moment I sat down until we landed, that's what I'd do. The worst parts for me was when I was the dummy and had to sit out the hand. I walked around the plane and would talk to people—obsessively, I see now. I was always asking questions, always attempting to get someone in a conversation, anything to take my mind off flying. I got over it, or at least came to accept flying without having to get out of my seat.

When we taxied at Logan Airport, we realized what the pilot was talking about. The biggest mob I had ever seen, estimated at fifteen thousand fans, was waiting for us. When the doubleheader had ended, the broadcasters announced what time we were getting back home. That was standard procedure, so that wives and friends could meet us back at the airport. Now, though, everyone else was there, too. Hundreds of people had gotten onto the tarmac, and there was no way we could get out of the plane and onto the buses that were waiting. So the plane moved over to the private aviation area away from the main terminal. There, we got into buses for the trip to the United Airlines terminal so we could meet our families and get our cars.

The fans wouldn't let us get out of the bus. They were shaking it, as if by grabbing a piece of the bus they somehow were snatching a souvenir. We were rocking back and forth inside the bus and didn't know whether to be scared or to laugh. Mostly, we enjoyed it. The next day O'Connell made a decision: "No more radio announcements about travel plans."

We dropped our first game back against the Angels. No matter. We won the next one and then staged a comeback that was a symbol of what we were capable of and were going to do repeatedly. My home run in the first and Scott's in the second gave us an early lead, but by the time the ninth started we were down by 5–2 as Jim McGlothlin had snuffed us. But Andrews led off with a single and Foy, who said later he was only trying to keep the ball out of the infield and a double play, homered into the screen. Now we were one run down.

The crowd was on its feet. They expected—maybe "demanded" is a better word—something to happen. I quieted them by flying out. But Tony followed with another shot into the screen. Tie game. In the tenth inning, Sparky came in. He gave a single to Don Mincher. My old friend Skowron, now winding up his career, drilled the ball to left center. This was my park, though, and I took off the moment I saw the direction he tagged it. I chased it and reached out my glove and speared it. Bubba Morton followed with a grounder that Foy misplayed and they had two on, one out.

Buck Rodgers then tagged a base hit to left. I saw it coming and I saw Mincher take off from second. I charged the ball and knew exactly what I had to do as I snared it one-handed. In a sense, I played it like an infielder as I took it out of my glove and threw the ball on a line to Gibby, who was blocking the plate. We had Mincher by a mile and preserved the tie. We still had a game to win, which we did in the bottom of the tenth. Reggie tripled and Adair, pinch-hitting, hit a little grounder to third, which usually wouldn't have scored the runner. But it took a funny hop past Paul Schaal and Popowski started windmilling his arms for Smith to run home. Which he did, of course. Another come-from-behind victory, another meet-me-at-home-plate celebration, another delirious crowd, followed by a locker room celebration and Conigliaro shouting, "We cannot be beat!"

Now my fielding and my throwing was in as much of a groove as my hitting was. I felt supremely confident in any situation I found myself in. I know that feeling was shared by a lot of the other guys, especially the younger ones who didn't have a six-year tradition of losing to get in the way. For all they knew, *Hey, this is the way it's supposed to be on the Red Sox.* Two days after our comeback over the Angels, we were in a tight game with the Twins. I picked up two more assists—throwing out a runner at third for the final out of the fourth, and nipping Ted Uhlaender at the plate after he tried to score in the seventh on a fly ball by Jim Kaat. It's a good thing I did, too. We went into the eighth trailing by one run, then pulled it out when Adair tied it with a hit and Jones, pinch-hitting, grounded a ball that Cesar Tovar couldn't handle and that scored the go-ahead run.

Even when we'd lose, we came off the field thinking we really were better than the other team. The next day the Twins led us by 7–1 going into the ninth. With two outs and a runner on first, we scored four runs. I got up with runners on the corners and just got under a pitch from Jim Roland. I hit a high pop-up between home and the mound. With the crowd yelling, the Twins couldn't hear who was hollering for the ball. Rich Reese and Tovar collided as they both reached for it. Could it be possible we'd pull it out again? Reese caught it, then lost it after bouncing off Tovar. As Reese fell, he stuck out his glove in a desperate lunge and the ball plopped into it. Game over. But we knew. Sometimes the magic doesn't work exactly the way it's supposed to. Funny, in the locker room we weren't heartbroken about it, we didn't second-guess ourselves. Instead, Williams said the Twins were "lucky." The thing is, we thought so, too. Now, that's confidence.

We entered August with a 56–44 record, two games behind the White Sox. The Tigers were third, four games out, the Twins and Angels were five behind. It was a month that prepared us for the stretch run—if that is possible. We were high and low in August, sometimes delirious with victory, other times shocked by adversity. All the time, though, we were prodded by Dick Williams, who seemed to have a plan that he would not deviate from. He had brought up Dave Morehead, a pitcher with us since 1963 but who had started the season at Toronto in the International League. In 1965 he had pitched a no-hitter for us, but couldn't complete a game after that. When the Sox called him up, Toronto was playing in Columbus. Instead of coming right to Boston, Morehead stopped off in Toronto to take care of some business.

"Maybe," said Williams, "he's not used to how we do things around here. Maybe he thinks it's like the old days." After Williams lashed him, Morehead was so fidgety in his first appearance for us that he couldn't get past the A's as we opened the month of August. But things looked better in the second game as Lyle, the rookie, took over for Lonborg in the sixth inning and saved the victory while striking out four. This is the time of year you need the bullpen, the dog days of August, when it's tougher to pitch complete games. In 1967, we had 41 complete games—roughly one in four. But that was only fourth-best in the league. Almost twenty years later, in 1986, when we won the pennant, we led the entire major leagues with 36. In 1967, you were still expected to finish what you started, but realistically we knew our staff was not going to do that.

There was one essential element that our team lacked for a pennant drive—someone who had been there before. With one move we took care of that, as well as getting someone who knew more about handling pitchers than any other catcher in baseball. We picked up Elston Howard from the Yankees for two "players to be named later." We knew he wasn't going to do for us what Babe Ruth or Herb Pennock did for the Yankees after the Sox traded them to New York. Ellie was thirty-eight years old. But he had class and he had been part of a winning tradition and he was ours. He brought in a record of nine World Series and nine All-Star appearances.

Houk, who was managing the Yankees, broke the news to Howard the morning of August 3. Ellie's first reaction was: "I'm quitting." He told me later that he started to feel differently while he drove to the Stadium to get his gear. The players came over to him, some to tell him they were sorry, others to congratulate him. Phil Rizzuto said to him, "I know you feel bad, but you're much better off than I was. You're going to be a contender. I was just dropped after thirteen years." However, the Yankees did hire Phil as an announcer after he was released.

We were in Boston, playing the A's, while Howard was packing. "Elston, would you come into my office?" asked Houk. "Mr. Yawkey of the Red Sox wants to talk to you." That was a good move on our part. Mr. Yawkey told him,

"We want you in Boston and we know that you can help our club, maybe win the pennant."

Haywood Sullivan also telephoned Howard to pump him up and tell him how much we could use him. It was a smart move. Even though the Yankees were down, Howard had been a fixture on their club for thirteen years. His life centered around New York. He could have been despondent. Instead, he was in a pennant race again, even though he was going to play in front of some of the same fans who had sent him hate mail after he broke up Rohr's no-hitter earlier in the year.

There was a powerful symbolism in Howard coming to Boston. Maybe it would help reverse all those down years. It certainly showed—once and for all—that we were up and the Yankees weren't. A few months before, Whitey Ford had retired at the age of thirty-eight. Over the winter, Roger Maris had been traded to the Cardinals. Clete Boyer was on the Atlanta Braves. Bobby Richardson and Tony Kubek had retired. Jim Bouton was down in the minors. Only Mantle was left—and he was thirty-five years old and playing on bum knees. Casey Stengel was managing the Mets, baseball's joke. There was another omen of change the day we got Howard. The American League voted to begin divisional play in two years, which would end the traditional pennant-winning setup. We were in the middle of the next-to-last classic pennant race.

I always thought Howard was the best catcher I had ever seen for calling a ball game. He could handle pitchers and no one was better at setting up a hitter. He knew us all. He was also one of the last links to another era. He and Hank Aaron and Willie Mays were probably the last players in the major leagues who had also appeared in the Negro Leagues.

Meanwhile, we won that day, with Morehead and Lyle playing a big role. It was only two days after Williams had growled at Dave, who had been shelled. Everyone on the club knew how miserably he was feeling from getting hit with both barrels—his manager and the A's. Williams knew this, too, and didn't give Morehead time to sulk. In a tight game, he called on him and this time he pitched five scoreless innings in relief against the A's, gave way to Sparky, who retired the only man he faced, and Wyatt preserved the lead. I didn't drive in any runs, but I helped keep us only one run back in the sixth, when we were trailing by 3–2. Mike Hershberger was on second and Dick Green singled. The ball took its time coming to me on the grass. But I snared it on the run and cut down Hershberger at home with a strike to Mike Ryan. It gave me four assists in the club's last five games.

Still, we were groping. After the big winning streak, we were only 6–6 on the homestand. Then we went on the road and lost four straight, including a perfect game to Dean Chance. Well, it was sort of perfect. It lasted only five innings because of rain. Chance seemed almost embarrassed when it was over. His first words to the press were "Gentlemen, that was a cheapie." But it was no fluke. Later in the month (on August 25), Chance pitched a no-hitter against Cleveland— but not a perfect game. That loss to the Twins dropped us to third place, two and a half games back.

Williams started to figure out a way to snap us out of a slump—if that's what it was. Maybe it was something worse, he wondered. Maybe we were . . . *choking?* . . . under the pressure. After we dropped the first game of a doubleheader in Kansas City, he sent Reggie to the bench. He put me in center and Norm Siebern in left. Adair replaced Foy at third. We were down by three, but tied the game in the seventh against Johnny (Blue Moon) Odom. Adair played a big role in the inning with his third hit of the game. Then we won it with three in the ninth and a two-out rally. Siebern had the big hit, a bases-loaded single for two runs. Here we were with two players coming off the bench to help break a four-game slide. Sometimes mirrors help in a pennant race.

Williams would try anything. It was close to midnight before the twi-nighter ended, but Williams said that Reggie, Scott, Foy, Howard, and Jones would have to show up at 10 A.M. for a workout, along with all the coaches. Howard couldn't figure that one out. He had been bothered for more than a month, before the deal with the Yankees, with a sore finger. Ellie had missed some time in New York. He was wondering whether Williams thought he was dogging it. The trouble, as Ellie saw it, was that Williams hardly spoke to him. Howard didn't know what to think. Neither did Scott or Foy. Dick kept yakking about their weight. Joe might have been a few pounds over, and Scotty . . . Scotty and his weight were a topic during his whole big league career.

He was still in the doghouse after the doubleheader. We didn't get back to our rooms until well after 1 A.M. No matter. That afternoon, Lonborg picked up his sixteenth victory— best in the majors—with Adair driving in three runs. The A's started to get to Lonborg in the eighth. I had to chase down and one-hand a shot by Harrelson, which signaled Williams that Jim was tiring. After all, he had flown in all the way from Atlanta on a two-day pass from Army Reserve duty. Sparky took care of the victory in relief.

Dick was from the school that if you tripped on the stairs in the lobby, and you lost that day, you had better not fall over those same stairs the next game. On our previous trip to Anaheim, we had lost the last two games by a run, and some of the guys had been caught staying out late. *Aha.* Dick had it. No late nights in California, our next stop, for a three-game series to close out the road trip. But we lost every game there by one run. First, Dick decided he was going to bench Scott again since he was a couple of pounds over his 215-pound limit. It didn't matter that Scott had tagged the Angels' starter, McGlothlin, for a homer the last time they met. Or that George was hitting better than .300 against Angels pitching. We were to learn that you could have a pennant on the line and Dick would still try to make his points—even if it might cost you a game. He had an unswerving stubborn streak that never permitted him to alter his beliefs.

The next game, Dick decided to put Foy back in the lineup if Joe was at his right weight. When Joe heard that, he was worried. He was five pounds over. That was a problem he

faced throughout his career. We were good friends. I had
invited Joe and his wife out to Bridgehampton when I was
being honored at a dinner and he stayed with us. I wish I
could have straightened him out. But he just didn't take very
good care of himself. What a waste of talent. This time he
went to a steam bath and in a few hours sweated off the five
pounds and didn't have breakfast. When they weighed him in
the trainer's room, he was right on target. He started. It didn't
help. We lost again—with Joe driving in our only run—and
fell to fourth. We couldn't do much against the Angels' Jack
Hamilton, who threw a spitball. In fact, Andrews almost was
thrown out of the game because he argued with Ed Runge,
the home plate umpire, that Hamilton was loading it up. One
more game before heading home and Lonborg, our stopper,
was starting. No good—for him, the team, and me. Another
one-run loss and we were all the way down to fifth, although
we were only two and a half games out of first.

Somehow I made it through the game, even though I was
knocked unconscious in the first inning when I hit the wall
going for a shot by Jose Cardenal. He got an inside-the-park
homer while I was on the ground, unconscious. In my last at-
bat in the eighth, runners were on second and third with two
out. I tried to look at this new lefty, Jim Weaver, that the
Angels brought in. I couldn't follow his pitches. It was as if I
was looking at something underwater. They came in blurred.
God. Was there something wrong with my eyes after hitting
the wall? Our trainer, Buddy LeRoux, told me he was sure I
was okay, but would make sure I'd see a doctor as soon as we
got back to Boston.

We just couldn't get on track, a three-game losing streak,
seven losses in nine games on the road trip we were ending.
Since that ten-game winning streak, our hitting—my hitting,
especially—had fallen drastically. We had eight wins and thirteen losses in the twenty-one games since that throng had met
us at the airport. The only "crowd" this time was composed of
wives, children, and friends.

Williams wanted us at the park three and a half hours

before game time as we opened a homestand against the Tigers. Dick had insisted that Scott go on the scales before every
game. That was Popowski's job—to weigh George. Whenever George was overweight, Siebern would start at first.

You have to hand it to Pop. He knew the way Williams
was and he knew how George was. George wasn't going to
lose weight and Dick wasn't going to back down about keeping him out of the lineup. So Pop, bless him, figured out a
way to keep everyone happy. He lied to Williams. He told
him Scott was at the required weight. It was Pop's and
George's secret. When Scotty finally got back in, he had a
heck of a stretch. He batted .350 in August, starting with the
very first game he returned.

Luckily, my eyes were okay, so I was playing left when
Morehead started against the Tigers. In the first inning, Scott
tagged a homer. I drove in a pair with a sacrifice fly and then
got hold of a ball in the eighth and hit it out of the park, more
than four hundred feet away to right center. The shutout was
Morehead's first complete game since that no-hitter in 1965.

Friday, August 18, marked two turning points in the history of the Red Sox. It started us on a seven-game winning
streak that positioned us for the greatest pennant race Boston
ever saw, and it effectively began the end of Tony Conigliaro's career as a slugger who could dominate a game.

He was one of Boston's own, a kid from Revere who
homered into the screen on his first pitch at Fenway as a nineteen-year-old in 1964. That's something the fans in a city
never forget. You break in like that, you're a hero forever.
Hamilton, the Angels' spitball guy, was pitching. His ball was
moving real good and we couldn't do much with him. Dick
complained to the umpires that he was throwing a spitter.
"Watch the guy," said Williams.

Tony had been one of the few players who was able to
get a hit off him. Then Tony came up in the fourth with two
outs and a scoreless game. Hamilton threw the first pitch and
it sailed toward Tony's head. Was it a spitter? I don't know,
but I thought so because of the way it acted. Guys who throw

spitters know how to keep them low or else they sail and then *no one* knows where it's going. This one went right toward Tony's face. He threw his hands up, but that didn't help. The ball was coming in with such velocity and lift that he just couldn't judge it. The whole park must have heard the crack the ball made as it hit Tony under the left eye. We all ran out as Tony collapsed in a heap at the plate.

"You're gonna be okay. It's gonna be fine," Rico kept whispering to him. You could hear Rico from five feet away because the place had gotten so quiet. Tony moved, but just a little. Someone finally brought a stretcher. Tony was awake but dazed and in pain. Lonborg, Foy, and Mike Ryan lifted him onto the stretcher and helped carry him into the clubhouse. I felt cold, and then I realized that I was shivering. It was as if someone had sucked the breath out of our whole team. We waited in the clubhouse for the ambulance to take Tony to the Sancta Maria Hospital, which was over in Cambridge. When I got back to the dugout, I started yelling at Hamilton for not controlling the damn spitter.

Tartabull pinch-ran for Tony and came on to score as we broke the ice with two runs. We won the game, which put us back in third, three games out. But my feelings were mixed with anger and sorrow. Hamilton was teed off that I was screaming at him and told a reporter, "He's got a hell of a nerve yelling at me. If he's such a great hitter, why didn't he do anything tonight?"

The next day we started hearing conflicting reports about Tony—he'd be back in a month, he was gone for the season, his eyesight was threatened. Hamilton tried to visit him in the morning, but the hospital turned him away. Tony missed the rest of 1967 and all of 1968 before he was able to return in 1969.

I don't know how he could stand watching us that first day in the hospital. He said he'd be rooting for us on television. We had a 12–7 lead over the Angels into the ninth. A pair of two-run homers later, though, the Angels cut it to a run and Williams had Lonborg warming up in the bullpen. We got the final out on a slow hopper that Rico charged and made a fine play on. Maybe luck was still with us, or maybe it was slipping away. Each game was becoming monumental, and we still had almost fifty to play.

Take a look at some of the silly things that happen in a pennant race. We creamed the Angels in the first game of a doubleheader the next day. But was that 12–2 victory enough to make Mr. Yawkey happy? Heck no. He was angry because the official scorer, Cliff Keane of the *Globe,* ruled that Andrews had committed an error on a ball hit by Rick Reichardt. After the game, Yawkey came in to the press room to complain. For many years he had stayed in his box, but this year he had fraternized more with the writers. Maybe he was feeling frisky about our better play. He wasn't happy about the writers this time, though. Until recent years they were the official scorers, paid by the clubs. Mr. Yawkey started yelling at Cliff that the hit should have been ruled a double all the way. Keane never wavered. It those days (that makes it sound like ancient history, but it certainly was before instant replay was a factor), official scorers would never reverse their decisions. Now, with the replay, sometimes you'll hear of a hit or error changed the next day. And why not? It's not like a horse race, where you have to put up the OFFICIAL sign immediately so people can get paid.

By the end of the second game, neither Tom nor anyone else in the park was in any condition to argue about anything. We became part of another bit of 1967 trivia—or maybe history would be more like it. We came back after trailing by 8–0. Do crazy things like that often enough, and you deserve the word "miracle."

Before we got to bat in the fourth, the Angels took an 8–0 lead as they chased Morehead with six runs in the second. Reggie faced McGlothlin in the fourth. In the first game, Reggie became the first man in Sox history to hit home runs in a game batting both right-handed and left-handed. He started things against McGlothlin by tagging another one out. No big deal: 8–1. Then I came up in the fifth with two on, and I homered. Suddenly, we were back in it. And if *we* didn't think so, the *fans* did. They wouldn't let us rest. I heard later that as soon as my shot cleared the fence, you could hear a cheer going down the South Shore beaches, since so many people had brought along portable radios.

They must have really blasted those radios the next inning. We tied it, and did it in style against Hamilton. Whenever he was ready to pitch, the crowd booed. Foy started it with a double and now the fans really gave it to Hamilton. He walked the next two batters. That knocked him out out of the game. Hamilton marched off to the longest, loudest, angry yelling I had heard at Fenway. Jones tagged a double off the center field wall against Minnie Rojas and now we trailed by only two. Tartabull hit a sacrifice fly, and Adair's single tied the game.

That man was one of the coolest clutch hitters I had seen. He came up again in the eighth with the scored tied at 8–8. In more than three hundred at-bats with us that season, Adair would hit only three homers. But Jerry hit one then—and we had the lead. I was the next guy up and I half-expected what came next: the brushback. Except it didn't brush me back far enough. Rojas got me in the elbow. This really got the crowd frenzied. Just two days after Tony's beaning, there I was, surrounded by the trainer and manager. It hurt like heck, but I wasn't going to miss this game. I didn't say a word to Rojas and went off to first. I heard someone yelling and turned toward the dugout. It was Williams.

"Cut somebody, Yaz! You damn well better go into second with your spikes high!"

The first base ump, Bill Valentine, shouted back at Williams: "Cut out that crap or you're gone." That teed off Williams even more and he ran over to me and started to tell me what he expected me to do—to knock whoever's covering second on his butt. Williams didn't stop there. He was standing between me and Valentine and spit. It landed right on the ump's shoes. "Dick, you're gone," Valentine bellowed.

"What?" screamed Williams. "I wasn't spitting on you. I was just spitting."

We didn't score, and took the 9–8 lead into the ninth. It felt pretty good with Jose Santiago out there. During the season, Williams had converted him into a reliever. Down the stretch he won eight straight games for us. And every one of those were in tight situations, games we still were in or were leading. He got us a little nervous this time, though. Don Mincher led off with a single and Rick Reichardt followed with a double. The runners held when Buck Rodgers bounced out, second to first. Santiago then struck out Bobby Knoop. Two down, runners on second and third. Popowski was managing since Williams had been ejected. Pop told Santiago to walk Tom Satriano. Bill Rigney, the Angels' manager, countered with a pinch hitter, Skowron. If there was one man in the park that day who knew about Moose, it was our catcher—Howard. They had been teammates on the Yankees in the 1950s and 1960s. I knew what Ellie would be telling Jose on the mound: "Low curves. He'll fish on the first pitch." Skowron did. Moose couldn't get a good piece of the low outside curve, and grounded into a force play. Just like that, we had salvaged a victory from an eight-run deficit. And we were only one and a half games out of first.

The new front office of the Red Sox still wasn't satisfied. They had a chance to improve the club even more the next day when Charles O. Finley released Ken (Hawk) Harrelson, who had been calling the owner a "nutcake." The Red Sox brass immediately started negotiating with Harrelson. Imagine, being able to get a quality slugger for free in the middle of a pennant race. Of course, the problem with that is you have to disrupt the club you have. And Scott had been hitting lately and was also the best-fielding first baseman around. At first, the front office was very low-keyed in discussing Harrelson, but the players knew we were after him. That night our streak continued and Ellie Howard became the latest hero. He came up against the Senators in the ninth with the game tied and drove in the winner. I was happy for him. Ellie had been struggling ever since he had joined us. His average was under .200 and he was 0 for 4 before his last at-bat. That night I also wore an ear flap with my helmet. Some people thought it was because of Tony's beaning, but I had been considering it for some time. I was being pitched very tight.

The streak reached seven, and we reached second, only percentage points behind the White Sox, with a doubleheader victory over Washington. The Twins and Tigers were right behind us, a game back. Our big play in the opener was a ninth-inning, Adair-to-Howard-to-first double play while we were holding on to a 2–1 lead. That play excited one of our listeners: Senator Ted Kennedy sent us a telegram congratulating us and wishing the best for the second game. That was nice, but Reggie's homer in the second game was even nicer. It was his sixth in the last ten games and capped our winning streak.

A few days later we headed for Chicago and a five-game series with the first-place White Sox, with their one-point lead over us. I discovered my friendship with Stanky, forged at first base in the All-Star Game, was short-lived. He went back to being his true self and I learned firsthand why they called him the Brat.

I picked up the Chicago papers in the morning, a few hours before we were to open with a doubleheader. Stanky was all over the papers, grousing about the Red Sox getting all the ink while his boys, his rinky-dink hitters, weren't getting respect. He told us to stop crying about Conigliaro's injury and he predicted that Lonborg wouldn't last four innings in the opener.

You can't retaliate with words against someone like Eddie Stanky. He'll always have the last one. So I knew we'd have to punch him out with our bats. We broke Chicago's back in the first inning, when I started a two-out rally with a single and we gave Lonborg a 3–0 edge. He lasted four innings, all right, and pitched a complete game. Even though we had a 7–1 lead, Stanky wasn't through. I was 3 for 3 when I got up in the seventh inning. When you're down by that much, it's unheard-of for a manager to change pitchers to throw to one guy with nobody on base. But that didn't stop Stanky. He walked to the mound and called for Wilbur Wood, a lefty, in the bullpen. Wood was coming in for one reason only.

Wood didn't even pretend he was trying to get the ball over. Four pitches aimed at my head, two of them behind me. Stanky figured that if Wood hit me, we'd be forced to throw at his guys and hit one of them. That would give the White Sox a base runner, and maybe start something going. They were such a light-hitting club—a .225 average, no one with 20 homers—he needed a hit batsman to start a rally. After I got to first, Williams took me out so I could rest for the second game. As I made my way into the clubhouse, Lonborg followed me. He was steaming that they were throwing at me.

"Who do you want me to hit?" he said. "Just tell me and I'll nail him."

No one knew that Jim had asked me about it, but I gave him the names of some guys I thought he should target. It was all very quiet, just between two ballplayers who had a world of respect for each other.

Technically, we were in first place, although we still had the second game to play. That didn't turn out quite right. We lost by a run and were back to second. In close games, people do funny things, or maybe you just notice them more than you would in a blowout. Usually, when the other team's pitcher is keeping you under wraps, you don't waste any scoring opportunity. But we did in the seventh. Rico was on second when Jones popped a ball into short left along the line. Pop, coaching at third, waved Rico home as soon as the ball was hit, but Rico hesitated. He didn't move until it dropped fair and then he could only make it to third. On the next play, Rico hesitated going home on a checked-swing grounder and was thrown out at the plate. Stanky filed that for his "I'm a better manager than you are" routine.

Saturday, August 26, 1967. For the first time since 1959, we were alone in first place so late in the season. We hadn't even been in sole possession in April. We grabbed a 5–0 lead while Jerry Stephenson pitched a no-hitter for five innings. By the eighth inning, Chicago was pretty well beaten. But that didn't stop Stanky from ordering Tommy John to throw at Adair. Stanky had been angry at Jerry since trading him, when Adair had accused Stanky of fiddling with the playing field and the baseballs. After almost getting hit, Adair told us that Stanky had commanded the pitch. When it was over, we were at 72–56, a percentage of .563, with half a game over Minnesota, and one game over Chicago and Detroit.

I didn't expect Stanky to be in a good mood after the game, but I figured he'd be gracious enough to let me get in some extra batting. I wasn't as loose as I wanted to be, and I asked the groundskeeper if I could bat for half an hour after the game. He checked with Stanky and said, "Sure." Something must have happened to tick Stanky off after he agreed, or maybe he was just being the Brat. I know that after the game he was trying to turn the tables on us. Here he was, the losing manager, but he told the press that if it hadn't been for dumb calls by Williams, the Red Sox would have won all three games we had played so far. I guess he was referring to Rico's indecision on running, which was not Dick's call.

Anyway, I grabbed some bats and went out to the field. I brought out one of the coaches to throw to me. Instead, I saw that Stanky was there with some of his players—and they were taking batting practice. I sat around for an hour. Finally, his guys left and I was ready to go out, but he shouted to me, "You can't take it yet." And he walked out of the dugout with his dog, a four-pound brown poodle named Go-Go he had bought as the team's mascot. He started walking around the outfield with the dog. There I was, sitting in the dugout, watching this scene as he went from left field to right and back again. For one hour. See, he was trying to discourage me, get me angry. But he also wasn't quite taking the field away from me. He knew if he did that, then we wouldn't let his guys get any extra batting practice in Fenway if they needed it.

He finally stopped walking the dog, went down the steps

into the dugout, and waved. It was more than two hours after the game. I got in only about fifteen minutes of hitting because it was getting too dark.

I don't know why that should have surprised me. Getting you angry was what he did all the time, any time. Stanky must have wondered how much his dog-walking strategy affected me. The next day, a doubleheader, I got to the park early and walked into the right field stands. I wanted to see if the wind was going to help me or if I needed to compensate in my swing. I was okay. In the first game, I smacked two home runs and we took a 4–3 lead into the bottom of the ninth.

Then came another moment of 1967 memories, another freeze-frame shot of a miracle in the making. Another image that millions of Bostonians will swear to having seen the moment it happened. Who's to say they didn't? Whenever you think of 1967, the reality and fantasy tend to blur.

Ken Berry led off the White Sox ninth with a double against Gary Bell. Hansen sacrificed him to third. Stanky sent up Duane Josephson to pinch-hit. Williams lifted Bell and brought in John Wyatt, our saver from the bullpen. Josephson, a right-handed batter, was fooled by the first pitch and he reached for it outside and hit a liner to medium right. Tartabull was playing right, one of three guys we platooned out there since Conigliaro's injury. Jose was a fine fielder, but had the weakest arm in the outfield. He hadn't thrown out a runner all year. He saw the ball coming and grabbed it one-handed on the run. Berry, like just about everyone else on the White Sox, could run fast. He tagged up and headed home. Jose's throw was straight, but high. Too high. "Be there, just be there," I said out loud as I watched the play in front of me.

Howard had positioned his left foot to the third base side of the plate. He leaped for the ball and made the only play possible. He grabbed it one-handed, no easy play with the kind of mitt catchers wore in 1967. He came down with the ball while his back was to Berry, who started his slide. Ellie's left foot got to the plate before Berry's shoe, pushing it off to the side. The ball still was in Howard's glove above his waist as Berry desperately lunged for the plate with his hand. But so did Howard. With a sweeping motion his glove came down and tagged Berry. Just like that. Double play. Game over.

Not to Stanky. Boy, he hopped over that top dugout step and practically beat us to the plate, where we all were headed to mob Howard. Marty Springstead, the ump who had made the call, was only in his second year. Did Stanky figure he could get the guy to change his mind? Or maybe the Brat thought he could set up Springstead for the next close play against Chicago, make him think twice before giving the "out" sign. After all, there still was another game to play that day.

The irony about that play wasn't lost on Adair. "I told you about how they keep the grass high and the field soft from watering," he told me later. "If that place hadn't been so muddy, Berry would have been able to get a better head of steam when he ran down the line. Stanky got his for messing with the field."

We dropped the nightcap, leaving us tied for first. Now we headed for New York, where they were giving me a "night."

About a hundred people, half of them named Yastrzemski and Skonieczny, were on hand from Bridgehampton. I donated most of the gifts, which included a cream-colored Chrysler convertible with plates that read YAZ-8 and a color television, to the Jimmy Fund. In the noisy locker room, I figured there was excitement going on because of my "night," with a lot of my friends coming around. Instead, there was a new man on hand—Harrelson had joined the Red Sox. It was Hawk's third team that season. He started in Washington before Finley wanted him at Kansas City. But Finley stopped wanting him after Harrelson had complained when the manager, Alvin Dark, was fired. Now, in our locker room, he was having a fine old time with the press, which mobbed him, and was being razzed by all of us. Kenny loved to talk and he loved the give-and-take of the locker room. You didn't need to say much to set him off. They loved him right off the bat.

Hawk told everyone how he came to Boston even though the White Sox offered $20,000 more, but his wife was a Massachusetts girl and that, anyway, he just loved the idea of playing for Tom Yawkey. Good old Hawk. Now he could take over all those questions from the press in the locker room.

I got us on the boards in the first, which was a nice touch in front of all my hometown fans. With runners on first and third, I hit a sacrifice fly to score Tartabull. I also got two walks but no hits as we shut out the Yankees. Sparky saved another, this time for Morehead. We were in another virtual tie for first, this time with the Twins, who had a point on us.

Hard to believe, but another doubleheader was ahead of us—our third in five days. When it ended, we had climbed back into first place, but mountains have been climbed faster —and easier.

The twilight doubleheader lasted almost nine hours, ending at a few minutes before two in the morning. The culprit was the second game, twenty innings of suspense and action that took six hours and nine minutes and ended with the Yankees on top. That gave us a split, but it also put us half a game ahead of the Twins and Tigers and two and a half games ahead of Chicago. Through that long afternoon, night and morning, though, I went 0 for 10. I hadn't had a hit since my second homer at Chicago, four straight games.

The opener was such a neat, quick game, a 2–1 victory by Lonborg over Stottlemyre as Jim drove home Reggie for the winning run. It took two hours and ten minutes. There wasn't much scoring in the second, either. But it took almost three times as long. We were tied at 2–2 after nine, with Hawk homering in his first at-bat as a Red Sox. Then we went ahead in the eleventh on a pinch single by Siebern. But with two outs in the bottom of the inning, Steve Whitaker tied it with a shot off Sparky.

In the fifteenth, the Yankees put two runners on, but Reggie made a shoestring catch on a looper by Bill Robinson. Bob Tillman then drilled a pitch into left center. But that

Stadium, bless it, had all the room you needed. I caught up to it with a backhanded stab, snared it, and tumbled to the grass. But I held onto it. In the seventeenth, we had Mike Andrews on third with one out, but Robinson cut him down at the plate after catching Smith's fly ball. The game kept going. We had another shot to win in the twentieth, loading the bases. The Yankees won it, though, when Horace Clarke singled off Santiago to score John Kennedy.

None of us had ever been so tired. And being in an 0 for 17 slump made me feel even worse. "Take tomorrow off. Come in whenever you're up to it. Hell, you went twenty-nine innings," said Williams. Actually, he meant "Take today off." We had another game at two o'clock that afternoon. Around one o'clock I dragged myself in and headed for the trainer's room. I wasn't worried about batting or fielding practice, just to be able to have the strength to suit up.

I took a nap after a rubdown. I woke up in the third inning, showered, and got into uniform and out in the dugout. It was the seventh inning and we were tied at 1–1.

"How ya feeling?" Williams asked me.

"Oh, I think I can pinch-hit, maybe go out in the field later," I told him.

"Fine," he said. "Relax now, but I think I'm gonna have you hit for Thomas when he's up."

George Thomas was due up in the ninth against Al Downing. In the bottom of the eighth, Williams took out Thomas and sent me to left. The next inning I went to the plate, dragging my body and an 0 for 17 streak. I knew I had been pressing, trying so hard to hit home runs because every game had seemed so monumental. It seemed as if my whole life had been geared for just this season, but now I was letting things slip away because I was lunging. I tried to be patient, to wait for my pitch, a fastball. But I got two strikes on me with the first two pitches and Downing came in with a slider. I popped it up to right field. But the swing felt good. The pitch didn't fool me and I got my bat around. Strange to think your confidence can return with an out, but it did. Still, I was 0 for 18. Foy brought my cap and glove out of the dugout for me as I headed for left field. "Joe, next time up, it's out of here," I told him.

My chance came in the eleventh with the game still tied, 1–1. Downing was still in there with his eleven strikeouts and only eight hits given up.

He had thrown me fastballs the first two pitches in my last at-bat. He was going to throw me another, I was sure.

The count regulated my batting life. Over the years I had learned to expect certain pitches at certain times in the count, and I geared myself to them. When it was 0–0, I was looking, *Fastball.* Not necessarily for it to be in my power zone, but for it to be a strike, a ball I could drive. I became an aggressive hitter at 0–0.

Because of my size, the count was very important to me. I had to look for a smaller zone for power than a bigger guy. If I was going to hit a home run, I had to look for a ball around the belt on the inside part of the plate, or the middle at most in order to pull the ball. If it was on the outside part of the plate, I wasn't strong enough to pull it or hit it out of the park to the opposite field.

So if I was thinking, *Home run,* I'd look inside if I was ahead in the count, from the middle to the inside part of the plate, from the belt area on up. That was my strength. But it also was my weakness when the pitch got to around the letters. I chased a lot of bad pitches up in that area. So if I got ahead in the count—say, 2–0 or 3–0 or 3–1—and I was thinking, *Home run,* I would give the pitcher the pitch if it was inside from the knees to the belt, even if it was a strike. I would just have to take it. I wanted his mistake to be in my power zone.

Now, if the count was, say, 1–1, I wouldn't be looking in the power zone. I would be looking inside middle, but I'd include the knees to the letters, where I could pull the ball and handle it well. But at 1–1 or 2–1, you're not thinking, *Home run.*

When the pitcher got me 0–1, 0–2, or 1–2, I would try to cover the whole plate and just get the bat on the ball, grind out a base hit—through the infield, over the infield. At 2–2, I would become a little more aggressive, look to drive the ball more, figuring the pitcher couldn't afford to be too cute and let the count go to 3–2. I'd be looking to drive the ball into the gaps.

At 3–2, you always see a lot of foul balls. But I became very aggressive because the pitcher would have to get the ball over the plate. He couldn't afford to be cute and try for the corners. I wasn't quite as aggressive as 2–0, 3–1, or 3–0, because I wasn't thinking, *Home run,* but I did think of hitting the ball hard because the pitch had to be a strike.

I anticipated fastballs at 0–0, 1–0, 2–0, at 3–0, 3–1, 2–2, 3–2. I wasn't even going to swing at a breaking pitch except with two strikes. And even then, I geared my thinking to fastball first, then hit the curve off of that. If you thought curve in advance, you'd never be able to get around on the fastball.

Because it's such a complicated thing, I always kept a black book of how pitchers threw me in every situation: What did he throw me with somebody on base, what did he throw me when there was nobody on, what did he throw me with a man on first, what were the counts, was he in and out? Right after the game, I'd write everything in the book and see if I could come up with a pattern.

It helped against Downing. He threw me another fastball on the first pitch. As soon as I saw it, I knew it was mine. I hit it into the bleachers in right center for number 35. Guess what? They mobbed me at home plate. We were starting to enjoy this sort of stuff. That run was enough, thanks to Wyatt's continued steady relieving, for a 2–1 victory.

The most tiring road trip of my life was over, along with one of my worst slumps. It was back to Boston, a series against the White Sox, and a September race. First, we had to get out of August. Chicago ended the month by beating us in the opener of our series.

12
AT LONG
LAST

On Friday, September 1, we had a half-game lead over the Twins, one game over the Tigers, and one and a half games over Chicago. Our record was 76–59. With my slump I had lost fourteen points in the month and I was batting .308, which placed me twenty-three points behind Frank Robinson. I led Harmon Killebrew by one homer and I also had an edge over him in RBIs, 95–90. Lonborg had the league's best pitching record at 18–6.

These are not numbers I thought about every day, although my dad constantly reminded me about them. He especially wanted that batting title. At the time I couldn't rattle off any of these figures. I didn't think it was proper to dwell on them. But I've got to admit that they're interesting to look at now. And they do give a perspective of what we had to overcome and what it took to get us the pennant. In our final 27 games, we won 16. We changed places fifteen times, slipping in and out of first, and as low as third, never behind by more than a game, but with never much of a lead, either. We had winning streaks and losing streaks. We played a whole new season in September (and one game in October), and a lifetime's worth of thrills. I knew that this was my time and I grabbed it. I had 96 at-bats in the final 27 games and got 40 hits for a .417 average. In those 27 games, I drove in 26 runs and scored 24. I raised my average eighteen points.

Our three opponents were three very different clubs. Stanky's White Sox had great pitching: the most shutouts, a team ERA of under 2.50. Joe Horlen won 19 games and he and Tommy John tied for the league lead in shutouts, Gary Peters won 16 games, Hoyt Wilhelm and Bob Locker were two of the best relievers in the game. The White Sox liked to steal bases, especially Tommy McCraw, Don Buford, and Tommie Agee, all with more than 20. And, of course, Stanky was there to make some mischief.

The Twins were an interesting case. They were playing .500 ball for Sam Mele when he was canned after fifty games. Then Cal Ermer, who had spent twenty-five years in the minors, took over and their percentage from that point on was just about the best. They had Killebrew, one of the league's best home run hitters. They had a rookie at second named Rod Carew who could stroke anything. There was also Tony Oliva, who already had led the league in batting. Dean Chance, Jim Merritt, and Jim Kaat were among the top pitchers in the league. The thing about the Twins was that no club had ever won a pennant after changing managers in mid-season. The 1988 Red Sox would eventually have something to say about that precedent.

The Tigers, under Mayo Smith, were after their first pennant since 1945. As the race roller-coasted along, Smith made me chuckle when he described managing as a disease, and suggested, "Maybe I ought to form a Managers Anonymous." He hated the pressure, but his club seemed to have everything—pitching with Earl Wilson and Denny McLain and Mickey Lolich and Joe Sparma, hitting with Norm Cash and Al Kaline and Willie Horton and Bill Freehan. Smith had a great philosophy: "When you smoke and drink, that tobacco doesn't mix with alcohol and you feel lousy the next morning. So I gave up cigarettes."

These were the teams to beat, and the only way you really could guarantee you would pass them was by beating them head-to-head. There were too many of them to hope that someone else would beat them. That was, however, just another theory that went down the drain in this crazy race.

Williams had to do some juggling. He wanted Harrelson in the lineup, but wasn't about to take Scott out and install Hawk at first base. What to do? Make a right fielder of Harrelson. Dick's first move in September looked great. We opened with a rout of the White Sox as Hawk, our new right fielder, hit a double, triple, and homer. But we fell into second by dropping the next two games to Chicago. I stayed late in Fenway after that second loss to the White Sox. That's right. Batting practice. The swing still wasn't right.

Then we left for a Labor Day doubleheader in Washington which we split with the Senators. Williams asked me how I was doing and I asked him, "why?" "Maybe you'd like to take the day off tomorrow," he said. "We'll see," I replied. Actually, it wasn't a bad idea. I had played in every game the last four months, started all of them except one.

The next night Williams asked me to see him in his office. "This is a good spot to take the night off," he told me. "They're pitching a lefty. You haven't been off since May. Take the day, and we've got an off-day tomorrow. You'll be able to get two straight days off. When was the last time you had that?" But I had changed my mind. I didn't want to take the day off. I had decided I wanted to start every game the rest of the season. Besides, I had discovered that sitting on the bench made me so nervous and edgy, I was better off using that energy in the game. I was able to do something unusual—change Dick Williams's mind.

We were both glad I did. I hit homer number 37 in the fourth. We had a big lead and everyone on the bench was pretty loose. They started to ride me.

"Oh, Yaz, Joe Coleman's warming up for you!" shouted Gibby. Coleman struck me out twice in our last meeting. Williams, though, figured I had accomplished what we needed, and offered to let me get dressed and leave.

"Uh-uh, not until I face the kid again," I said. "He just got lucky the last time. How could he strike me out twice?"

In the seventh, Coleman did come in. I got to the plate and went through my gyrations and I imagined what he was thinking. I thought to myself, *He caught me on fastballs the last time. He'll do the same thing again.* I was certain. I could hear the guys laughing and cheering while I got set. The fastball came in and I hit it out. Number 38.

We had an off-day before a series against the Yankees at Fenway. I visited Tony C. in the hospital, where the news was not encouraging. It was confusing. The doctors were divided over whether he could play again that season, or whether he needed surgery. Originally, they told him he could start hitting a few balls by now. At home, I started getting phone calls from people who wanted me to order World Series tickets for them, the first such requests I had ever received. Baseball Commissioner William D. Eckert had given all four clubs in the race the go-ahead to start printing. The bleacher seats were going to cost $2. A box seat was $12. *Imagine, $12 for a baseball game,* I thought. But in Boston, right then, you didn't ask the price. You asked how many tickets you could buy. We also voted World Series shares. There had been so many changes on the club that only seventeen players and Williams took part in the voting. We agreed that the Jimmy Fund would get one full share. Meanwhile, we heard that the Twins had voted out Sam Mele, who had been their manager for fifty games until he was fired.

The calls for tickets increased the next day when Lonborg took number 19 against the Yankees. We were now only a percentage point behind Minnesota again. That .001 started to take on a life of its own. It could look as big as 1,000 or as small as, well, a decimal point. It depended on where you were in the standings, whether you had just won or if you had lost. I don't think I had ever before thought of the difference between, say, a winning percentage of .563 or .564. Now, all of New England was learning the new math.

In his victory Lonborg got another hit, a ground-rule double. On days he wasn't pitching, he asked for more time than the other pitchers in the batting cage. "What the heck, Yaz," he told me. "Who knows when I might be in a situation that needs a hit? Maybe I can help us win a game along the line." Jim wasn't stopping there. He gave up some of his swings in the cage to practice bunting. In the days before the designated hitter, every pitcher had to be a pretty accomplished bunter because they usually were asked to move the runner along if there were less than two outs.

Good old Boomer Scott gave us a laugh with another one of his razzle-dazzle base-running exploits. At least, when you win you laugh. George already had been called out twice on appeal plays for leaving third base too soon on fly balls. This time, he was on first when Smith hit a ball to right. Scott was sure it would be a hit, took off, and was chugging into third when Pop frantically raised his arms to signal: *Stop! Go back!* Steve Whitaker had caught Reggie's shot. Scott had to recircle. Instead of going all the way to first, though, he stopped at second. The throw to first got him.

"George, why the hell did you do that? Why'd you stop at second?" Dick asked him when he got back to the bench.

"Trying to make them think I belonged at second," George explained. "I didn't have a chance in the world of getting back to first. I thought they might forget what base I had been on." We poked one another in the ribs on the bench.

See what I meant about those decimal points, those little half-games? We lost the next night to the Yankees—the Yankees of ninth place, where we used to be—and fell to third. Now it was the Tigers' turn to tie Minnesota for first, while the White Sox were fourth, only one game back. We were beaten by Monbouquette, who had been our pitching star of the early 1960s, back when we were going nowhere. I'll bet he probably figured then that he would love to pitch for the

Yankees instead. Now Bill, who had been our leader in victories and innings pitched and complete games when it really
didn't matter, was toiling for the Yankees—when it didn't
really matter, either.

The next day Carol learned about pennant pressure and
superstition. For the first six years she had attended games,
usually at nights or weekends. But now she vowed she would
be there every home game in September. For the first time,
she became animated in talking about the race. She started
conversations at dinner about what happened that day and
who the Sox were playing the next game. At breakfast a routine began.

"Do you think we'll win today?" she asked.

"Yes, of course," I said. And every day I was home
would start with the same question. So on Saturday, of course,
she was in the stands for our game against the Yankees. She
usually got hungry midway through and went downstairs for a
hot dog. While she was on line she heard the crowd roaring.

"What happened?" she asked.

"Yaz hit one out."

Carol figured, just like any other smart baseball person,
that because she was under the stands at that time, getting a
hot dog at that moment contributed to the homer. She stayed
under the stands the rest of the game. And for the remainder
of the season, every fourth inning she went under the stands,
ordered a hot dog, and waited there for the game to end.

"How can you stand it?" I wondered. "You mean you
just hang around the hot dog stand?"

"I feel as if I'm part of it," she explained. How could I
argue with her?

We closed the Yankee series with another decision and
another symbolic milestone: victory number 82. That guaranteed our first winning season since 1958. An 82–80 record? If
you had asked us in spring training how a .500 season would
make us feel, it would have made us ecstatic. But far more
than a .500 record was at stake now. This only proved to the
rest of the baseball world we were winners. Everyone on the

team already knew that by then. Gary Bell pitched a complete game, giving him an 11–6 record since we got him from Cleveland. And Dick made another of his moves, or rather was smart in not making a move. We held a 4–1 lead when Mike Ryan, a catcher who was hitting under .200, came up with the bass loaded in the sixth. A fan could argue that it was a spot for a pinch hitter. But Dick left Ryan in. He hit a triple —one of only two he hit in 1967—to put the game on ice. That hit, worth three runs, accounted for more than 10 percent of his RBI total for the season.

Conigliaro went to the ballpark the next day. It was his first time there since the beaning. We were off, but Williams and some of the coaches were on hand. Tony put a bat in his hand for the first time in almost a month and got into the cage to face his brother Billy, who was throwing batting practice. Billy was in our minor league system, but would be up with the Sox himself within two years.

Tony took a dozen swings and didn't rocket any of them. Here was a kid who had 20 homers and 93 ribbies the year before—and 20 homers in 1967 before the beaning—and he was having trouble getting the ball to the Wall. After BP, he moved to right field and shagged some flies from Billy. Then Tony got back in the cage and told his brother, "Throw hard."

A couple of Tony's shots hit the Wall. Still, when he was finished, he walked off the field, muttering, "It's just not good. Just not good." He wasn't getting headaches, which was a good sign. His vision wasn't blurred. But Tony explained that his problem was depth perception. He could follow the ball coming in, but was unable to tag it at just the right moment. Instead of feeling good about his first workout, he felt lousy.

Tony was in the stands the next night, though, when we got back into a first-place tie. Since 1953, we had only one 20-game winner—Monbouquette in 1963. Lonborg became the second by stopping Kansas City in a pitcher's duel with Jim (Catfish) Hunter. Catfish was a superior pitcher with a losing team. That year he had five shutouts. He always gave up a lot of homers, though, because he was always around the plate with excellent control. Reggie ripped him for one in the fifth. We were tied in the bottom of the eighth at 1–1, with Lonborg up and a man on first. He faked a bunt and the infield charged in. Suddenly, Jim swung away and hit a fastball to deep right center. It went for a triple and drove in the winning run. It was a great way to win number 20, especially how he escaped a bases-loaded, none-out jam, as well as a pair of first-and-third, one-out situations. Nobody was cooler than Lonborg that year. He felt the way I did. He wanted to be the guy who was there in every key game, each big moment.

Our latest winning streak reached four the next game with another victory over the A's. Rico was the big man this time by driving in three runs, the last two after they intentionally walked Harrelson with a runner on third. Guess who was called out for leaving third too early on a fly ball?

We learned the next day that Conigliaro definitely would not play any more that year. But at least we were tied for first when we faced the Orioles in a three-game series to end our homestand. Then we dropped all three and fell into a tie for third with the Twins, a game behind the Tigers. Lonborg was frosted in one of the games after Williams removed him with the score tied 1–1 in the seventh—just because Jim had hit the leadoff batter. Jim stormed off the mound. But it wasn't much of a weekend for any of the contenders, Detroit or Chicago or Minnesota—a grand total of five victories against seven losses. We, though, had a three-game losing streak and were going on the road. After 150 games, only one game separated the first four clubs. There were twelve games remaining.

America was getting caught up in the pennant race. The Cardinals were running away from the Giants in the National League, so everyone focused on us. More than sixty writers were traveling with the Red Sox. We had become the darlings of the sports world. I know that a big deal, deservedly, was made out of the 1969 Mets. They went all the way from ninth to first. Well, in a way, we were the Mets before there was a

"Mets." They had seven years of being laughingstocks. The Red Sox had a history of failure, or of coming close and just missing, or being also-rans. We were about to become the first team to finish first from so far back. It was just this possibility —this break from the past—that also symbolized what was taking place all around the country, that made us instant darlings. Even Baltimore fans were rooting for us. When we dropped our third straight game to the Orioles, the result was announced in Baltimore at the Colts' football game. The fans booed.

We moved on to the pennant-mad Detroit for the start of an eight-game road trip: two against the Tigers, two in Cleveland, and four against the Orioles. We would close out with four home games, two each against Cleveland and the Twins.

The Tigers' Kaline was already thirty-two years old and I knew he was becoming frustrated. This was his best shot so far. He had captured the batting title eleven years before as the youngest player ever to win it, but that was about all he had ever won. Still, the Tigers had that collection of outstanding pitchers, combined with power. It probably was the most respected lineup in the league. They drew more walks than anybody.

We opened on a Monday night. It was tied going into the eighth, but the Tigers went ahead. I got up in the ninth with one out and the score 5–4. Tiger Stadium was my favorite home run park. A home run was what we needed just then. Fred Lasher, a right-handed fastball pitcher, was on the mound.

I had been bearing down all month. I was on a roll. It was getting to the stage where I honestly believed that there was nothing that could come up that was beyond me. It got to the point where my confidence level was so high, I'd go to bed at night and think of different situations when I could come up and win the game in the last inning. The thing was, something always *did* seem to come up. And then I'd imagine a new situation the next day, and I just knew I'd be there, be the guy who had to do it or we'd lose. It almost got to be psychic. I wanted those situations. That last month, it was almost as if I was setting up the situations, not the team, that I was beyond what my surroundings dictated. You start thinking that way, that it's up to you and sure enough it is. After a game I'd always think, *How can I help the Red Sox win the game tomorrow?* I wanted to be put on the line every single time.

So I got up against Lasher and said a little prayer. I guess I started that ritual with about a month to go. I don't remember the situation, but I said a "Hail Mary." I got a hit and I kept it up. Grandfather Skonieczny was looking over me, I just knew he was. Before every at-bat, I said a little prayer to him. Then I turned to Lasher. He was out of the strike zone with the first two pitches and I thought, *Fastball.* When he threw it, I got my bat around as sweetly as if it was in my dream. The ball shot into the upper deck for my fortieth home run. We were tied. What the heck. Somehow, we all knew something like this would happen, wouldn't it? It was my third hit of the night and second RBI. But Jones did me one better. In the tenth, he walloped one out, too, his fourth hit and the decisive one. Santiago got the win—the first of four victories he recorded in our final twelve games.

Now three teams were tied for first at 85–66—Detroit, Minnesota, and Boston, while Chicago, which had played one more game, was at 85–67, half a game back.

The next night, it was another ninth-inning comeback against Detroit, this time when we were down by 2–1. Consider that when I got up in the eighth, Lolich had struck out thirteen batters and yielded only five hits until Adair opened the inning with a hit to right. Mickey hadn't walked anyone when he faced me. But he walked me on four pitches. Scott then singled home Jerry to tie the score. Was this game like a championship? Mayo Smith, the Tigers' manager, acted as if there was no tomorrow. Earl Wilson, who had won 21 games —tops in the league—was brought in as a reliever for the only time in the season. I came in on his wild pitch. That gave us the lead. Boomer soon followed on a sacrifice fly. We took a 4–2 lead into the bottom of the ninth. Santiago must have been tiring. I had to make a sliding catch of Don Wert's low liner, and then Jose walked a couple of guys. We eventually pulled it out, though, for a sweep of the two games, both won by Santiago. That second straight ninth-inning rally kept us in first, sharing it only with Minnesota. This was as close to an actual confrontation for the pennant as we had come, and we won with some style and, yeah, some luck.

How many games could we pull out in the ninth inning? How many ya got? That's what we believed. So the next night in Cleveland, with the score tied at 4–4 and two out, I got my fourth hit, took off for second on a wild pitch, and scored on Reggie's single. Minnesota and Chicago also won.

There was something else about our victory. Williams showed he would make his point no matter what the situation —even in a pennant race, even if it would cost us the game. Remember that four days earlier Lonborg growled at him for being taken out after giving up only one run? This time Jim pitched seven innings, gave up three home runs, and yielded four runs before Williams lifted him. Some of the writers questioned Dick about leaving Jim in so long.

"I wanted to teach him something," claimed Dick.

Even at the risk of losing in a pennant race.

We almost didn't get to play that game. It was raining so hard that the Indians were thinking of calling it off. The American League office had already told them that if they did, the game would be rescheduled for Boston. That would have been great for us, and actually good for the Indians. Because it was their "home" game, we were going to split the receipts. That certainly would have given them more than they got from the forty-five hundred fans who showed up, leaving seventy-two thousand empty seats. But hand it to the Indians' management. They tried to get the game in and they did. We almost blew a 6–1 lead, but led by 6–5 going into the ninth. It started raining and it delayed the game for an hour. That didn't bother Wyatt, though. He set down the Indians in order for his save number 16 to go with 10 victories. Our final road trip of the season, four games in Baltimore, was next.

You never know where help will come from. We got lucky and Detroit unlucky in two more accidents. First, there was the one in June when Kaline hurt his thumb. Then, in the final weeks of the season, Mathews and McLain had freakish things happen to them. Eddie, who had been purchased after Wert got hurt, and went on to hit five homers, tripped on a stairway in his home and tumbled down twelve steps and was unable to play. Then McLain, a 17-game winner, didn't realize his foot had fallen asleep while he was sitting at home, watching television. When he stood up, the foot buckled under him. He dislocated his toes.

We had our injury jinx, too. There was Tony's—about as bad as you could get. And Rico had missed a month after getting hit. His fielding didn't suffer, but he had been batting close to .300 when he was injured. His hitting tailed off when he returned.

We split a doubleheader with the Orioles to open the series, with Santiago picking up his third victory in five days. This time, Jose was our starter in the second game. He had only completed one game all season, and picked a pretty good time to get number 2. Some monumental base running by Reggie helped us in the second game after we were blown away, 1–0, in the opener. We were trailing by 2–0 when we scored five runs on only three hits, two errors, and Smith's running. I started the inning with a single, but the big play came when Harrelson hit a grounder to Aparicio at short with Scott on third and Reggie at second. Aparicio threw to third to head off Smith, who retreated toward second. That allowed Boomer to score, but Smith then ran back toward third, giving Hawk time to reach second. We produced a five-run rally.

Still, the game we lost allowed the Twins to take over first. Kaat was pitching back to his 1966 form for them, when he won 25 games. He defeated the Yankees for his sixth straight.

Frank Robinson was playing in only his eleventh game of the season against us the next day. But he hit his seventh homer against us to give Baltimore a 4–0 lead. We battled back, of course, and we even went ahead by 5–4 when I hit number 42. But Brooks Robinson retaliated with a two-run shot of his own. With a week to go, we were now third, only half a game back. In fact, only .007 percentage points separated all four clubs, with the White Sox in fourth, only one game out.

Lonborg just *had* to win for us as we ended our Baltimore trip on Sunday. He came through with one of his finest performances. This time he didn't complain when Williams took him out after six innings and only two hits. He knew that Dick was saving him so he could get in two more starts over the final four games. And anyway, we had a 7–0 lead. Adair, Jones, and Scott came through with four-hit games.

On our day off on Monday, I took some batting practice, and we inched back into a tie for first with the Twins. They were clobbered by the Angels. Zoilo Versalles, the Twins' shortstop, complained that the Angels' manager, Bill Rigney, had hot-dogged it by sacrificing two runners along with a 7–2 lead. Pennant races make you say nasty things. Versalles was batting only .202, just two years after he was the league's MVP.

Well, this was it. The start of our final homestand: two games each against the Indians and Twins. We were still half a game back of Minnesota. Dick planned to open the series with Bell, then start Lonborg in the second game. But we also were playing "scoreboard baseball," a game that drives players and fans crazy.

The papers were filled with stories, edging out Boston's primary election for mayor. We knew that the state was rooting for us, of course, and all of New England. But we also had become America's Team before the Dallas Cowboys. I remember when the Yanks' Monbouquette had beaten us a few weeks before, he had said he was praying for us to "win for Mr. Yawkey." A week later after Moe Drabowsky of the Orioles pitched well against us in relief, he said, "This is my job. But I've always been a Boston fan." To make sure everyone knew what was going on with the Twins, one of the stations arranged to beam their broadcast back to Boston.

We came back flat. The Indians started Luis Tiant, who would give me lots of laughs one day. But no one was smiling at him then as he shut us out with his fastball through six innings as they took a 6–0 lead. In the seventh I tagged him for a three-run homer, 450 feet into center field, for number 43. It was a historic shot, but didn't mean much else at the time to me because we lost the game. It tied me with Ted Williams for the most ever hit by a Boston left-handed batter. That number did have some magic around town, I must admit. The club record actually is 50, which Jimmie Foxx hit in 1938. But the right-handed Foxx was hitting into the Wall, and Ted's 43 had always seemed more impressive. On the scoreboard, though, we could see that the Twins were getting even with the Angels. Killebrew socked a pair to tie me for the league lead at 43 and Kaat came through with another clutch victory. He had won seven straight in September. Now the Twins had a one-game lead. We were tied for second with the White Sox, who were rained out, while the Tigers were one and a half back. They remained alive thanks to Lolich, who shut out the Yankees, 1–0, with Mathews driving in Kaline on a sacrifice fly. The Twins could win it all by taking two of their last three games.

After what happened next, I thought it was all over for us. The Indians—a sixth-place club we had beaten seven straight times, and twelve of fifteen on the season—stopped us for a second straight game. We were so tight and they were so loose. Lonborg didn't last after starting with only two days' rest. We were shut out with only six hits. *The best, the absolute best we can do now,* I figured, *is a tie for first.* And even that was a reach. My folks had a disappointing drive home. They had left the farm, at the height of the potato harvest, to drive to a beach on Long Island Sound, where they could pick up the Connecticut station that was broadcasting our games.

In the locker room, I went over to some of the guys and

congratulated them on the great season we had. As far as most of us were concerned, it was all over.

"Way to go, Jimmy," I said to Lonborg. "You kept us in it."

"Thanks, Yaz, you did, too," he told me.

I went over to Rico and Adair, and Boomer. Guys came over to me and patted me on the shoulder. I was already thinking about what we had to do next year, how this had set us up as legitimate contenders and what we needed to do to get to that next level.

But a little while after our game was over we heard some good news—the Angels beat the Twins almost the same way the Indians had defeated us. Chance was knocked out after starting with two days of rest. The big moment for the Angels —and for us, it turned out—was Killebrew coming to the plate with the bases loaded, in the seventh, the Twins trailing by 4–0, and the count run up to 3–0. Ermer let Killer swing, and he flied out. Maybe the Twins were getting tight as well. And the Angels were loose. They also were madder than you would want a team that already is out of it to be. The day before, a couple of the Twins' benchwarmers, Sandy Valdespino and Jackie Hernandez, had been giving a pretty good ribbing to the Angels during Minnesota's victory. That had really ticked off California, which went on a crusade as a spoiler. After beating Minnesota, the Angels were going into Detroit to end the season with a four-game series.

Even with the Twins' loss, when I went home I told Carol, "Honey, this is it. We're out of it." The White Sox were playing a twilight doubleheader with the last-place A's. If Chicago won two, they'd be in first. Still, I thought, *Ah, what the heck.* So I called the Boston papers for the scores. Every ten minutes. First, it was scoreless. Then the A's took a 1–0 lead. I called again. They led by 3–0—against Gary Peters, whom I always thought was their top guy. And then they won the first game. In the second, it was Hunter against Horlen. I kept jumping out of the living room chair to make a phone call. It was scoreless through three, through five, then in the bottom of the sixth the A's got four runs. They swept the doubleheader. *Maybe,* I thought, *this is meant to be for us.*

We were going to be off for two days, Thursday and Friday, before the Twins came in for their final two games. Minnesota was a game in front at 91–69. We were a game back with Detroit at 89–69. The White Sox were one and a half behind with a record of 89–70.

In the first three days of the final week of the pennant race, the four contending teams played nine games and lost seven. Because of the last-minute craziness, the league had developed a formula in case of three-way ties (a four-way tie wasn't possible). There would be round-robins involving Minnesota, Detroit, and Chicago—or Detroit, Chicago, and us. None of that looked very possible to us. Even if we swept the Twins, we needed the other clubs to collapse. If we split with the Twins, it was all over.

On Thursday, another break, or was it? The Angels' game at Detroit was postponed because of rain. That set up a doubleheader for the Tigers, but it could also give Sparma another day of rest. Meanwhile, a few of us worked out at Fenway, while the Twins flew in that night.

The agony continued on Friday, at least halfway. The White Sox were eliminated by the eighth-place Senators, who scored an unearned run and won by 1–0. The Tigers never had a chance to play. They were rained out for a second straight day, which meant they were going to wind up with doubleheaders on Saturday and Sunday. Williams gave us his lineup for Saturday's opener against the Twins. It was going to be Santiago starting. Also, Hawk was the cleanup hitter, playing right. Adair was at third instead of either Foy or Jones.

When I got home after practice, the place was mobbed. All my relatives had come up from Long Island and they were shoehorned into every corner of the house. I told Carol that we couldn't stay there. I called the Colonial and got us a room for the two nights.

I didn't sleep much that night. You plan for a lifetime to be in a situation, and then, all of a sudden, there you are.

Tossing and turning can't describe it. It was as if every possibility in the world was on my shoulders, in my hands, and I had to handle it.

I flashed back—

—to the garage in the winters, bundled up in my shearling coat, swatting at a ball on a string.

—to the fungoes I hit with rocks in the potato fields.

—to the nights and weekends on the White Eagles, playing alongside Dad.

And I also considered our present state, how we had to handle a Minnesota club that had kicked the crap out of us all year, beating us eleven out of sixteen. All we had to do now was win two straight. But I also continued to imagine that I was going to be the key man again. It was a conviction I couldn't shake, didn't want to lose. This was a reprieve for us. Only two days earlier we were shaking hands and practically saying goodbye. Some of the guys were actually packing their stuff so they wouldn't have to do it at the last minute on Sunday.

I got out of bed at six in the morning, got dressed while Carol was sleeping, and walked the whole golf course. For two hours all I did was think about what was coming up, and what my role would be in all of it. I thought about all the events that had brought me to this moment in time. Alone on the course, I saw some squirrels hopping across the fairways. I could hear birds chirping in the trees. My senses were very sharp, almost as if I was the only person in the world just then, and that I could control everything. The first golfers of the day were getting ready to tee off when I made my way back toward the clubhouse. Then I went to the ballpark early.

My biggest worry was how the players were going to respond. Two days before we were real low. *Now,* I wondered, *can we get back up?* I spent fifteen, twenty minutes just talking to them, telling them, "We're back in this thing. We've got to go."

"Jose, you know we're all behind you," I told Santiago.

"I'm fine, Yaz," he told me. "I called home to Puerto Rico last night. The whole island's rooting."

Jose had not had a winning season since 1963 with a relief win to finish 1–0 for the A's. But there he was, riding a seven-game winning streak in the middle of a pennant race and enjoying the heck out of it.

Jose made me a promise.

"I promise you that Killebrew isn't going to hit any out of the park off me today, okay?" I was tied with Killer for the home run lead at 43.

"Jose," I replied, "You stop him and I'll make sure I hit one out for you."

"A deal," he said.

We had been in a pennant race for a month, and fans and players had become accustomed to that special pressure. But that Saturday brought a different atmosphere, a level of intensity I had never seen or felt before. When we went out for batting practice, the stands were loaded with people standing up and cheering. I had never experienced yelling like that before the game even started. Vice President Hubert Humphrey (rooting for the Twins, naturally), Senator Ted Kennedy, governors of half a dozen states, and every official of every hamlet in Massachusetts, it seemed, were on hand. Kids climbed billboards beyond center field, hanging on and watching us. I took batting practice, went into the trainer's room, and took a nap for twenty minutes and was ready to go.

Jose got tagged early. But if you wanted this game to symbolize the season for us, you got it. They scored a run off him, loaded the bases with only one out, but then Carew lined out and Jose got Uhlaender—after going to 3–1—on a grounder.

A break. But Kaat was pitching and he was tough, going through the best streak of his life with seven victories in the month. I had tagged him for a single in the first, but he left me stranded. Then another break. Luck? Bad luck for them? All of the above. Kaat had one out in the third. He already had fanned three batters, then mowed down Santiago for his fourth. Suddenly, he felt something pop in his left elbow. He called "time." Then he tried pitching to Andrews. He threw two balls and then Kaat signaled that he couldn't continue. Jim Perry came in, threw for ten minutes, and finally was ready to pitch to Mike. He walked him. But Perry got out of the inning by striking me out.

I got another chance against him in the fifth. Reggie began the inning with a double, then Dick pinch-hit for Gibson, bringing in Jones. Dalton hit a grounder to Carew at second, an easy play. The ball took a bounce when Rod didn't expect it, though, and hit him in the shoulder. Adair soon tied the game by looping a hit over Carew to score Reggie, with Jones going to third. That brought me up. I rapped the ball sharply into the hole between first and second. Killebrew dived for it and couldn't reach it. Carew dashed over, though, and came up with it. But no one was on first for his throw. Perry had stood flat-footed on the mound. While he watched, Dalton scored. We were in the lead.

The Twins tied it in the top of the sixth and Scott put us ahead with a 450-foot homer in our half of the inning. So we were nursing a 3–2 lead in the seventh. Andrews got on with a roller in front of the plate, and then Adair hit an apparent double-play ball back to the pitcher, Ron Kline. He wheeled and threw to second—but Versalles dropped the ball. Everyone was safe and I came up with two runners on.

The noise factor was monumental all day. Each time a player's name was announced, the volume almost hurt. And it wouldn't stop. As I got up out of the batting circle, it grew even louder, still rising as I stepped into the box. Finally, it would tone down, but it wouldn't stop, and you almost wanted to say, "Shut up, let me think." But I was able to block it all out. I'd take a pitch, and go through my ritual, step out of the box, hitch up. Touch my helmet, my belt, my shirt. I'd pull on my pants, unconsciously. I guess what I really was doing was buying an extra second or two to talk to myself. Maybe I was talking out loud, as Stottlemyre insists, but I had the ability to block it out, just as you block out 35,000 screaming people. You could see the fans, see their lips moving. But I didn't hear them.

Ermer didn't want Kline to face me. He brought in Jim Merritt, a southpaw. In Minneapolis, with its shorter right field area, Merritt threw me sliders. I thought that he might change his mind in Fenway, though, figuring that even if I tagged his fastball, it would be hard to get it out of the park. I got up, thinking, *Slider.* I took the first pitch, a high fastball with no movement. That made me feel better. The count went to 3–1. *High fastball,* I thought. I had the count my way and I knew the kid was going to throw it in the strike zone. He was one of the best control pitchers in baseball. In the whole season he had walked only 30 batters in more than 220 innings. *Sure enough, high fastball.* I lashed at it and I knew, just knew with that split-second recognition, that I had done it. It headed for the bleachers—those stands 380 feet away that I never thought I'd ever reach—and a roar started. It built as I circled each base, continued as the 3 went up in the scoreboard to show we had a 6–2 lead, and the noise didn't end for three minutes. It continued long after I had gone into the dugout. On the bench, our trainer, Buddy LeRoux, asked Santiago how he was feeling. Jose told him, "I'm getting tired. But don't say anything to Dick."

Santiago kept his promise to me. He stopped Killebrew from hitting a homer. But he also got lifted in the eighth after walking the leadoff batter. Bell came in for him. Gary was not a reliever. He got out of the eighth, though, and even had two outs in the ninth. Then Cesar Tovar lofted a fly down the line to me. I knew I could get it. But I didn't account for the wet grass. I couldn't get a solid footing and had to chase it for a double. Ironically, that gave Killebrew life. Although Howard was now catching, Dick was signaling the pitch selection from the bench. Gary's first pitch was off the plate. Williams ran out to the mound. I knew exactly what he was telling him. He didn't want Gary to walk Killebrew at any cost, not with Tony Oliva coming up, and Bob Allison following him. Bell threw a 1–0 fast ball—which Killer had to know was coming

—and ripped it. I just stood there as it hit into the screen for his forty-fourth homer. Yeah, I was annoyed. I allowed myself that much, even though we still had a game to win and a pennant to fight for. He was tied with me for the home run lead. But Bell got Oliva, and we had a 6–4 victory. While we were all whooping it up in the locker room, Williams came over to me and said, "Don't blame Bell or Howard. I called that pitch." Even later, when he saw me leave to meet Carol, he left the locker room and told her, "Carol, I'm sorry about that pitch. It was my call."

Now get this. The Tigers were on the verge of practically wrapping it up. While we were winning, they defeated the Angels in the opener of their doubleheader. They were in first place by percentage points at 90–69, while we were tied for second at 91–70. Then the Tigers were leading, 6–2, in the eighth inning of the second game—and they blew it. A victory would give them a half-game lead going into the final day. Instead, the Angels produced a six-run rally in the inning and won.

Carol and I and everyone from both families celebrated that night. My uncles and cousins and Mom and Dad, her folks, her brother, friends. There were probably thirty of us at Stella's, an Italian restaurant in the North End. When we were ready to leave, the owner warned me that a few hundred people were mobbing the front. We sneaked out through the kitchen. Back at the Colonial, I told Carol I couldn't attend a party that was planned for the families, and I went up to the room by myself. I read some of the papers and dozed off. Strange, but this time, instead of imagining all the great things I was going to do, I became fearful. I worried about Chance and his sinker, and about how the Twins had handled us during the year. I wasn't starring in my imaginary movies. I had this peculiar feeling that we didn't deserve what we were on the verge of accomplishing. About three in the morning, I got up, and I had to get out. I started to dress and Carol woke up.

"What's the matter?" she asked. "Where are you going?"

"I have to go for a walk," I told her. She had seen me often enough over the years reacting like a caged animal. She understood.

Back I went to the course. It was the first day of October and cold and damp. *What's the wind like?* I wondered. I was almost shivering in my light jacket, but I knew I didn't want to go back to the hotel. I still had to be alone. I got in the car and gunned it north on Route 128. I drove to Gloucester, which was still asleep. Then I headed back. Even though I grabbed something to eat at the hotel, I realized how stupid I had been. Here we are, on the day we can win the pennant, and I'm going sight-seeing without any sleep. What the hell kind of shape would I be in just a few hours later?

That last Sunday, this is the way the standings looked:

	W	L	Pct.	GB	To Play
Boston	91	70	.565	—	1
Minnesota	91	70	.565	—	1
Detroit	90	70	.563	1/2	2

About ten-thirty, I got to the park, as usual the first player there.

"How ya doing, Carl?" Fitzie asked me. Good old Fitz, the first guy on the Sox who had a smile for me. Still good to me after all these years, still concerned.

You come in for the game of your life and everything is heightened. Or should be. I tried to snap out of it. Usually, I would take either batting practice or fielding practice. I thought that this time I'd try both to try to get into the swing of things. It didn't help. Batting practice was lousy. Out in the field the ball felt heavy on the thick grass.

I walked back to the dugout and tried to gather my thoughts. *Let me continue the routine,* I said to myself. I sent the bat boy out for lunch, which he always brought down from the press room. I still had this nagging feeling that it was

going to be a rotten day. I took my pregame nap in the trainer's room and knew Fitzie would wake me up fifteen minutes
before game time, as usual. Tony C. was in the locker room,
trying to be part of it and yet not wanting to intrude.
Lonborg, who was going to start against Chance, had changed
to a hotel room with Harrelson at the Sheraton in Boston
instead of staying at home. Lonborg had been worried about
his career record against the Twins. It was 0–6, including an
0–3 record in 1967. We all were concerned with rituals: Were
we doing the right thing, the kind of thing that helps you win
pennants?

We started out shaky. Killebrew walked and Oliva hit a
drive toward the Wall. I ran up against it, my back to home,
leaped, and couldn't grab it. It caromed off toward center.
Reggie picked it up, and I was surprised to see that Billy
Martin, the third base coach, was waving Killer home. Smith
uncorked a relay throw to Scott and thought we had Killebrew at the plate. But Boomer's throw was high and Killebrew scored.

In the third, I was involved again in the field. With Tovar
on first, Killebrew got a hit in front of me.

Stop Tovar from reaching third, I thought to myself, and I
decided to charge the ball on a dead run. But the field was
muddy, and the ball hit in one spot where the dirt was
scooped out. It rolled underneath me and Tovar came home
on the error. *Uh-oh,* I thought. *Now I'm going to hear it.* But the
fans in left were great. Some of them even applauded me and
I heard someone yell, "Way to try out there, Yaz."

Still, I steamed for three innings. Chance was pitching
great and I thought, *How can I atone for this?* I didn't think it
was going to be the sixth inning with Lonborg leading off. I
thought to myself, *Here's an out,* even though Jim had singled
earlier off Chance. But Dean was pitching a four-hitter. I had
singled in the first, Rico got a hit in the second, Lonborg in
the third, and I had doubled in the fourth, just missing a home
run near the top of the Wall. Still, Chance was protecting that
2–0 lead.

All of a sudden, everything changed. Jim noticed Tovar was playing back at third. It was one of those decisions a guy makes and it changes a life around. Lonborg bunted. He laid it down neatly along the ground and Tovar couldn't make the play. Then Adair got on with a hit just past Carew, and Jones singled just past Tovar after fouling off a bunt attempt, and—*boom*—it's bases loaded and here's my chance.

As I walked to the plate, I started to pound it into me: *Keep it under control. This is the situation you've wanted time and time again.* I knew that what I didn't want was to start thinking, *Home run.* Chance had that hard sinker that was always tailing away from me, so it was almost impossible to hit a home run. I walked to the plate with almost a defeatist attitude. I told myself I couldn't hit the home run, which every part of me would have loved to do, which the crowd, chanting "Go! Go! Go!", was demanding. Instead, I was beating myself mentally to think, *Base hit. Go up the middle.* But that's going against all my instincts and background. There was a war inside me. I knew I had to think, *ground ball up the middle. Base hit.* I was even thinking of going to left field, but again I thought, *A single's only going to tie it.* Only. I had imagined myself the ultimate hero in just this situation. Logic won out. As I put dirt on my hands, I started a litany: *Base hit, base hit, base hit. Up the middle. Don't try to pull the ball.* My confidence had returned. At that moment, I felt I was back in the spot I had wanted.

Chance had a 20–13 record, and he had real nasty stuff. He had a hard sinker that tailed away from left-handed hitters and moved in on right-handed hitters. A right-handed hitter was dead against him. If you were left-handed and tried to pull it, you'd just hit into a double play. He just kept coming at you, no letup, no finesse, a hard, 90-mile-an-hour sinker pitcher. He wouldn't give in. Ever. Here it was, just him against me.

The first pitch was a ball inside, and I was ahead in the count. I stepped out. It flashed in my mind that: *Maybe he's got to make a pretty good pitch. Swing for a homer?* No, I had to still keep thinking, *Up the middle. Base hit.* Sure enough, he came in with that sinker that started to tail away. Except I knew just where it was headed, and I drilled it to center for a single that scored two runs. I stood at first listening to the crowd roar, watch the streamers swirl from the stands as if it was a parade, and wondering how Carol was enjoying her hot dog under the stands. But I wasn't real happy about the single. I wanted to hit a home run, especially because of the error I made.

Hawk followed with a bouncer to short that Versalles threw home, trying to catch Dalton at the plate. It wasn't a wise move. Dalton was in ahead of it, and we had the lead as I ran to second. That was it for Chance. Al Worthington came in to pitch to Scott, but threw two wild pitches and I scored. A few batters later, Reggie singled in Tartabull, who ran for Harrelson. We had scored five runs on only four hits, a walk, a fielder's choice and two wild pitches.

We took that 5–2 lead into the eighth. Rich Reese singled, but Adair started a wonderful double play by grabbing Tovar's grounder at second, tagging Reese and throwing to first. But Reese spiked Jerry, who had to limp off the field while the crowd stood and roared for him and another of his clutch plays. It all changed very quickly. Killebrew and Oliva singled and suddenly Allison was up. The tying run. Allison stroked the pitch cleanly and hit it toward the corner, my corner. I couldn't let it get in there and rattle around and clear the bases.

With that instinct I had developed out there, I moved almost as soon as Allison had swung, and raced over for it and scooped it up on my backhand. Killebrew already was heading home and Oliva was taking third. *Stop Allison from getting to second,* I thought. He would tie the game if he scored from there. I wanted to make it a hard throw and I used that good ole grandstand Wall to set my right foot. The throw went on a line to Andrews at second. Allison was hook sliding, but Mike nabbed him with the tag. It was a throw I'll always remember. Three outs.

We gave the fans one last tingle in the ninth as Uhlaender

led off with a grounder to short that suddenly hopped up and hit Rico under the eye. *This can't be,* I thought. *Not Rico, too.* For a few moments he was on the ground. He got up, though, and said he was ready to play. Carew, up next, hit a grounder to Andrews, who was playing second because Adair had been hurt. Mike snared the ball, and started to make an almost-identical play to Adair's. Andrews tagged Uhlaender, who spiked him, but Mike was able to get the ball off to Scott. It was a low throw that he dug out of the dirt. Double play—two down and one to go. Then bedlam as Rich Rollins hit a pop fly to Rico at short. I charged in behind him in case he dropped it. When it hit his glove, Fenway exploded. How the fans got to Lonborg before Rico or I did I'll never know. This was in the days before fans routinely charged the field after a big victory. The police were caught by surprise. Why would anyone expect a few thousand people to run out and mob us? But there Jim was, hoisted on their shoulders, people tearing at his shirt for a piece of flannel, shredding it while Jim was smiling, not showing how really scared he was of being passed along, bobbing up and down like a cork in the ocean. I dashed for the backstop, then worked my way from there to the dugout. People were reaching for me and tearing at me. Some guy who was trying to pat me on the shoulder connected with a shot to my jaw instead.

Ten minutes later, Lonborg escaped. He came in looking shaken. In another part of the locker room, Conigliaro was crying. I looked around and saw my dad there, standing with Uncle Mike and John.

Tom Yawkey came over to my locker and said, almost crying, "I don't know how to thank you."

"You know," I told him, practically shouting in his ear so he could hear me above the roar, "you and I are the only ones left who realize what this means."

I looked at him and laughed. I had gotten his clothes soaked.

The scoreboard showed that Detroit had won its first game by 6–4. We didn't wait for the second. We didn't break

out the champagne, of course, but we took out the beer and
shook it up and sudsed everyone. I took shaving cream and
swirled it around Rico's face. Conigliaro, who had been allowed to watch the game from the bench, seemed happy but
somehow out of it. Even though he was on the bench, he
wasn't allowed to needle anyone.

"Thanks, Yaz. You had a fantastic season," Williams told
me. Then he thanked Mr. Yawkey for giving him the chance
to manage. Tom was crying.

And yet, we actually hadn't won anything yet. All we had
clinched was a playoff if the Tigers won the second game. But
if they lost, it was ours.

So a couple of the guys went into the trainer's room
where LeRoux had a radio, which was bringing in the second
game. It was supposed to be on TV, but NBC switched to the
AFL game between the Raiders and Chiefs. None of us left
the locker room once our minicelebration ended. We waited
for the results at Detroit.

How could the season end easily for us? We had nothing
left after we had beaten Minnesota, yet we had to wait out a
game most of us couldn't hear. Instead, there'd be a whoop
out of the trainer's room and someone would run out and tell
us who singled, or who grounded out.

The early news wasn't good. The Tigers took a 3–1 lead
in the second, but then the Angels came back with three in the
third to go ahead by 4–3, then three more in the fourth for a
7–3 lead and another in the fifth and it was 8–3.

I got so excited, I yelled, "That's it! Put the champagne
on ice!"

"No no, not yet," someone said. It's a good thing. We
would have gone crazy putting the champagne in and out of
the ice. The Tigers came back in the seventh for two, and
going into the bottom of the ninth, the Angels held an 8–5
lead. We were all gathered near the radio and in the doorway.
Bill Freehan, the Tigers' catcher who had been behind the
plate for all thirty-six innings in the two weekend doublehead-

ers, led off the ninth with a double. A shock went through my body.

"These guys are going to win it," I said to nobody in particular. "It's fate." Somehow, I was thinking that the same Impossible Dream that had come true for us was about to evolve for the Tigers. Wert walked and suddenly it became possible for a home run to tie the game.

The managers did some juggling. Mayo Smith sent up Lenny Green to hit for Lolich and Rigney countered with George Brunet, who had lost 19 games, the most in the league, but was a guy who pitched in tough luck that season. Brunet replaced Minnie Rojas, and I said a "Thank you" to Rigney for fighting this thing all the way down to the wire. But Smith didn't let Green bat and replaced him with Jim Price, a right-handed hitter, against Brunet, a southpaw. Price hit a fly to left.

"That's one," someone in the locker room shouted.

Dick McAuliffe, the next batter, hit a grounder to second.

"One!" we screamed as Bobby Knoop, the second baseman, threw to Jim Fregosi for the force.

"Two!" we yelled as Fregosi completed the throw to first for the double play.

We started our second pennant celebration, only this time we brought out the champagne. We had done it, brought Red Sox fans their first pennant since 1946, their second since 1918!

It's not the celebration that I remember. It's the intense feeling surrounding it. Guys are always celebrating a pennant when they clinch it. The Cards had a champagne party of their own a week before. But this . . . this was a victory for the underdog. No, that's too simple. It was a victory for a city that didn't think it had one left in it.

"Say something, Yaz. Speech."

I stood on a table while Fitzie was holding my ankles nervously, hoping I wouldn't fall.

"Thanks for not quitting," I told the guys. "Thanks for giving me the thrill of my life."

• • •

The next day I was able to put into perspective my own role in the whole affair.

I wound up the season with 6 straight hits, and 7 hits in my last 8 at-bats in the two games. As we won eight of our last twelve games, I connected for 23 hits in 44 at-bats (an average of .523), hit safely in eleven of the games, drove in 16 runs, scored 14 and hit 5 homers. They enabled me to win the Triple Crown with a batting average of .326, 121 runs batted in, and 44 homers. It was only the eleventh time it had been done. I admit I wasn't sure it was mine.

"Tell me," I asked a writer when the game ended, "do I still get the Triple Crown even though I'm tied for homers with Harmon?" When I heard I did, it was especially satisfying. For good measure, I also led in slugging average with .622, in total bases with 360, in runs with 112, in hits with 189, and I finished third in doubles with 31.

Maybe wishing had made it so, those dreams I had of putting myself in the clutch, where it was up to me and where I would come through.

And maybe, what we accomplished made people forget about some of the bad things that had surrounded the Sox over the years. I know I thought we had a hell of a future.

"I just had a feeling we'd do this," Bobby Doerr told me. "It was like what the Yankees did to us in 1949 by winning the last two. When the weekend started, I knew we'd be able to do the same thing ourselves."

It just took us a few more years.

Outside, we were greeted by a constant blare of honking horns. Firecrackers exploded. Traffic was snarled. I thought that NBC learned a lesson in all this. Sure, football was becoming the Sunday television sport. But when there was a pennant race on, nothing was more important to Americans than baseball.

· · ·

In the 1967 World Series, Roger Maris was on one side and Elston Howard was on the other. And neither was playing with the Yankees. That said a lot about how the game had started to change, and how its new era was under way.

We had been formed, mostly, from our farm system: Rico, Reggie, Andrews, Scott, Lonborg, Foy, Tony C., all of us were career Red Sox players. We added Bell, who had been an Indians' starter, in midseason; Santiago and Wyatt, whose careers were going nowhere at Kansas City; Adair, who had lost starting jobs at Baltimore and Chicago; Harrelson, somehow set free from the A's, and Howard.

The Cardinals were an unusual collection, in that so many of their key players were not homegrown: Orlando Cepeda was acquired from the Giants, who had given up on him the year before; Lou Brock was obtained from the Cubs; Curt Flood originally was Cincinnati property; and Julian Javier belonged to Pittsburgh. Maris was traded by the Yankees in the off-season for a giveaway, Charley Smith. Only Tim Mc-Carver, the catcher, and most of the pitchers were developed by the Cardinals, along with Mike Shannon, Dal Maxvill, and Bobby Tolan.

They had won 101 games with Bob Gibson disabled for two months with a broken leg. Now Gibson was ready to face us. But we had Lonborg. The problem was that Jim had started our last game and could not start again until Game 2. If it went seven games, he had would have to start that last game with only two days' rest. Gibson was rested, since the Cards had coasted the last month.

That string of great breaks ended before our first Series game even began. Someone messed up the pregame schedule and our batting practice was cut from forty-five minutes to twenty. We got only half the swings we should have received. I had about a third, and felt rusty. And we needed them after the emotional turmoil we had gone through for a solid month. The two days off barely had given us a chance to get into a

different kind of groove. It would have been good to get the
BP in and get accustomed to swinging again. I had only half a
dozen, and when I went in to relax before the game, I just
didn't feel ready. I don't know how many of us did. Just getting to that point was such a tremendous accomplishment—
after all, we had just won the tightest pennant race in history
—that no matter how hard you try, you can't always get yourself in gear automatically for the next hurdle.

Except that as soon as I faced Gibson the first time I was
ready. We had a pretty good thing going between us.

Gibson used to talk to me. I got into the box the first time
and he shouted from the mound, "I'm going to strike you
out." He didn't stop there. Every at-bat he hollered at me,
and I'd yell back at him, "Bull, throw that crap at me." We
carried it over in spring training. I knew his reputation for
throwing at guys, but he never threw at me. Oh, he was mean,
all right. But I think that Gibson saw me as a one-to-one challenge, and he was going to go with his best against my best,
with no distractions.

He got me out with a foul pop in the first. I came to bat
in the fourth feeling good. I had just cut down Julian Javier at
the plate to end the inning for the Cards. I was pumped when
I faced Gibson, but all I got off him was a grounder to second.
That frosted me because he had hung a slider and I should
have pulled it hard to right. I figured it was time to quit screw-
ing around. I left the bench and found Fitzie inside and told
him, "Get the ground crew ready after the game, I'm going to
take batting practice when it's over." Then I went out to left,
determined to remain alert in the field. I didn't have to wait
long. Curt Flood led off the fifth with a high, twisting shot
toward the line that I leaped for and caught backhanded.

My next two at-bats I floated two balls off Gibson to left.
We lost, 2–1, as Santiago hit a homer and pitched a hell of a
gutsy game, in and out of trouble, ten hits in seven innings,
but giving up only the two runs. Brock, who had four hits,
scored both of them on groundouts by Maris. Gibson went all
the way and struck out ten.

After I spoke to the writers, I asked Foy if he would pitch to me. When Rico and Hawk saw what I was doing, they asked if they could come out, too. Rico had struck out three times and Hawk also was 0 for 3. The ground crew rolled the cage out of its cave along the left field foul line. People started streaming down from the press box to see what was going on. They said they had never seen anyone take batting practice after a World Series game.

Well, this was only my first Series game. Taking batting practice after games had become such an accepted way of doing things for me, I never thought it was unusual. Doerr stood behind the cage as Foy got set to deliver.

"Hands high," said Bobby. "Quick hands now."

The workout lasted almost an hour. We took turns pitching and batting. I had forty-seven swings and knocked my last three over the right field wall. When I finished, I was feeling good, and said said to the club photographer, "I'm going to hit two out tomorrow."

I felt good about our chances, too, although that extra game that Gibson would have against us was on my mind. No one gave us much of a chance against the Cards, who were 3–2 favorites. They liked to talk big, too. I thought how much better our chances would have been if Conigliaro could play.

Jim was our starter in Game 2 against Dick Hughes, a twenty-nine-year-old rookie. I had a world of confidence with Lonborg out there, and I was feeling good that the two of us could make something happen. I didn't even take batting practice, thinking I had been in a groove the day before. *Let me conserve my energy.* I was no Killebrew.

Lonborg didn't mess around. Brock had killed us the day before with his four hits, two stolen bases, and two runs. Lonborg went straight for his head on the first pitch. We never heard from Brock again that day. He was 0 for 4. But no one else did anything against Jim. He pitched one of the greatest World Series games ever, a one-hitter. Along the way, he also brushed back Flood, Maxvill, and Hughes.

Meanwhile, I had told Doerr that I was going to be

swinging from the heels against Hughes, a righty. We needed something to shake us, and to demoralize them, and there's nothing like the long ball to do that.

When I got up in the first, I swung just in front of the pitch and whacked it out of the park but foul by a few feet. Hughes walked me. In the fourth, after Lonborg had retired his twelfth straight batter, I came to bat in a scoreless game. I didn't expect to see Hughes's slider anymore—that's the pitch I had hit foul but long. This time he fed me fastballs, and ran the count to 2–1. His next pitch was hard and low, but over the middle. I drove it on a line into the right field stands. I felt so good about that fat 1–0 lead that when I got into the dugout I said to Lonborg, "Go get 'em, big guy. That's all you'll need." And that's all he did need.

This was not a superstitious guy. The rest of us respected that old baseball tradition, and none of us talked about the no-hitter. But Lonny was challenging each of us when we trotted onto the field each time: "C'mon, guys, I want that no-hitter."

He retired the first nineteen batters, but with one out in the seventh, Curt Flood fouled off two pitches with the count at 3–2, then took a ball that was just outside. That didn't faze Jim, working with only a 2–0 lead, and he set down Maris and Cepeda. Before the Series, we had sent out people scouting the Cardinals. Frank Malzone had given me a good report on Joe Hoerner: "Don't worry about the breaking ball. He tries to jam left-handed hitters by throwing it past them. Also has a good sinker." It the bottom of the inning I got my chance to see if Frank was right. With runners on first and second, manager Red Schoendienst brought in Hoerner. *Fastball* went through my mind. That's what he fed me. The count reached 3–2 as he missed on a fastball, low and outside. The next one was coming in high and tight, I was certain. And there it was. I was all over it and sent it ten rows back in right. That was the first time anyone had hit two in a Series game since Mantle in 1960. At that point, the Babe had been the only one ever to hit three.

Now, with a 5–0 lead, we could all think of Jim's no-hitter. That gave him some room to relax, too. In the eighth he got two groundouts, bringing up Javier. But Lonborg hung a curve and Javier got around on it and drove it into the corner for a double. There went the no-hitter, but not the game.

You always wonder after a game like that what the other manager and pitcher are planning. Lonborg had brushed back four of their guys. I had gone 3 for 4, with two homers and four RBIs. It made sense to me that Nelson Briles, who was going to start Game 3 in St. Louis, might have some thoughts of retaliating. You don't want to do it late in a World Series game that you're trailing. But you might want to do it right away in the next game.

I knew it was coming even though they didn't tell me. Eddie Bressoud, whom I had been good friends with when he played for the Red Sox, was on the Cards. He told Fitzie that they were going to throw at me. Fitzie never told me until after the game was over. I had the ability to avoid being hit, and I never got hit in the head. Fitzie thought that if he warned me I might try to get out of the way with an unnatural movement.

Briles was a Cinderella story himself. He was in the bullpen in July when Roberto Clemente hit a line drive off Gibson's right shin, breaking a bone and promoting Briles to the starting rotation. He won his last nine in a row. I faced him with two out. He threw a hard one behind me. Those are the kind you can't avoid. I didn't, and it plunked me in the left calf. No way I showed any emotion.

"Thank you," I called to Briles as I trotted to first.

But Williams tore out of the dugout to confront the home plate umpire, Frank Umont.

"What are we gonna have here, a throwing contest?" shouted Williams. "I know that was deliberate. He threw behind him. Two can play this game."

By then Schoendienst was out there, too.

"What the hell are you talking about?" said

Schoendienst. "Lonborg was bragging that he brushed back our guys the last game."

"No more," said Umont to both managers.

It sure was a different time back then. In the 1960s, guys threw at you all the time. If someone hit you, it was practically written into your contract that you'd go down to first base as if it didn't hurt. In the meantime, you're dying. Don't even count the times they threw at you after a home run. From 1967 to 1970 I lost track of how many times I'd been knocked down. It would come at least once in a series, and sometimes once a game. I'm not talking about throwing at your legs. They threw behind your head. In 1967, Kaat threw a ball that must have been half a foot behind my head. On the next pitch, I said the equivalent of "The hell with you." I singled. That is the great equalizer a hitter has when a pitcher throws at him. I started the 1968 season hitting a home run against Earl Wilson in Detroit. We only played one game because of a rainout, so then we went into Cleveland. Now, remember, I hadn't even faced Cleveland yet, but in my first at-bat, two outs, nobody on, the first pitch from Steve Hargan knocked me down.

Gary Peters became one of my best friends when he was traded to the Red Sox, but when he was on Chicago, he used to wait for me. He'd watch batting practice from the bullpen and when it was my turn in the cage he'd walk by me and say, "I'm gonna get you today, somewhere I'm gonna get ya," and he'd continue walking. After he was traded to us, he told me, "Stanky used to tell the pitchers that if there was one guy on Boston we had to get, it was Yastrzemski."

What must have bugged Stanky was that I never had fear. Or, at least, never showed it. The hardest pitch to avoid is when they threw behind your head. Everyone always falls backward. It's an instinct, you shy away from trouble, don't poke your head toward it. But I always fell forward, so the idea of getting hit in the head never bothered me. What hurt, and got me angry, was getting hit in the elbow. That affected my swing. I got nailed there against Minnesota once after somebody had hit Killebrew. I was up all night squeezing a tennis ball, trying to keep the swelling down, trying to keep the feeling in my arm. Two days later we were playing Texas. I got taped up, put a big pad on the elbow. We were kicking the crap out of the Rangers. Billy Martin was managing. A left-hander came in to pitch to me and jeez, on the first damn pitch, he hit me right on the elbow. I went down to first, but I was sick inside. I wanted to throw up. Martin came out to the mound and started yelling at the pitcher, "Hit him in the back, but not in the elbow, dammit." Billy understood that you could put a guy out of commission that way.

Still, hitting guys was accepted then. There was a reliever, I think for the Angels, who got me a few times, always when I never expected it. He'd tag me when I was ahead in the count, 3–0, 3–1. That's when I figured I could set up, and that's when he hit me in the side. Yet, when you had a big day back then, you kind of expected it.

Then, all of a sudden it changed. When the Players Association came in, it was as if you didn't want to hurt your fellow union member. Nobody threw at you anymore. It became very comfortable getting into that batter's box and hitting. The union brought the players together, and then once there was a strike, where everyone went out, the richest and the poorest, that solidified an "all for one and one for all" philosophy. Your brother can hardly be your enemy.

Now when someone gets thrown at, he runs out to attack the pitcher. The umps warn everyone if a few players hear chin music. If these guys had played in the 1960s, there would have been ten fights a day, that's how many guys were throwing at you. A pitcher automatically unloaded on you. I understood that and accepted it. If the guy in front of me hit a home run and there were two outs, I knew I was going to get drilled. That's why I kind of hoped they'd throw at my head. I knew I could get out of the way. But when the pitch is behind you, like the one Briles threw, you freeze.

Yet, I had so much confidence when pitchers threw the ball just under my chin, many times I wouldn't even move. I would just kind of raise my chin a little, which drove the pitchers nuts. Here the manager probably ordered them to brush me back, and all I did was just a little head bob. But that's how much confidence I had in my quickness. I loved it when guys threw at me, especially when I wasn't swinging the bat well. The elbow, the hand—I didn't like getting hit there. Those injuries slowed me down for a couple of days. But if I got hit in the side, the leg, the butt—that would get me mad.

So I stood on first against Briles, steaming. Cepeda relieved the tension for me. The first baseman asked, "Did you get your $100,000 contract for next season?" There had been a lot of talk about it in the paper. A $100,000 deal was a rarity. Mantle might have been the only one in the American League with one. After we won the pennant, O'Connell told me during the locker room celebration that I had it.

"Yeah, I got it," I told Cepeda. "Did you get yours?"

"No," he said, and turned his attention back to the game.

With Scott up, Briles threw one in the dirt. It skipped a few feet from McCarver, not really a wild pitch, but I thought I could catch them by surprise. I took off for second, but McCarver's throw nailed me.

The next three times I faced Briles I was trying to unload. All I got out of the at-bats were grounders to second. The only satisfaction I had that game was nailing Javier in the second when he tried to stretch a single. We didn't do much else and they beat us, 5–2.

That brought us back to Gibson again in the fourth game to pitch against Santiago, who had become a starter. I loved to play behind Jose because he pitched so fast. His attitude was "Gimme the ball." He also was a heck of a defensive player. Also, if he got beat and you pulled a prank on him, he wouldn't get mad. But the Cardinals had an edge in starting pitchers. This time Jose didn't have it. In fifteen minutes he was gone after yielding six hits and four runs. That was plenty for Gibson. We got only five hits, although I singled and doubled, yelling right back at him each time he threatened to blow me away. But I was the only Sox runner who reached second.

I know it's hokum and it's the kind of thing they do in the movies. But in baseball we really do have locker room speeches before a big game, and the manager really does put stuff on the bulletin board, figuring you'll get angry if you read something negative.

DEAD SOX was the headline on Jim Murray's column. Williams held it in front of him and snarled it out.

"Is this what you guys want everyone to think of you?" he asked. "Who is this guy, Murray, anyway to say this crap about us? We're the guys who were 100–1 shots." Then he tacked it up on the board, and we all sauntered over to it and gave it a quick look. Things like that used to get some of us angry. Of course, you only hear about the ones that the manager used that actually work. How many other times did the manager read some negative story to fire us up, and it didn't mean 2¢? To tell the truth, the married guys were more ticked off because their wives weren't treated very well in a hospitality suite set aside for both teams' wives and friends. Then before the game, someone told us that the Cardinals didn't even bring their luggage to the stadium because they were so sure this Series wasn't going back to Boston.

Our backs had been pressed up against the wall so often that we had developed an immunity to fear in those situations. Jim had a slight cold for a few days, but kept a paper horseshoe a fan had sent. How could the Cards compete against that, even with that hard-throwing southpaw, Steve Carlton, starting for them? Lonny retired the first seven batters before Maxvill singled over second base. The only other Cards' run of the three-hitter was Maris's homer with two out in the ninth. Even McCarver appreciated what Lonborg was doing. When Jim got to the plate in the seventh, the catcher said to him, "We're really ripping you, aren't we?"

"Yeah," said Jim, who had given up one hit the last game. "I knew your hitters would do better with the background in this park."

Good for Jim. Flood had complained after the one-hitter that the shirt-sleeved background in Fenway had aided Lonborg.

By the time Maris hit his shot, we had a 3–0 lead. I had gone 1 for 3, but didn't figure in the scoring, although I got the fans on me when I flung my helmet after Carlton struck me out in the third with Foy on second base. Harrelson scored him with a hit, though. In the ninth, Howard looped a hit in front of Maris with the bases loaded, driving in a run, and the last one came in on Roger's throwing error.

We were back in Boston, and for the second time in eleven days facing the exact same situation: we had to win our final two games.

There were more than four hundred telegrams waiting for us in the locker room for our off-day of practice. The longest one came from Notre Dame and was addressed to me. It was signed, somehow, by six thousand students. *We need everyone's good wishes,* I thought. Dick was starting Waslewski, who, I learned by reading the papers that day, was going to become the least-experienced pitcher ever to start a World Series game. He didn't even start the season with us, and then, after he came up in June, was demoted back to Toronto. After the International League season ended, he was brought up to replace Darrell Brandon, who developed arm trouble. Waslewski had a 2–2 record with us, but had pitched three strong innings in Game 3. Here was a kid who didn't even figure to get a full Series share and he was starting a game. Dick was playing one of his hunches again.

That Fenway noise was all around us again. I didn't think that last weekend of the regular season could ever be eclipsed, but I didn't know about Boston at World Series time. The crowd wasn't letting any of us concentrate. Doerr was hollering to Rico in batting practice, "Chop down, you're hitting under it." Rico was 0 for 10. Yet, Waslewski came through for us. And so did Rico. Gary mowed down the first six batters, giving him a string of fifteen straight over two games. Rico staked him to a lead by homering in the second. In the third the Cards reached him for a pair and they led by 2–1 when we batted in the fourth. That's when we set a Series record of three homers in an inning. That's when each drive shook Fenway. In the dugout, you could feel the benches swaying, your teeth chattering.

I had singled to right off Hughes in the first, and I thought he was going to keep it away from me when I led off the fourth. I saw one on the outside corner and I went with it, crushing it hard enough to land into the screen in left center to tie the game. With two outs, Smith homered into the right field stands, and then Rico was up. It seemed as if everyone sensed what was going to happen next. And Rico did it, hammering the ball over the Wall. The lead didn't hold and they tied it in the seventh. Gary had been taken out in the sixth after walking two batters, but he had kept us in the game and with that effort, he became a part of that 1967 magic.

You've heard of the seventh-inning stretch? That day our fans gave it a dimension of warmth and cheering and expectation few people in baseball had ever experienced. Here we were, tied at 4–4, needing to win to keep the Impossible Dream alive, and the crowd acted as if it just knew we were going to turn it on again, as if we were some drama they had seen before, knew the ending, but still wanted to see it again. The funny thing was, in the dugout we expected it, too.

With one out, Jones pinch-hit. I could see a wild look in his eyes and I told him, "Dalton, calm down. Think up there." Dalton had been storming before the game when he saw the lineup card and that Foy was playing third base. Jonesy couldn't understand why. He was hitting over .300 for the Series. He ran into Williams's office and asked him, "What the hell's going on?" Dick tried to calm him down and said, "We need Foy's glove today." That helped only a little. Despite that crazy look when he picked up the bat, he singled. Then Foy hit a liner to left that Brock chased. But good old left field. The ball bounced away from him and toward the infield. Popowski signaled for Jones to hold at third, but Dalton was in his own world by then. He raced right through the sign, rounded third, and slid into home, beating the throw. Bedlam. We got three more runs—I got one of my three hits and scored my second run—and took an 8–4 lead into the eighth with Bell pitching. With one on and none out, Mc-Carver drilled the pitch to left center. I had been there before, though. I was able to spot the ball when he hit it and on the dead run I hauled it in against the Wall. They loaded the bases, though, but with two out Dave Ricketts hit a ball deep that I was able to get under. The threat ended, we got out of the ninth, and we were in a seventh game to decide the World Series.

For the first time we got the matchup we had wanted—Lonborg versus Gibson. The problem was that Jim had only two days rest against three for Gibson. It was only the third game Dick asked Lonny to pitch with two days' rest. The first time he hurled a shutout, the next time he was shelled.

It was asking too much to go against a team like the Cardinals under those conditions. Jim had taken care of Brock in the two games he pitched, but right off the bat I could see that Jim wasn't keeping the ball low. Brock led off the game with a liner to left that I had to race for and barely caught. I thought, *If we can get something going early against Gibson, before the big guy gets into a groove, we'll have a chance against their bullpen.* In the first I came up with Foy on second, but I popped out. They got a pair of runs in the third, the second scoring on a wild pitch. Then they added two more in the fifth. We didn't even get a hit off Gibson until the fifth, when Scott tripled. Boomer scored on the wild relay home.

With the 4–1 lead, they got the first two runners on in the sixth and Javier was up. Dick called "time" and went to the mound. He wanted to take out Jim. But Lonborg practically pleaded with him. "Okay," said Dick. "Javier's probably going to sacrifice anyway." You stop the sacrifice bunt by pitching high. Jim did and Javier crossed everyone up. He swung and hit the ball into the screen. We were down by 7–1. All we could do after that was get a man on base each of the next three innings. I led off the seventh with a walk, but nothing developed. Rico opened the eighth with a double and reached third on a wild pitch, but was stranded. *Maybe, one last time?* I led off the ninth with a single. It raised my Series average to .400. But Hawk hit into a double play, Scott struck out, and the dream suddenly was over.

But it hadn't died.

You can't kill what we had and what we did just because we lost one game in October. It remains a part of people to this day. They call it the Impossible Dream or the Miracle of Fenway. For me it always went beyond a slogan. It wrapped me up forever with New England. No matter what, I would always be a part of them, the fans, the team, the city. It became our permanent connection to each other, like a family tie. And nothing could ever break that. Not to a Yastrzemski.

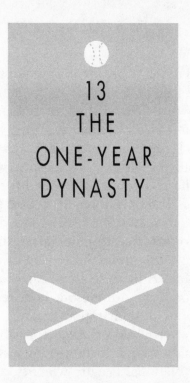

13
THE
ONE-YEAR
DYNASTY

You know it won't last forever. But we changed things around in Boston that year. Attendance more than doubled, and it hasn't been under a million since. Everyone believed that each year we could be in contention. After all, if 1967 could happen, then anything was possible.

The season lingered for months. I didn't want to forget it and neither did anyone else. One morning a dump truck pulled in front of our house filled with sod. It was left field. I had asked them to let me have it, since every season they always put new grass out there because stands were added in left field when the Patriots played football and tore up the old grass. This time, though, I wanted a permanent souvenir of 1967. That was not an era when people ran all over the field and tore it up after a big victory, so there was plenty there for me.

I also brought home some awards: the American League's Most Valuable Player trophy. Also, the Hickok Belt for Pro Athlete of the Year. I beat out Bart Starr, the quarterback of the Green Bay Packers, for that one. The baseball award was the big one. It sets you apart as the guy the team needed most and to many people it signified that you were the best player in the league. I was hoping to get it unanimously, a rare honor. Only three players had done that in the American League. I did win it by a wide margin. Two writers from each city voted, and I captured nineteen votes for first. But it wasn't unanimous because a Minnesota writer voted for Tovar. At least the guy could have voted for Killebrew. Still, MVP, something that only three Red Sox players ever had won—Foxx, Williams, and Jensen. I scooped up a wonderful assortment of honors and trophies after the season—Gold Glove Award, *Sports Illustrated* Sportsman of the Year, the Associated Press Male Athlete of the Year. Baseball writers in Boston, New York, and Minnesota honored me at dinners and presented me with their top awards.

A few days after my MVP Award, Lonborg received the Cy Young. It was the first time the trophy was split into American League and National League winners, and Jim ran away with it in our league. He took eighteen of twenty votes, which surprised none of us who had been part of his 22–9 season and his clutch pitching.

It was important for me to share my honors with the public. One way I realized I could do this was by giving the trophies to someone in public life so that others could always see them. That winter, Carol and I, along with Dick Williams and his wife, Norma, and Joe DiMaggio, visited President Lyndon Johnson. I presented him with my *Sports Illustrated* Sportsman of the Year Grecian trophy. I also gave a baseball Writer's trophy, a two-foot clock, to Senator Ted Kennedy, whose brother Jack had always been special to me. And I handed the Hickok Belt, as America's top professional athlete for 1967, over to Mr. Yawkey. He kept it in a display case in his office, along with a silver bat that Ted Williams gave him. I want the Hickok Belt in the Hall of Fame now, but with a plaque under it that will tell the public I had given it to Mr. Yawkey so they'll understand the affection I had for him.

The excitement of the off-season was shattered one day in December.

A few weeks earlier, Lonborg had signed a new contract, and told O'Connell he planned to go skiing. Dick had asked him not to. There was nothing in the contract that prevented Jim from going, though. Dick was so concerned that he warned Jim that if he were injured, he would risk losing his salary for 1968 since it would be a nonbaseball accident.

"Don't worry," Jim replied. "I'm in good shape. I won't get hurt."

But on Christmas weekend it happened. He was skiing at Lake Tahoe when he tried to stop short. Instead, he tore ligaments in his left knee. I just couldn't believe it. My next reaction was anger. I was ticked off. We won a pennant by one game with a 22-game winner—and now we had lost him. You don't know before a season that you're going to win, but dammit, you want to compete. And when I heard about it, I didn't think we could even compete. It hit me: *The season's gone.*

It was, too.

After Jim, it was all downhill—and frustrating as hell to take. We had lost our doormat image, and then all of a sudden we lost Lonborg to a skiing accident, for God's sake. We lost Conigliaro to the beaning—he sat out all of 1968. And then Santiago, who had that big winning streak at the end, hurt his elbow. You lose three top talents and now you're crap again. You're back where you were in the early 1960s.

Think about it. Tony C. was just coming into his own. He was always a good offensive ballplayer, but in 1967 he became a good defensive ballplayer. He was built like DiMaggio, with size and grace. Selfishly, I thought we'd have him for the next five years—a young Conigliaro, a young Petrocelli, a young Lonborg, a young Reggie Smith, a young Yastrzemski —you think you've got a future. You come up your first few years and the Yankees are beating the hell out of you and now you've got the young players, and you think: *Now it's our turn.* Not only did those injuries hurt the team, it took a big emotional thing out of you. You know you can't replace someone right away. Oh yeah, down the road maybe, but how do you replace a Conigliaro? And you can't get a pitcher out of Triple A to replace Lonborg.

Santiago was 9–4 when he got hurt in 1968. That means that over a twelve-month span he was 21–4 for us, a better record than Jim's. Jose got hurt during a rain delay in Minneapolis. He went four innings, then we all sat for more than an hour, waiting for rain to end. When he started to warm up again, he complained his arm was a little tight. He went in anyway, and on his second pitch—*pop!*—his arm went, just like that. You could hear it at first base.

That's how it went that season. It didn't happen all at once. But things just didn't pick up and I started having problems with Dick. The guys who had helped him win the pennant in 1967—Adair, Scott, Tartabull—wound up in his doghouse, and I stuck up for them. There were other signs. You'd go into the trainer's room and Adair would be there sleeping, and you wonder, *What's going on here?* I saw things slipping back—maybe it was just me, but I didn't want to go through it again. And the way Dick complained about the players was demoralizing. I told him, "I don't care if you call guys in your office and yell at them. But no one wants to live in a city where your manager says things about you in the press."

Dick wouldn't let up. He continued to be all over Scott. Boomer was a great competitor, all baseball. Dick tried all sorts of things to get him going, either by jumping on him when he got heavy, or by figuring out ways to get him out of a slump. One time Dick tied a rope around Scott's leg in a special practice. Boomer was in a slump and Williams figured that if he could get Scott to hit to right, he could break the habit. But Scott wouldn't do it. He used to move his front leg, which Dick thought was at the root of the problem. Dick said if he could stop Scott from kicking that front foot out, he'd slap the ball to right. So Dick put the rope on Boomer's right foot, and every time he moved it, Dick would yank on the damn rope and it would knock Boomer on his butt. Now, this wasn't like a simple batting practice. Dick wanted game conditions. So we had a catcher behind the plate, wearing full gear.

Lonborg was trying to come back from his accident and pitched as if it was a real game.

Mr. Yawkey and I sat in the stands watching this and just cracked up. There was Lonborg throwing heat, not holding back at all. He must have hit Boomer ten times. "Boomer should be wearing the catcher's protective equipment," said Mr. Yawkey with a laugh.

With Lonborg ineffective and Santiago lost to us, we still wound up with a respectable record. In fact, we won 86 games, only 6 fewer games than in 1967. Hawk was the league's MVP, the leader in RBIs, and I was the batting champ at .301. Detroit was not going to be caught in 1968, though. McLain won his 31 games and the Tigers ran away with the race, winning 103 games.

In 1968, the pitchers overpowered the hitters. That's why I was the only player in the league to hit .300, in fact the only one to hit over .290. The league had its lowest average in sixty years. One out of every five games was a shutout. I was hitting about .270 going into the last month of the season. At that point, nobody in the American League even was at .300. Yet, I had a feeling I was going to get hot. I told George Scott, "Boomer, I'm going to hit over .300." To raise your average thirty points when you've got so many at-bats is tough to do. With only a few weeks to go, I had raised my average to .289. Danny Cater of the Oakland A's had been leading, but I was able to tie him.

So we were even when the Sox started a three-game series at Oakland, where the Athletics had moved after the 1967 season. In my first at-bat of the first game, I singled. Cater was playing first base. When I got there, I told him with a laugh, "Danny, when we leave here in four days I'm going to be hitting higher than you are." I went 9 for 14 in the series while he went 3 for 12, lowering his average to .288. In my last at-bat, I singled. With a four-hit game, I had reached .300. When I got to first, Danny said, "Well, thanks a lot for letting me smell the batting title, anyway."

The next year, 1969, they lowered the mound five

inches, from fifteen to ten inches high, thinking that would help the hitters. Actually, I hated to see that happen. It seemed to me that 1968 was just one of those flukes, a pitcher's year. But when they lowered the mound, that brought in a lot of players who became sinkerball pitchers, I didn't want that. I wanted the fastball pitchers, all those guys trying to blow the ball past you. Instead, the finesse guys started to come in with their sidearm moves, their sinkers. The hard throwers were almost obsolete because they couldn't make the adjustment. I was a a great fastball hitter and I wanted the fastball. I'd rather have the mound high and them trying to strike you out.

Dick Williams and I almost had a fistfight in 1969. That was another year when just about everything happened to us. Unlike 1967, though, much of it was bad. It began on one of the most emotional highs Boston had experienced since our dream season. Tony C. returned for our home opener, his first appearance at Fenway in twenty months. When he got to bat for the first time, the applause was so overpowering that umpire John Rice stopped the game so Tony could just stand there and wave to the crowd. The nice thing about that day was Tony driving in the winning run against the Orioles. What did it matter that it was an infield tapper that traveled forty feet? Tony came back with a 20 home run season.

Pitching was what we needed, though. A few days after Tony returned, we appeared to have the pitching, and to have inherited more turmoil. We traded Harrelson, the league's MVP, to the Indians. They were going to send us a couple of pitchers and a backup catcher. And guess who we were playing the next game? Cleveland. Hawk promptly quit. Good old Hawk. He played the power game perfectly. Players never quit in baseball when they were traded, at least not in 1969. Kenny had a lawyer whom I was to become friends with some years later. His name was Bob Woolf, a man I had heard about with some interest because he had been Earl Wilson's attorney and agent when Earl was with us. Earl was the first player I

knew who had an agent. Now Woolf had called a press conference for Hawk.

"Kenny is shocked," Woolf said. "We've decided Kenny
has too much to lose by leaving Boston. How much? At least
half a million." And Kenny announced he was quitting.

It's true that Hawk had become a celebrity in Boston.
There was going to be a recording out soon called "Don't
Walk the Hawk." Hawk was firm. He refused to report to the
Indians, even though they were managed by Alvin Dark,
whom he had defended against Finley at Kansas City. Ken's
refusal to report was fouling up the deal, and players from
both sides didn't know which locker rooms to go to. Was it a
deal if Hawk backed out of it? Finally, they were told to report to their new teams, and get dressed—but not play. So the
next day five of the guys in the deal were in uniform, except
for Harrelson. He was still retired. He said he was prepared
to work in his sandwich shop, which he claimed brought him
$1,800 a week.

The Cleveland players in the deal, Sonny Siebert, Vicente
Romo, and Joe Azcue, put on their brand-new Sox uniforms
while the players we traded with Hawk, pitchers Dick Ells-
worth and Juan Pizarro, went to the Indians' locker room.
Hawk even came to the game that night. But only as a spectator.

"I couldn't get through the mob," he told me. He was
laughing.

Of course Ken eventually joined the Indians, but not until he renegotiated his contract and jumped into the $100,000
class. Which is what he wanted all along.

One of the last major acts Williams performed for the
Red Sox was benching me, which made front-page news. He
claimed I wasn't hustling.

We were in California, playing the Angels, and I had a
bad ankle. I wasn't running well. But I played in every game
that season. The next day we were in Oakland and the whole
damn outfield was out, injured. Dick knew I had the ankle
problem, and he asked me if I could play.

"I can play," I told him, "but I can't run."

I taped it up tight, and played. There was an unusual play in the first inning. I was on third with two out, when Scott hit a little ground ball back to Blue Moon Odom, who was a pretty good fielding pitcher. He came up with it on the third-base side of the mound, saw that he didn't have a play at first but that he might get me, limping toward home. He threw home instead of going to first base. I couldn't slide and the catcher tagged me out. I went out to left field, but when I came back to the bench in the second inning, Williams started screaming at me, "Goddam it, you can't run any faster than that. You can't slide. I'm taking you out of the lineup!" At first, I thought he was kidding around when he walked away. I sat down and I realized he wasn't kidding. He told Joe Lahoud to take my place. I jumped up and ran over to Dick and said, "What the hell are you talking about? You knew before the game I wasn't even planning to play."

We started going round and round. He asked if that was the fastest I could run, I told him, yes, he said it wasn't good enough and I shot back that maybe old age was catching up with me. He shouted, "Say one more word and that's $100!" And I screamed, "Hell, make it $200!" Next thing I knew, it was $500.

I headed for the locker room, angrier than I'd ever been in my whole career. He fined me in front of the whole team. After the game I stormed into his office and said, "Dick, let's go at it right here and now." And he said, "We're not doing anything like that."

I had a beer in my hand. I fired it against the wall and walked out. A month later, Dick was gone.

He never finished his third season. He was fired over some dumb thing, but it showed how stubborn he was. A reporter asked Mr. Yawkey who he thought were the greatest managers since he'd been in baseball. He named Casey Stengel, Connie Mack, John McGraw.

"What about Dick Williams?" the writer wondered.

Mr. Yawkey replied, "He's only managed a couple of

years. You can't put him in the same category as someone who's managed twenty years."

Williams read the article and he got ticked off. He demanded a meeting. Popowski told me that when Dick was going up to see the old man, Pop said to him, "Dick, don't do it. He's the owner. I've read the article, and it's nothing against you. Don't do it."

Williams wouldn't listen. He stormed into the office. The next thing that happened, he was gone. O'Connell announced there was "a communications breakdown between Williams and the players." All the things that had riled the players about Dick began to surface. Pop managed the last two weeks of the season.

No question that Dick Williams was the right man for us in 1967. His attitude helped turn around a team and brought the Sox a sense of accountability. He was wrong, though, in ripping guys in public and in keeping them in his doghouse. I know that I had a hard time getting over that speech he made in front of the team. The day he was fired I hit two homers and drove in four runs against the Yankees.

You see, I was a guy who always played with injuries. That year, in fact, I was the only player on the team who was in all 162 games, and was one of only a few in the whole league who didn't miss a game. If you add up the games in my career (3,308), my seasonal average comes to 144 a year. For my first twenty years I never missed appearing in at least 100 games, and in my twenty-three years I dipped under 100 only once, in 1981 during the baseball strike when we played only 105 games. I was in 91. When I retired I had played in more games than any player in baseball history, with the most 100-game seasons.

It had always seemed to me that not playing, whatever the reason, was a signal that you didn't care. Probably, that idea goes back to the farm, maybe back to playing alongside my father when he was forty and had to throw sidearm because of his shoulder. I was always impressed with that. He would never miss a game. Maybe it was a symbol of weakness.

Yes, that could be it—that he could never show how he really felt or how he was really hurting.

All in all, I was on the disabled list only once. I don't know whether it was luck that had kept me off or that I just refused to yield to the pain and injury. For a guy my size, an injury was more serious, since I didn't have the brute strength to compensate for it. I knew I wasn't as effective when I was injured, but I always tried to figure out ways I could get around it, maybe with an adjustment in my stance, or being taped extra-tight. My one time on the disabled list came in 1972. I slid into home in Anaheim. My spikes caught up in my shin guards and I tore the cartilage and ligaments in my knee. The doctor, who happened to be the Rams' surgeon and was familiar with these football-type injuries, wanted to put me in the hospital and operate the next day. Instead, I told him to put the foot in a cast and send me back to Boston. But back home, the doc there wanted to operate, too. Even though it was early in the season, I knew we were going to be involved in a pennant race, and I didn't want to miss it. I asked him about the options, and he said he'd put a half-cast on it and see how that would work along with special exercises. He didn't like the idea of doing that, but I insisted, even though he warned me that on my first day back everything in the knee could go. I worked with weights and I had a heavy brace put on, designed especially for me at Harvard. And thirty days later I was back playing.

There were many times over the years I shouldn't have played, couldn't play. But I also knew I could draw a lot of walks, and that was an offensive tactic as well. In the later innings, especially, pitchers would tend to walk me in tight games. I led the league in walks twice, and I actually drew more intentional passes in my career than Ted Williams did.

There were many times I returned to action sooner than I should. In 1980, eight days after my forty-first birthday, I fractured my ribs by crashing into the cement in left. I missed 32 of the last 35 games. Another season I played only because Tom Yawkey unintentionally made me feel guilty about being on the sidelines. I had sprained the ligaments in my left wrist and couldn't swing a bat. The club left me back in Boston and I was miserable. They were on the Coast, and I'd go to the ballpark every day for treatment. Mr. Yawkey was there with his batting practice and he would ask me, "How ya feeling?" One day I took batting practice and he watched me and said, "You look pretty good. Why don't you take a flight out there?" I couldn't say no to the man, even though that batting practice had made the wrist worse. He had never asked me for a thing before. I joined the team, and they put me back in the lineup immediately.

"Tape the wrist so tight I won't even feel it," I told the trainer, "Then tape my hand to the bat." I figured that at least I'd be able to follow through without losing the bat. And that's how I played, with the bat taped to my wrist.

My first time up, there were men on second and third. The pitch came in and I swung and missed and the pain was so awful, I felt like saying, "Take me out now." But I hung in there, and on the next pitch, I got lucky—I hit it off the end of the bat, and blooped it over third. As I ran to first, I unraveled the damn tape so the bat wouldn't stick to me, dropped the bat just before getting to first, then I rounded the bag and barreled into second with a double, knocking in two runs. Then I took myself out of the game.

It wasn't so bad if my injuries were to the leg or the side, but if I was hurt in a hand or an arm or a wrist, it would screw up my swing, not just for the couple of days or whatever time until I healed, but since I had gotten into a bad habit, it would carry over and affect my swing. After I hurt my wrist in the summer of 1971, I didn't hit a homer for almost twelve months. In three of the four years before the injury, I had hit at least 40 home runs. All of a sudden, I had lost my power. That forced me into bad habits, trying to compensate. It was so tough that I was swinging practically one-handed. Halfway through the swing, the pain would be so bad I'd have to take my left hand—the power hand—off the bat.

The most significant injury, though, affected the last third of my career. My average tumbled after my shoulder injury in 1975. It was never the same for the rest of my career, yet I played for eight more seasons. I changed my stance and dropped my hands. My original injury led to other shoulder problems. One thing I knew, and that was my body. When we clinched the 1975 pennant on a Saturday, I told Darrell Johnson, our manager, that I was going to take the week off before the American League Championship Series. First, my mother had been stricken with cancer, and second, I needed the rest. I could use the Florida weather, give me a chance to heal. He told me, "You can't leave the team."

"Darrell," I replied, "If I don't get to where it's warm, I won't be any good at all to the team." Before he could say anything, I just left. That created a lot of speculation in the papers, especially because I didn't play that final Sunday. People thought Johnson had benched me, and that I had been annoyed so much that I didn't show up. No, that wasn't it at all. I just needed to take care of myself.

I took five days off, didn't swing the bat all week. Then, when I took batting practice, I felt great. I had a pretty good Series, too. The rest gave the shoulder a chance to heal. Still, those last eight years, I changed my batting style every year because of that shoulder injury. I couldn't use that big swing anymore for power, so I was just trying to get it down. I don't believe anyone was aware of it. Up until then, I still had been hitting a few home runs to left center. But from then on, I never hit a ball to left field. If I did, it was an accident. I couldn't even hit a ball to center. If I was to hit a home run, it had to be pulled sharp. That's why in my later years I loved going to Detroit and New York. In Fenway I just knew I lost maybe twenty feet with the change in swing, and if any type of wind was blowing in, I couldn't reach the fence. I had a shorter swing and rolled my top hand over quicker to pull the ball. Come to think of it, I played my last eight years under a handicap of not being able to hit the way I had earlier, with bad shoulders, not as much power, and with just the wrong kind of home ballpark for the power I did have.

In those last eight seasons—from 1976 to 1983—I hit 67 homers at home and 68 on the road. Until then I had hit 170 at Fenway and 147 on the road.

I was healthy in 1970, though. In many ways it was my most productive season. And it was the first year I played a lot of first base for the Sox. But it was also another year of finishing third. The Orioles again dominated our league with three 20-game winners in Mike Cuellar, Dave McNally and Jim Palmer, and John (Boog) Powell and Brooks Robinson and Frank Robinson. We seemed to have settled into the role of permanent third place, despite a season in which we led the league with 203 homers, with seven players in double figures. The Orioles ran away with the division by generating 108 victories. I almost won the Triple Crown again. But when you're not in a pennant race, nobody notices.

For the last weeks of the season, I was battling Alex Johnson of the Angels for the batting title. It brought some interest to the Sox. Even though we had a decent season, we were just too far behind the Orioles. But I could win the batting title. I probably would have if he didn't con me. I read a story in the Boston papers that he wasn't going to sit out, that he'd play a full game if the title was on the line. In my last game I got a hit in my first at-bat. That put me at .330. Eddie Kasko, our manager, wanted to take me out right then. In order for Johnson to catch me, he'd have to go 3 for 3 or 4 for 5. But I said no, that if he played a full game, I'd play a full game, too. I made out my next three at-bats, wound up 1 for 4 and was batting .329. Johnson had a game remaining the next night. He was hitting .327 going in. He went 2 for 3, then took himself out of the game. We both finished at .329, but when it's that close they bring it out to four decimal places. And Johnson beat me for the title in the second-closest race in history: .3289 to my .3286. "Now," Ted Williams told me, "you know how *I* felt." In 1949, Ted lost out to George Kell of Detroit by .0002.

That .329 was to be the highest average of my career. There were other accomplishments that season. I played in

161 games, I led the league in scoring with 125 runs, I hit 40 homers and I drove in 102 runs. I also led with a .592 slugging average. For good measure, I even stole 23 bases. That not only was the most on the Sox (no one else even had 11), but was good enough for eleventh in the league.

I was thirty-one years old and felt good. I still had confidence in the club and thought that Kasko could get us moving again. We needed some pitching. I had just completed a four-year stretch in which I batted over .300 three times, won two batting titles (missing out on that third by a margin I can't even imagine). I hit at least 40 home runs three times in that stretch and drove in 100 runs three times.

Then I hurt my wrist the next year, and it virtually finished the season for me and the team. But we had made a move that was to help change the club's future—and its personality. We got Luis Tiant, who was considered washed-up by Minnesota because of a bad shoulder. He didn't do much for us in 1971, but he helped transform the club the next year. We were going to be back as contenders again.

14
FUN AND
GAMES

Remember the fun the 1967 team had? We were starting to get it back again. We had a streak of pranks and craziness in the clubhouse that lasted for almost five years, until baseball changed again with free agency and a more serious locker room returned. But it was great while it lasted.

The Sox of my early years were somber clubs. Winning changed that, but Tiant helped make us nutty. I know that I became a different character in the locker room. In 1971 we got not only Tiant, but the great Luis Aparicio, who was the best base stealer in the American League when he was younger. Doug Griffin also joined us, and the locker room atmosphere changed overnight.

When did it start? Maybe with the first hotfoot. Maybe with the first scissored tie. Come to think of it, some of the stuff we did was scary, maybe even dangerous. But it was great fun.

With that big cigar, with that crazy Cuban pronunciation that I'm sure he did for effect, Luis was a presence in the room. "Cheet," he'd say. And we knew he was angry. "Hey,

Luis," I'd shout, "don't give me any of that bullcheet." He would roll that cigar in his mouth and laugh.

Luis had a ritual. I don't think he ever went to the bathroom at home. He'd come in and say to me, "Hiya, Polack." Then he'd go to his locker, get undressed, put his baseball shorts on, light a big cigar, pick up a newspaper, and go to the bathroom. You wouldn't hear from him for about twenty minutes. Then you'd hear him flush the toilet and yell, " 'Bye, Tommy Harper!" Everybody would start laughing.

Tommy would mutter, acting as if he was teed off, and Tiant would come out of the bathroom with a big grin, but Harper would say, "I'm going to get you."

"Me? What for, Tommy? I treat you good. I flush you down the toilet every day."

This went on day in and day out. We were all waiting to see what Tommy would do. Boy, he did it. It was a Saturday day game, and as usual I was the first one in. But Harper came in pretty early, which surprised me. He took a bucket of crushed ice and walked into the bathroom. Then he hid behind the stall, which had a ledge over it under a window. Tommy figured Luis would be there soon. So I told all the guys and we'd peek in the bathroom and then look for Luis. But Luis was late that day and Tommy must have been up on that ledge for an hour and a half.

Finally, Luis came in, and all the guys in the locker room almost burst from holding our breath. We sneaked glances at one another, but tried not to laugh. He walked in with the same routine: "Hiya, Polack. How ya doin'?" He got the cigar, the newspaper, went into the bathroom.

The place was suddenly quiet. All of us waited outside to see what Harper was going to do. Luis was the only guy there who didn't know a thing. We were all dying until we heard that flush. All of a sudden, there it was. Then we heard Luis say, " 'Bye, Tommy . . ." and before he could get "Harper" out, Tommy dumped the whole bucket of watery ice on him.

We jumped up and down screeching, and Luis started

shaking and yelling, "You no-good son of a beetch," and then shouting in Spanish.

That triggered a sort of mass hysteria, like an epidemic of pranks. Soon someone was doing something every day. It got so bad that you'd be afraid to wear good clothes into the locker room because someone was going to cut them up. That's when I started wearing only khakis or jeans because I just knew that somebody was going to get me. We'd cut up people's clothes, cut the legs off pants. A guy would be sleeping and we'd throw a bucket of cold water on him. Or give a guy a hotfoot. There was a lot of fun in the clubhouse at all times.

But once batting practice started, that crazy stuff stopped. It kept everybody close, and relaxed and happy. So did Luis. He'd pitch a 1–0 game, and win, and be fine. That's easy. But if he got knocked out, he'd sit for a while and then jump up and say, "I'll get them next time," and snap out of it. Ballplayers will respect a guy who acts okay when he's going bad. It's easy to be a good guy when things are happening for you. So having fun on the club helped us over the times we'd get into a bad streak or run into bad luck. I don't want to make it look as if we never had fun before. In my earlier years with the Sox, fellows like Dick Radatz and Bob Tillman knew how to make things lighter. It's just that the pranks we pulled on each other didn't become *serious* fun until much later.

Aparicio helped. Luis was an immaculate dresser. In the 1970s everyone wore a golf sweater over a shirt and khakis. But Luis wore tailor-made suits. He was already thirty-seven by the time he joined us. His first nine years in the game, though, he led the league in stolen bases, and he led the shortstops in fielding eight times. A classy guy. That meant we had to get him. One night in Minneapolis, I went out to dinner with Gary Peters, who had been traded to us, Smith, and Lahoud. And there was Luis with his back to us. He was sitting at the bar next to a priest. I came up behind Luis and tore the whole suit behind the back. As I was doing it, the priest looked at the scene with his mouth open. I said to the priest,

"Father, you hang around with this guy and I'm going to do the same to you." I walked back to the table, but turned around and saw the priest leave.

The four of us started to have dinner. I was sitting there, enjoying life, relaxed, wearing my golf sweater. Luis tiptoed up behind me and all of a sudden he ripped a sleeve off of my sweater. Then he walked back to the bar. I just sat there with the sweater hanging, one sleeve off, since I couldn't wear shirt-sleeves in the restaurant. We started to joke about it. From there, somehow, we got into a conversation about our childhood, and Reggie and Peters started talking about throwing knives. Reggie was bragging about how he grew up in Watts and how they threw knives on the street. Gary was raised in the country in Pennsylvania. He could handle a knife, too. He knew how to skin animals. They began to argue about who could throw a knife better.

"It was tough in Watts. You had to learn how to handle a knife," Smith said.

"Reggie, you're full of it," replied Gary. "If you're so hot, let's see you throw this knife into the wall."

Reggie grabbed the steak knife out of Gary's hand and threw it at the wall. It bounced off. Gary took the knife and— *boom*—stuck it right into the wall. They started to stare at each other, and I watched both of them, amazed. A few hours before, we were pals. Now Peters was so ticked off at Reggie that he said to Lahoud, "C'mon, Joe, let's get another table."

They took one right next to us, with their backs to Reggie. Reggie had a temper, and he began to get angry because Peters was razzing him from the other table: "Yeah, hotshot from Watts. Great man with a knife. Jeez, I'm trembling over this guy."

Suddenly, Peters turned and took his steak knife and stuck it under Reggie's throat. Gary took the point and rubbed it there until a trickle of blood appeared. Reggie was a strong guy. He put his hands around Gary's. "Take your hands away and I'll put the knife down," Gary told him.

When Gary put the knife down, Reggie stormed out of the restaurant.

Reggie should have been a hell of a player. As it was, he had a good career. But I thought he had the ability to come damn close to being a Hall of Fame ballplayer. He put too much pressure on himself and he would explode. Maybe it was because of the comparisons people always made. He was a switch-hitter and Mantle's name always cropped up. But Reggie had more ability than anybody I ever saw. He could run, hit, throw, switch-hit with power. He just never channeled it.

Luis was watching the scene with the knife from the bar. Now he figured it was safe to come over. So he ripped my shirt. Everyone laughed. I got back to the hotel with my shirt and sweater torn. When I walked into the lobby, I found myself at the tail end of a Miss Minnesota Pageant, part of the Miss America competition. The girls were congregating in the lobby, all the runners-up, and a few of them were crying.

Peters walked over to them and said, "Don't feel bad. Look at these guys. I just dragged them off the street to have a meal."

No one was safe—at any time. I had a Ford agency in Lynn, Massachusetts, which got quite a bit of publicity. But we'd be on the bus driving somewhere and pass a junkyard. Tiant would get up and shout, "Hey, there's Yaz Ford. Nah, that can't be it. Those cars look better than the ones you've got."

There were other ways we stayed loose. Once the team got a reputation for having fun, it infected everyone. Even Mr. Yawkey.

I was a creature of habit. Because so much of my life was spent at the park—more than anyone else, I'm sure—I wanted to make it as easy on me as possible. At the beginning of the season I would buy three pairs of khakis, three pairs of jeans, six golf shirts, a couple of sweaters, a sports coat, underwear, socks, and put them all in my suitcase. This was my road clothing. They were always ready to go. I used to tell the equip-

ment guys, "Make sure you give my suitcase to Vinny." He
would send my jacket and pants out to the dry cleaner, and
he'd wash my underwear and socks. So when I came in for a
road trip, I'd throw everything in, put the dry cleaning in,
take the bag Vince had prepared. *Boom,* it was done.

Tom Yawkey used to watch me. He was fascinated by my
routine and before every road game he would stand next to
my locker and watch me pack. Then he started to time how
long it took me to get everything ready. He came up with a
time of one minute and ten seconds as my best. One day after
a game we were getting ready to go to the airport. We had
only about forty minutes to make the plane. Yawkey went to
Vince and announced, "I'm going to pack for him. Get the
stuff ready."

I didn't know this, but as I walked through the door I saw
Mr. Yawkey running around. He scurried into the bathroom,
grabbed my shaving stuff, took the jacket out of my locker,
threw it in, took the laundry from Vince, shoved it into the
suitcase, and then slammed it. He was huffing and puffing.

"Well, Vince, how'd I do?" he said, very satisfied.

"Nah, you're twenty seconds off, Mr. Yawkey," Vince
told him, giving him back his watch.

On another trip to Minneapolis, I went fishing on the
Mississippi with Lahoud and Reggie and Peters. It was an off-
day, and we told everyone we'd be back around four in the
afternoon and have a fish fry. The night before, I had gotten
the key to Peters's room from the front desk. Ken Tatum, a
relief pitcher, was his roomie and was hanging around. I had
my fishing knife with me. I cut all of Gary's clothes up, put
them back in his suitcase, and I turned to Tatum and said, "If
you tell him I did it, I'm going to get you someday, too." I
knew Tatum was kind of scared, and he'd do something
weird. I went back to my room and peeked out the door, and
sure enough, there was Tatum, coming out of his room, with
his suitcase. He checked out and went to another hotel.

The next day we went fishing, but Peters never said a
word. I thought that was strange, but I wasn't going to say

anything. Well, we came back to the hotel, invited the other players, and had our fish fry at four. It was over about six, and I felt like getting a steak at Harry's. "You guys wants a steak?" I asked Reggie and Joe and Gary. "Yeah," said Peters. "But I got some things to do first. I'll meet you over there." The three of us went to Harry's.

I was having my salad, waiting for Peters, when all of a sudden it hit me: *The creep is in my room.* "Hold my steak. I'll be right back," I told the waiter. I jumped in a cab, got to the hotel, opened the door to my room, and damn, it was on fire. Peters had taken all my clothes, placed them in the center of the room, and set them on fire. But he couldn't put the fire out. So he took the bedspread and snuffed it out with that. The whole mess was still there, smoldering.

I didn't want to keep the guys waiting, so I straightened up quickly and got back to the restaurant. Reggie and Lahoud came back with me and helped me clean it up a little. But the next morning I checked out about seven. I wanted to be out of there before the maids came by. I got to the ballpark so early I was the only person around there. But just as I walked in, there was a fire chief and a police chief and Jack Rogers, our traveling secretary. "We want to see you in private," Jack said. "What happened in your room?"

I thought quickly. I told him we had fish, and room service had brought up cans of Sterno to keep it warm, and someone knocked a can over and it caught fire and the only way I could put it out was by putting the bedspread over it. The fire chief lectured me about the danger to everyone in the hotel, and I thought that was the end of it. But then the hotel manager showed up, too. He handed me a bill for $700. "What? For a little hole?" I said. "We've got to replace the whole carpet," he replied. I didn't want to pay and they threatened to take me to jail. Jack didn't want that. "Okay, here's a check for the $700," said Jack.

You think we'd have learned a lesson with close calls like that. No way. We'd see Aparicio, the immaculate dresser, and we just knew we had to get him. Luis was a hero back home in

Venezuela. Every time he'd go back there after the season, they had a huge welcoming committee for him at the airport, with a band and officials.

We hatched a complicated scheme. It was a Saturday, the last weekend of the season, just before batting practice. Luis was sitting in front of his locker, but his clothes weren't there. I tried to figure this one out. Reggie and Griffin were sitting next to me and I said, "There's no clothes in Aparicio's locker." Kasko came up to me and said, "Luis is leaving after the game because he can't get a flight to Venezuela on Sunday." Then Eddie added, "By the way, he shipped his clothes out of here yesterday. So what he's got here are the only clothes he can wear."

Hmmm.

But where were the clothes? It dawned on me—he locked his stuff up. It was time for infield practice, but he didn't move. He just sat in front of his locker. But he also was staring at this storeroom, where I knew his suitcase was, where Vinny always locked up the trunks for the trips. Luis was making sure that no one could get at his suitcase.

Before the game started, I went over to Vince and Fitzie, all the clubhouse kids, and the players. "Here's what we do. Whenever Luis's at bat, we're going to rush into the clubhouse, get the key, open the locker, and get to his suits and tear them up. Someone comes in and tells us when his at-bat's over, and we get back out of the room."

That's how it went. We'd run in and I'd slit his pants in sections. We had developed this to a fine art. There's a special way you slit a guy's clothes so he doesn't realize it. It's the way you tape them from the inside after you cut them. So after I made the cut, other guys would be taping them together from the inside, so the tape wouldn't show. When we heard he made an out, we'd run back outside. But he would go back to his locker, standing guard, as soon as his at-bat was over. He wouldn't even watch the game when we were up. He'd listen to it on the radio, and when he heard it was the third out, he

ran out of the clubhouse and onto the field. When the inning
was over, he'd run back in front of his locker.

His next at-bat, we got his coat, then shirts. Now it was
his fourth at-bat, and we were really into this destruction. I
said to Vinny, "Get me an ax." He found something for me
and I cut Luis's shoes in half, and then I nailed them to the
floor.

The game was over. Luis didn't say a word. He ran into
the shower and then ran back to his locker. He draped a towel
around his waist. "Goodbye, you guys. I'm leaving today for
Venezuela. See you next year," he said, very happy. He figured he got away with it. He headed for the storeroom to get
his clothes. Nobody said a word. We just sat and watched. I
wanted to explode, but I had done this often enough to know
I had to control myself, that the least unusual movement
would give the whole thing away.

Luis looked at his clothes. Obviously, they were okay
because they still were hung up neatly. Luis was singing, "See
ya next year," as he put on his underwear. All of a sudden it
fell off his body. Then he took his pants and tried to put them
on, but half of them fell on the floor. He sat there with half his
pants on the floor, looking around. He was boiling, so mad
that he was almost crying. Finally, I said to him, "Luis, is that
band gonna meet you when you get home today? What're you
gonna wear, buddy?"

"I'm gonna get you," he screamed.

He began running around, looking for clothes. He
couldn't find any. But the clubhouse boy, who was just about
Luis's size, was wearing a pair of old cutoff jeans and a beat-up
T-shirt. Luis asked the kid, "How much you want for the
jeans?" I told the kid, "Don't sell them cheap." The kid said,
"Give me $100."

At least, Luis figured, he had his shoes. He bent down
and tried to get a shoe on, but I had nailed them to the floor.
He yanked it up, and when he finally pulled it up, it came in
half. He looked around, seething. He bought a pair of old
sneakers from another clubhouse kid for $25.

———

Luis never said a word, not a goodbye, to any of us. He walked out to that brass band in Venezuela, resplendent in cutoff jeans.

We weren't afraid of getting the coaches or managers, either. I once got Johnny Pesky. We were in Detroit on a Sunday. I was being rested that game, and Ken Coleman, an announcer, asked if I could go up in the booth with him to do some broadcasting. Don Zimmer said it would be all right. "But don't leave before the game's over. I'm going to check on you. Every couple of innings I'm going to look up there." After about three innings I got antsy. I wanted to get back to Florida because our season was already over. So I decided I'd leave early and grab the plane for Fort Lauderdale. I ducked out about the fifth inning, but went into the manager's office first. I cut the arms and pants of Zim's clothes, and then I cut Pesky's clothes, too.

Well, they figured it was me because I was the only guy who could have gone in during the game. So Pesky, who was furious, couldn't wait to get back at me. He didn't have to wait long. My luggage was going back with the team, even though I was headed for Florida. When the plane arrived in Boston, Pesky was there, waiting for the luggage to be unloaded. When he saw my bag, he opened it up and started giving away my clothes. "Here's a Yaz souvenir!" he shouted, and people started grabbing them. Some fan was taking Polaroid pictures of what Pesky was doing because it was so unusual.

After the season was over, I went back to the park and asked Vinny where my stuff was. "Gee, Yaz, all your clothes are gone." There was nothing I could do, so I absentmindedly opened my mail. I opened one letter and there were three Polaroids—of Pesky giving away my clothes. *So that's what he did,* I thought. All of a sudden, Pesky walked through the door.

I said, "Woody, you know, I just came to take my clothes home and I don't have any."

And he said, "Is that right? What happened to them?"

"I heard you gave them away."

"Aw, Yaz, I wouldn't do anything like that. Just like no one would cut up my clothes when I'm going home from a road trip, and I had to wear a Red Sox jacket and baseball pants coming into Logan."

"Nah, Woody, I wouldn't do that."

And then I brought the pictures out, and said to him, "Well, then, what the hell is this?"

"Oh," he replied, "I'm trying to take them back from the people."

Zimmer, meanwhile, had never said a word about any of this. I forgot all about what I had done to his clothes, too. About a month later, a truck pulled up to my house. The guy said, "Special-delivery package from Don Zimmer."

"Okay," I said, "give it to me."

"It's a C.O.D.," the guy said.

"How much is it?"

"$148."

"For what?"

"Well, it weighs a lot and it was sent express."

My curiosity got the better of me, and I wrote him out a check for $148. *Now,* I thought, *what the heck's in a $148 package?*

It was wrapped in all sorts of plastic and boxes, like a gag gift. I waded through this thing, peeling off the layers. All of a sudden, the smell hit me. Jeez. He had packed dead fish, and guts, and dirt and rocks. All that crap cost me $148.

The players also got me. When I was on the road, I often would come into the park early and tell the clubhouse kids I wanted to take a nap. But I had helped create a climate of nuttiness. It became dangerous to sleep where the other guys could see you. So I gave the kid $20 and told him to let me into one of the locked rooms but not to let anyone know where I was.

You can't keep secrets for long in the locker room. While I was sleeping, some of the guys got a tub, filled it with ice water, and poured it over me. I woke up in such a shock that I screamed for twenty seconds, or thought I did. I couldn't make a sound. When I finally got myself together, I looked for the kid and asked him how the hell they found me.

"They told me they'd tear up my clothes if I didn't turn you in," the frightened kid told me.

In those years, everyone tried to outdo the next guy in the clubhouse. Take the thing with the radio. They would blast it. Luis would want his kind of music, and someone else would get up after a few minutes and say, "I don't want that crap." It was a noisy clubhouse, people always yelling and screaming, hotfoots, water being poured, uniforms being cut. But once we took batting practice, that was it. Everything was silent again.

Once the game was over, the radio would be blasting again. If we lost, it would be quiet for five minutes, then Tiant would say, "What's this, a morgue?" and he'd turn the radio on. "We'll get 'em tomorrow," he'd say. That's why we respected him. If he won or lost, "We'll get 'em tomorrow." And that's the way the team thought. It became very close. Rarely did anybody ever get angry at another guy or hold a grudge.

Tiant used to be in his glory during a game when somebody got jammed and broke a bat—sawed-off. The guy would be mad, and he'd throw the bat in two pieces. But Luis would take the two pieces and tape them up. The guy would be sitting there grumbling, and Luis would hand him the bat and say in his accent, "You wanna use this bat again?" and that usually brought the guy out of it.

I knew as a hitter how much it meant to get sawed-off, so I'd laugh when Luis did that sort of stuff. One time, somebody got me sawed-off and I was ticked and fired the bat down the runway. I could see Tiant out of the corner of my eye just laughing his butt off. I went to the bat rack and punched it and slammed some bats, but one of them was sticking out and hit me in the head. I was furious while everyone else laughed. I was waiting for Tiant to do that thing with the tape. He surprised me. He didn't do it. I forgot about it and went to the outfield. I came in after the inning and as I headed for the dugout I saw it. He had gotten me, after all. He not only had taped up the bat neatly, but he had the damn thing hanging from the top of the dugout like a flag.

"Hey, Polack, you gonna use this bat again?" he asked.

Luis would do that sort of stuff to me whenever I was vulnerable. After a bad swing, I'd take a step out of the batter's box, and there he was, laughing. He'd wave his hands as if he was lassoing you and he'd shout, "Get back in here and let somebody else hit!"

Luis wasn't the only one who liked having fun with me. Ted Williams enjoyed getting me riled. When Ted managed the Senators, he always seemed more intent on getting me out more than anyone else. I sensed that he just couldn't stand to see me get a hit. But I always did hit well against the Senators. One game he started a left-handed pitcher. We shelled him and I got a couple of hits. The game was out of control, and you figure it didn't matter what happened from then on. But every time I came up in the game after that, Williams brought in a left-handed pitcher to face me, the same way Stanky did that time, only not to try to hit me. He'd stop the game and take out the righty who was pitching. Once there was nobody on base and two outs and he was being slaughtered—and he lifted the pitcher for a lefty. The whole club was laughing. And after that, in almost every game we played, Ted would bring in a southpaw to face me. Just to get me out. Maybe he was trying to test me, to see if I had learned his instructions to "Be quick, dammit. Be quick."

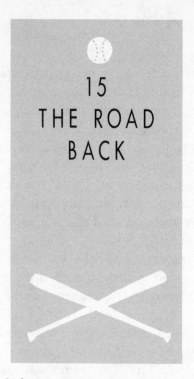

15

THE ROAD
BACK

We scrapped and fought and almost won a division in the 1972 strike year with a club that really wasn't distinguished. But the Tigers played one game more than we did—they lost six games to the strike, we lost seven—and beat us out by that half a game.

In some ways, losing that way is tougher. You get so close with guys who are giving their all, who weren't as good as the talent on Detroit or Baltimore, and then miss out. Kasko did a good job managing us. He was in the same mold as Houk, whom I thought was the best I played for. Eddie kept everything inside, would never chew you out in front of everyone. We never had top-flight pitching the four years Eddie managed us. Sure, we were in the 1972 race, but we had to start two Triple A pitchers the last two weeks. That was our first year without Lyle. In 1971 he saved 16 games for us. And then we traded him to the Yankees. That was not as bad as the time we traded Babe Ruth to them, but Sparky became the top reliever in the league in 1972 with 35 saves. We didn't have anyone who got us more than 5 saves. But Eddie knew baseball, and got the most out of his players.

Tiant was the big guy who produced in 1972. We called him El Tiante, which made him sound like some sort of magical bird or god. He was mean in Fenway, just the sort of pitcher we needed to have—a right-hander who could handle the other teams' right-handed hitters to neutralize the wall. Luis already had a long career by the time we had picked him up in 1971. People didn't realize that in Denny McLain's 31-victory season of 1968, Luis had the best earned-run average in the league. But he was thirty, with shoulder and rib problems, by the time he joined us. But in 1972, he was 13–2 down the stretch for us. I also got over my wrist problem, and in September—after missing a month earlier with my bad knee—we were battling the Tigers for first place. Almost half the season went by before I hit my first homer. I got only 12 for the year. But in September, I hit 10 of them, while batting .350. It reminded me of 1967.

You could look at what happened as another of those "Red Sox lose again" stories. Or you could see it, as I do, as the beginning of building another championship team, and failing because we weren't quite there yet.

The fact is, it got down to the final two days of the season. We were that close. We even had a one-and-a-half-game lead with five to play.

That season excited Tom Yawkey so much that at the end, going into Detroit, he went on his first road trip since the 1940s.

No wonder he was into it. The season had driven fans and players a little bit screwy. In June we blew a four-run lead to the Tigers in the ninth inning, when they scored eight times, but we won our next seven. When I returned to the lineup on June 9, our record was 18–23. The rest of the season we were 67–47. On August 1, we were seven games behind the Tigers, but in five weeks we took over first place. When we were at our low point, Fisk claimed the Sox weren't getting "leadership" from the veterans, specifically me and Reggie. What could I say? How do you defend a negative? Pudge and I always got along great. Fisk had the same intensity I did. He wanted me to be a rah-rah guy, but that was the manager's job. I led by example. I'd go out and play hurt, tape it up, and play. Get a walk, anything, to help the ball club. It wasn't in my nature to go around and tap everybody on the back and say, "Let's go." I had enough problems trying to hit the baseball. When Fisk said that, Reggie was more annoyed than I was. All the years I had been there, everything I had heard and read and seen, had insulated me to this sort of flare-up, which I always regarded as minor, anyway. Reggie, me, Fisk, and Kasko had a closed-door meeting about it.

"I'm not a rah-rah guy," I said. "You want to do that, go ahead," I told Fisk. He believed that since we were the veterans, we should be going around to the players.

"That's the manager's job, not mine," I said. The meeting lasted about five minutes, and as far as I was concerned, it was over. Sure, I was ticked when we didn't play well, but I wasn't going to go around the clubhouse telling all the guys, "Hey, I am a leader and you had better start doing this and doing that." Then we played the Indians. I had a stomach virus and felt crummy. Our team physician even told me to sit it out, but I thought I should play this particular day. I did, and took myself out of the game after hitting into two double plays. Maybe my leadership returned when my wrist got better.

So with ten games remaining we were tied with the Tigers and sent Luis to the mound against them. He won, as he did so often down the stretch. Luis Aparicio was a giant for us also. He missed six weeks with a broken finger. When he came back in early August, we were one game over .500. Luis and I hit our stride together. The rest of the season we were 36–22, which is .621.

We had to play our final six games on the road—three in Baltimore, three in Detroit. We left Boston with an 82–67 record, one and a half games better than Detroit, at 81–69. The Yankees were three and a half games behind us with only five games remaining, while the Orioles were four back. Everyone realized it was going to be Detroit or us.

The trip opened in Baltimore on a Friday night, and, I swear, it really was 1967 again that night. Imagine, Tiant against Palmer, tied after nine innings at 2–2. There was a man on when I got up in the tenth.

Earl Weaver went out to talk to Jim. I found out later that Earl asked him, "Do you want to walk him?"

"No, I'll pitch him high and outside," Palmer replied. I think I had hit only one home run off him, and that was a few years before. So while he respected me, he wasn't afraid of me.

The funny thing is, he got the pitch where he wanted. It was a little high and a little outside, and I went with it. I tagged it to left center. At the wall, Don Buford leaped, but it was over the ten-foot fence. I watched it sail over just as I was headed for second base. "Yeah!" I shouted and exuberantly raised my right hand, my second finger pointing toward the sky. At that moment, I felt we were number one.

I had been in the majors for twelve seasons. We had won some big games, had won a pennant. I had captured a host of individual honors. And yet, when there were bad times, I often became the focus. Some fans, and some writers, always thought that I needed motivation, that if I happened to do poorly it was because I lacked the drive when the Sox were out of it. I don't know how you can prove that—or disprove it. But I think that what happened as the years went by was that I had become so identified with the Red Sox that my fortunes mirrored their fortunes. I somehow became the symbol of their bad times and their good times. I didn't run out a grounder when I was limping? Well, then, I was dogging it. I made a throw to the wrong base? Sure, my mind's not in it. Did I become the "old" Yastrzemski in the clutch September drive, as opposed to the Yastrzemski singled out by Fisk? No, it's not that simple. Life isn't that simple. I know this, every fiber in my body was tingling in September and my awareness of everything going on the field was so high I felt as if I had ESP.

And so, the next night in Baltimore, it happened again. I

hit another homer, this one in the eighth inning after singling in a run in the first, and we won by 3–1. It kept us one and a half games up with four to play. We needed to win two of our final four games to clinch the division title.

We didn't get out of Baltimore with a victory, though. The Orioles beat us on getaway day and we headed for Detroit with the race this simple: whoever won two of the three games there would win the division. To give you some idea of the kind of team we had, and the ridiculousness of our situation—we were starting three rookies in a game that would put us one victory away from the pennant. Dwight Evans, a twenty-year-old, was in the outfield. A first-year southpaw named John Curtis was on the mound against Lolich. Curtis was being handled behind the plate by Fisk, another rookie. Aparicio was at shortstop, and he was going on thirty-nine.

Luis, one of the greatest base stealers in history, and I would figure in a base-running play that helped close the noose around us. Irony is part of losing, I guess. Luck is part of winning. But Aparicio falling is part of the losing lore of the Red Sox—like Enos Slaughter, like Bob Gibson, like the Big Red Machine in 1975, like the Yankees and one Russell (Bucky) Dent.

We were down by only 1–0 in the third with one out. Harper and Aparicio singled and we had runners on the corners. And then history—or at least a historical memory. When I hit the pitch, I thought it was in the stands. It went over Mickey Stanley's head in center, and when I saw it bouncing around and Stanley chasing it, the only thought on my mind was: *I'm going for an inside-the-park homer.*

My head was down and I headed toward third. There was no way the relay was going to beat me home. But I didn't count on a crazy thing happening. Luis, the most accomplished base runner of his time, fell after rounding third. I couldn't believe it. He was scrambling to his feet and trying to get back to third.

No, Luis, no! I shouted to myself. *Go home, dammit!*

People don't remember what happened next. When he

headed back for the bag, I actually pushed him. I said, "Go!"
He started running for home again, but then he fell a second
time. Even though he fell, if he had kept running he would
have scored. I would have, too. Instead, he ran back to third.
They tagged me in a rundown, and then Lolich struck out
Reggie. So instead of having a 3–1 lead with one out, and
Lolich on the ropes, we had simply tied the score at 1–1.

This was not the year we had a second chance. They beat
us the next day, with Tiant pitching, to clinch the pennant.
When it was over, I sat at my locker and cried. Fisk cried.
Tiant cried. At that moment, it was the toughest defeat of my
career. Mr. Yawkey came up to me, put his hand on my shoulder, and said, "Don't worry, we'll get them next year."

Well, we didn't, and Eddie Kasko was gone. Eddie probably preferred being in the front office anyway, running the
scouting operation. Considering that we never really had a
group of top-flight pitchers, Eddie had done pretty well with
us—two seconds, two thirds, never less than 85 victories. But
the front office wanted us to get over the hump, and the top
brass was impressed with the job that Darrell Johnson had
done in the minors.

By now, I had been together with Bob Woolf since 1970.
He had become as much of a Boston celebrity as the clients he
represented. Bob was the man I needed to help me make the
transition from baseball to business. It's not that I really
thought I'd ever retire (well, maybe deep down I did), but I
had wanted to begin building a base and to learn more of how
the outside world works.

We had an unusual deal. Bob was sensitive to my relationship with Mr. Yawkey and never intruded on it. So while
he was my attorney, and became one of my best friends, he
never was involved in any contract talks with the Sox. Sure, he
handled all my outside activities, and they were becoming
increasingly important and time-consuming. But he never directly spoke to anyone on the club about how much I was
getting paid or how they'd do it.

One day he called me and said, "How'd you like to do a

commercial in Japan? We'll all go over—you, me, Carol and Anne." *Well, sure, why not?*

And that was the start of our Great Japan Escapade, involving the Democratic Whip, relations between Japan and America, and the state of baseball. It also slightly affected my future in the game.

We went over more for a lark than anything else. The commercial was supposed to be for the Japan market only, so I didn't make a big deal about it. Not many people knew I was traveling there. And then, when we stopped in Honolulu, who did I see but my old friend Tip O'Neill?

"Where ya headed?" he asked me with that booming, good-natured voice.

"Japan. We're going to talk some deals," I told him.

"Boy, that's great, Yaz," he replied. "I wish ya luck."

Of course, I knew that baseball was popular in Japan. What I didn't know was . . . so was I. For when Tip had returned to Washington, he had innocently told a writer, "Yastrzemski is going to Japan to sign a contract." Well, to most people, that means a baseball contract. The word got back to Boston, where the papers suddenly reported that I was off to Japan with my attorney to play baseball.

The word then traveled to the Orient. As soon as I landed in Japan, I was besieged by newshounds and photographers wanting to know if it was true, that I really was coming over.

That would have been a first, in a way. There had been some good American ballplayers who had gone to Japan, but usually they were at the tail end of their careers, or hadn't had the success I did. Also, there was an agreement between the Japanese and American big leagues not to raid each other. If any deals were made, they had to be quite formal. But all of a sudden, there I was in Japan.

Funny, but I wasn't even thinking of baseball in Japan, at least not then. And neither was Bob. Yet, it seemed strange to me that when we were told to check into the Imperial Hotel, we were asked to use an alias. We were shepherded around

Japan by a mysterious Mr. Matsui, who had been educated at MIT and whom I had met in Boston. Essentially, every place I went, I used his name—for restaurant reservations, at hotels, on trains. He introduced us to Premier Kakuei Tanaka and every other high-ranking dignitary he could think of. I began to think that perhaps the people who had brought us over really had something other than a commercial in mind.

That was obvious after one dinner when the owner of the team in Nagoya, a city of two million, met us for dinner. And when we left, the place was swarming with photographers. I hadn't noticed any of them in the restaurant while we were having dinner, but the next day our pictures were in one of the papers. I learned they had put together a composite photograph. Not only that, the story with it said I was signed. That led to another story in Boston, with the *Globe* reporting I was about to sign a four-year deal worth than $1 million. Funny, though, about that dinner—I hadn't mentioned one word about playing baseball anyplace except Boston. The owner of the Nagoya team never even brought up the possibility that he might be interested in signing me.

Still, I had become a celebrity and an object of curiosity. Not only did crowds follow us, but people began to hold up three fingers when they spotted me. "What the heck is that for?" I asked our interpreter.

"Your Triple Crown," he explained. Only it came out more like "clown."

Eventually, it became clear that the object of our trip really had been about baseball. The Nagoya people wanted us to visit their city.

"What do you think, Bob?" I asked Woolf.

"Yaz, you owe it to yourself to listen to them," he said.

Bob was right—from his standpoint. As my lawyer, he always had to think of my best financial interests and long-term plans. Yet, Bob also was sensitive enough to my feelings to know there was a line there when it came to the Red Sox, and he never stepped over it. Still . . . I had to hear what they were going to tell me. Reflecting on that now, I realize I

never was interested. I went along as much for Bob's sake—
when he got into negotiating, he was at the top of his game,
and *loved* it—as out of curiosity.

We met in Nagoya a few times with them, and each meeting seemed to have been telegraphed in advance. We got so
much publicity that the commissioner of baseball in Japan
spoke to the Nagoya owner and told him that he had heard
from Bowie Kuhn's office in New York. The American baseball commissioner was not happy about this possible raid, that
it was going against the traditional baseball ties between the
countries.

When Bob heard that, he was concerned about what effect this would have on my image in Boston. He didn't want it
to look as if we were carpetbaggers, and in fact, that had
never been our intent. He said we ought to get out of Nagoya
as quickly as possible.

We figured the train back to Tokyo would be the best
way. Lose ourself in a crowd. Still, I didn't want to take a
chance being spotted. It was becoming embarrassing. So I
bought a false mustache and put it on and got through the trip
without any herd of picture takers. Instead of the deal being
over, though, it seemed it was going in a new direction. Now
the Nagoya people called our hotel in Tokyo and said they
wanted to sit down and talk contract. The team's owner
showed up wearing a white surgical mask. He didn't have a
cold, but was trying to disguise himself.

Bob had already given the Japanese some ground rules in
our discussion. He told them I wouldn't consider leaving for
less than $300,000 a year for four years (which was about
$100,000 more than I could have signed with in Boston), but
in addition wanted Nagoya to pay all taxes and living expenses and schooling for the kids. I even got into the spirit of
the thing.

"Jeez, why don't you ask them for a car?" I said. "Maybe
they'll guarantee me some commercials, too." I could understand how high-level business deals could get your blood boiling. It was like some game I was playing. It was like . . .

well, like my dad negotiating with the Phillies or the Tigers, fifteen years before, coming up with an outrageous demand after they had already agreed to a point that was beyond your dreams. The fact that the Japanese called back indicated that they were willing to deal.

They came in at $150,000. But when Bob insisted on $300,000, they smiled and nodded.

"What does this mean, Bob? That they agree?" I asked.

Bob had done some studying about Japanese negotiating techniques, and their way of life.

"No, Yaz, it only means that they're being polite," he explained. "Their style is never to insult you by flatly refusing your offer. But even when they agree to a deal, it's never finished until they get a board of directors to approve it. A lot of Japan's business works by group decision."

They came back a few days later and said they would pay me a salary that would net me $175,000 a year *after taxes,* they would give me a free apartment, living expenses, and schooling for the kids, and they would give me a car. *Hey, I'm not too bad at this negotiating business,* I thought. But that was just stuff for my ego. It wasn't what I really wanted.

"Let's go back home," I told Bob. I realized that I never was interested. Maybe I had enough of negotiating fifteen years earlier. Maybe I was just a farm boy at heart. We heard what they had to say, but as far as I was concerned, I was going to finish my career with the Red Sox.

When I got back to Boston, I didn't even telephone Mr. Yawkey to tell him I had been in Japan. I didn't want to use it as a bargaining lever.

You know who was the most upset that I had been to Japan? My mom and dad. I was surprised at how angry they were. It wasn't because I was thinking of leaving the States. But their memories of World War II still were strong. They felt it would have been unpatriotic of me to play in Japan.

The day after I got back, Mr. Yawkey called. I knew something was on his mind. The only other time he ever called was at Christmas. We got the niceties out of the way, and then there was silence.

Then Mr. Yawkey suddenly asked, "What's this I read in the paper about Japan?"

"Aw, it's nothing," I told him. And it was.

Besides, how could I miss the chance to play for still another Boston manager, my sixth? Darrell Johnson came on board in 1974 and learned that you never took anything for granted on the Sox.

We held first place for fifty-three days, from mid-July, all of August, and into early September. The 1974 season was my fourteenth. I batted over .300 for the sixth—and last—time in my career. At the age of thirty-five, I led the league in scoring with 93 runs. At times, it had a magical feel. We had cut Aparicio, as well as Orlando Cepeda, who played only one season. Pudge hurt his knee in training camp and Rico pulled a hamstring the first month. Yet, we had climbed to the top.

Our lead was as high as seven games in early August. It never got above that although I thought we could increase it at Anaheim, against Nolan Ryan. The American League record for strikeouts had been 18, which Bob Feller had set in 1938. Ryan entered the ninth with 17. I opened the inning with a walk. But he got Rick Miller on a curve and then struck out Bernie Carbo for number 19.

Still, that fat lead prompted memories of 1967. The *Boston Globe* began running a day-by-day recap of our 1967 pennant run. If it was August 15, say, the paper would run the August 15 results from 1967 as well. On August 23, we were riding a five-game winning streak, with Tiant pitching a shutout, and I had a nine-game hitting streak. Luis not only had won nine straight games, but his timing was remarkable. Each of those victories followed a loss the team had suffered the previous game. Each time he went to the mound, he halted a potential losing streak. But for the club, it suddenly stopped working like 1967.

We put together an eight-game losing streak as part of a stretch in which we won eight games and lost twenty. One month later our seven-game lead not only had disappeared, we were five games back. Season over. We all stopped hitting in the stretch. In one nineteen-game span, we hit two homers. Flat? We dropped a three-game series in Baltimore that knocked us out of first. We totaled eight hits—all singles—in that series. How about a thirty-eight-inning string without an earned run?

The front office tried to strengthen us at the end of the season by bringing up a pair of rookies from our Triple A team at Pawtucket: Fred Lynn and Jim Rice. Fred only got to bat 43 times, but he hit .419, and Jim drove in 13 runs in 67 times at the plate. Despite the team's fade, we knew that 1975 was going to be a much better year. All we had to do was not break any bones. When I say "we," I'm talking about the Sox. The rest of baseball conceded the pennant to the Orioles or the Yankees. We didn't make any off-season deals, as we were content to go with those two rookies.

I knew about Lynn and Rice because I had seen tapes of them when they still were at Pawtucket. I had discussed them with Mr. Yawkey. In those days—the year before free agency —you developed your own players and so you were anxious to know about the talent in the farm system. Rice and Lynn— heck, I'd been following them for more than a year. Just as I'd been following every guy who had come up to us over the years. It was as if you were bringing new relatives into a family.

These guys were different. You see kids come into training camp every year, but these two were exceptions. Rice was raw power. If he just made contact, the ball was going somewhere. And Lynn—he never did any extra work, never any extra hitting, never shag any extra fly balls, he wouldn't break a sweat and still he'd get three base hits. I'd look at him and think, *Goddam, here I am busting my butt trying to get a hit and this kid does it without even trying.* He was a tremendous talent on offense and defense. He'd get into a slump and come into Fenway and he would get three hits to left, two off the Wall. Fenway was made for him.

I was going to be thirty-six years old during the season. I made the official switch to first base, where I had been playing, on and off, since 1968, and Rice took over in left. It continued that left field mystique. For all of the 1940s, 1950s, 1960s, 1970s, and 1980s, although other players filled in at times, only three players *anchored* left for the Boston Red Sox —Ted, me, and Rice.

We had a fine young outfield with those rookies and Dwight Evans in right. Yet, we lost Fisk in spring training with a broken arm. We weren't sure how Rico would come back after a beaning he had suffered in September. Rick Burleson became our new shortstop and anchored the position. Rico returned to play third. Cecil Cooper was a .311 hitter for us as the DH and backup at first base. I was pretty comfortable playing first, in fact hitting better than .300 for more than half the season. Luis was pitching great before he got hurt, and Rick Wise became our big winner. We got into first place in late June, beating the Yankees three out of four in a big series at Fenway.

The one game we lost, I hit two homers, but even though I was playing left field in the game, all my knowledge about the Wall didn't help me. Walt Williams hit a mean shot that hopped off Rico at third. The ball skipped out to left and found the one spot where I couldn't handle it. Did I tell you about the door? Well, there's one out there, recessed about two feet. Imagine a roulette wheel when you toss the little pill in and it bounces off the side until it settles. That's what happened to Williams's hit. The ball got in there and bounced back and forth a couple of times. If I had been able to reach the ball and cut it off, they wouldn't have scored. But once it started rattling around, there was nothing I could do. Williams's hit knocked in the winning run. But the next day we won, got into first, and never left it.

We did some magical things—how many "miracles" can you have in a career?—as we produced a ten-game winning streak sandwiched around the All-Star Game. We trailed in one game by 7–1 and won it, 9–8, on Cooper's homer. We

♦ *Remember the "I want my Maypo!" commercials? That's my mom and me in 1969.*
(COURTESY CARL YASTRZEMSKI)

- *My bubble-gum card for the 1967 season—with the signature that Ted Williams thought was illegible.*

• *Hit 3,000—September 12, 1979, at Fenway. They stopped the game to take pictures.*
(COURTESY ROBERT G. WOOLF)

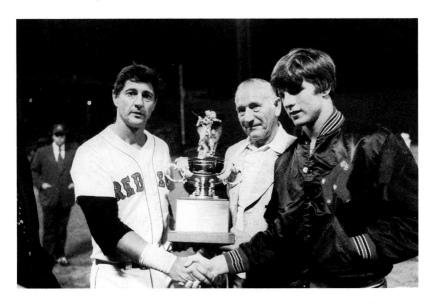

• *Then they presented me with a trophy, as Dad and my son Mike shared the moment with me.*
(COURTESY BOSTON RED SOX)

♦ *One of the 3,000 questions I answered at the press conference after hit number 3,000.*
(COURTESY BOSTON RED SOX)

♦ *President Jimmy Carter was a fan of the Georgia Peach, Ty Cobb, but he honored me by accepting a jacket and shirt commemorating my 3,000 hits and 400 home runs. That's Carol and me with the President in the Oval Office.*
(COURTESY THE WHITE HOUSE)

• *I don't remember when I popped this, but I was looking into the bleachers after the swing.*
(COURTESY BOSTON RED SOX)

• *A family portrait from the early 1980s—left to right, that's Suzanne, me, Carol, Carolyn, Maryann, Dad, and Mike.*
(COURTESY ROBERT G. WOOLF)

♦ *My final weekend, 1983, and final wave.* Thanks for the memories, *I thought.*
(COURTESY BOSTON RED SOX)

• *My last bubble-gum card, for the 1983 season. They gave me thirteen extra pounds in the stats.*
(COPYRIGHT © THE TOPPS COMPANY, INC.
COURTESY FARRELL SHAPIRO)

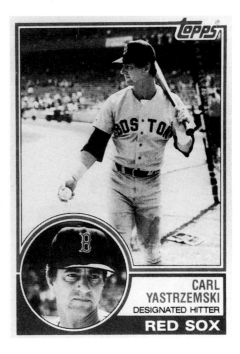

• *No one expected it, but I decided to touch as many people as I could. . . . I ran along the Wall that had been my backdrop and I ran alongside the stands in left, where they had been my closest and best critics. I knew there were tears in my eyes but that didn't matter any more.*
(COURTESY THE BOSTON GLOBE/BILL BRETT)

YAZ
• • •

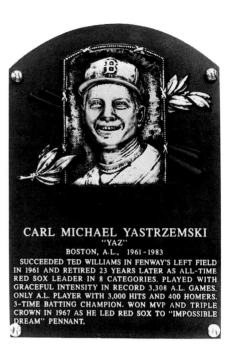

CARL MICHAEL YASTRZEMSKI
"YAZ"
BOSTON, A.L., 1961-1983
SUCCEEDED TED WILLIAMS IN FENWAY'S LEFT FIELD
IN 1961 AND RETIRED 23 YEARS LATER AS ALL-TIME
RED SOX LEADER IN 8 CATEGORIES. PLAYED WITH
GRACEFUL INTENSITY IN RECORD 3,308 A.L. GAMES.
ONLY A.L. PLAYER WITH 3,000 HITS AND 400 HOMERS.
3-TIME BATTING CHAMPION. WON MVP AND TRIPLE
CROWN IN 1967 AS HE LED RED SOX TO "IMPOSSIBLE
DREAM" PENNANT.

• *I loved the Hall of Fame plaque.*
Getting in on the first vote meant so much
to me—it put the "official" stamp on my
career and accomplishments.
(COURTESY NATIONAL BASEBALL HALL OF
FAME)

• *They retired my number in*
1989. I guess that 380 sign in
right wasn't so far away after all.
(COURTESY BOSTON RED SOX)

blew a 5–1 lead and won, 6–5, and we lost a 7–4 lead in the ninth but won, 8–7. We had another big series against the Yankees in July, and brought a five-and-a-half-game lead into Shea Stadium, where they were playing while the real Stadium was being rebuilt. We split the first two, then Lee won the opener of a Sunday doubleheader by 1–0 against Hunter as Lynn made a great catch on a Graig Nettles shot. We knew when we won the second game that we had knocked the Yankees out of it. George Steinbrenner must have thought so, too. He fired manager Bill Virdon and brought in Billy Martin. Then it was the Orioles' turn to make a run at us.

They came in only four and a half games back, but Luis, who had been hurt the second half and only won two games, stopped them with a shutout. I wasn't doing so well during the second half after separating a shoulder. My average after the break was .212. Lynn and Rice had taken over from me and Rico as the hitting stars of the Sox. Still, the Orioles edged closer. Then, on the next-to-last Sunday of the season, Jim broke his hand in Detroit. We had a three-and-a-half-game lead with a week to go, and the Orioles weren't losing games —playing better than .600 for more than two months, 14–3 in their latest streak—while we were just hanging around .500 for almost two months.

That's when Johnson asked me if I could play left, and I told him, "In my sleep."

No one knew how seriously hurt I was with a shoulder injury that was to affect my slugging for the rest of my career. Maybe in a career of twenty-three seasons you shouldn't speculate about "what might have been." After all, when you play that long there are going to be setbacks. But I can't escape the fact that I was having a heck of a year in 1975 until the shoulder. Two days before the All-Star break I was 5 for 5 with two doubles. I was batting .313, I was second in the league in runs scored to Lynn, I had 10 homers.

It had happened in Milwaukee, around the same time my mother was being operated on for cancer. I was at first base that night, and made a sweeping tag. The runner hit me, and I pulled all the ligaments in my shoulder. The next day, I couldn't move it.

I flew back to Boston to see a doctor, and it was the same day my mom was having her surgery. I visited her in the hospital. She looked up from her bed, surprised, and said, "What are you doing here? The team's in Milwaukee."

"Mom, I hurt my shoulder," I told her.

"No, you didn't," she insisted. "You came all the way back to see me. Well, I'm fine, and you better get back with the club in Milwaukee." I did. I had to. I didn't want her to think she was so seriously ill that I had left the club. So I went back, but Mrs. Yawkey would visit her every single day.

Now, in the final week of the season, I was glad we had Lynn, at least. I wished we could clinch the damn thing so I could take a few days off before the American League Championship Series, and give my shoulder a chance to heal. We beat the Yankees to start the week and our magic number was down to four. It rained for three days, so we went into the last Saturday not knowing whether the season would continue by having to play the rainouts, or whether we could clinch it. We clinched it the hard way. We lost to the Indians, but the Yankees swept the Orioles in a doubleheader. We had won our first divisional title.

That's when I took off for Florida to rest my shoulder. "Where's Yaz?" people asked. Because I had been benched in the pennant-clincher, a lot of fans thought I was pouting. Johnson had decided not to use me because of the second-half problems I was having, especially against left-handers. But I knew this: I wanted to start in the ALCS against the Oakland A's, who had won three straight World Series.

With that benching, the speculation began. Would I play against the A's, and where would I bat? Johnson made a midweek decision. Yes, I would play—and I'd bat third. That surprised everyone. Third is where you put your top hitter. Off my recent performances, that hardly would be me. For the season, I had driven in only 60 runs, hit only 14 homers, batted only .269.

I got back to Boston refreshed and very happy. My mom was going to be able to see the American League Championship Series. When she left the hospital, her ambition had been to see the playoffs. She was a tough woman. She didn't know she had cancer until after the playoffs. When she was told she had cancer, I visited her in the hospital, and she broke down. I couldn't move in my chair. I was just frozen. She snapped me out of it.

"Okay," she said, "what do we have to do to beat this?"

They said she had up to six months to live, but she survived almost three years, taking chemotherapy and radiation treatments, overcoming the spread to different parts of her body. Her optimism helped me. She had something to look forward to, and now I did, too.

Since 1967, I have been asked about the clutch, and how I've reacted to it. I know this, strange as it sounds. If I was the opposing manager, I wouldn't have come in with my best pitcher against Yastrzemski. In the tough situations, whether it's a question of rising to a higher level, or my ability to block everything out—the noise, the situation—I could do it. I think it might have come down to the fact that my first year produced the most pressure I ever had. After that, it didn't bother me. That's why I was able to shrug off rumors of turmoil on the club, why I never responded to reports that had something to do with a manager being fired or a player traded. I became hardened to what was said about me and the club. I learned too quickly that there was nothing I could say or do to squelch a rumor or a false report in a newspaper. So I didn't say anything. Maybe some reporters took that to mean I was standoffish, or that maybe what was written was the truth. No, it simply meant I wasn't going to fight or argue. And after a while, it really just rolled off my back. The Red Sox are such an important part of Boston life—of New England, really— that small details get analyzed, a player's inflection is examined. You get an idea of what that 1967 pennant meant to Boston when you look at the attendance figures. Fenway is the smallest park in the American League. But that year we led the league in attendance, and went on to lead again five times in the next eight years. From 1967 on, we never dipped under a million again and often went over two million. No one can respond constantly to this sort of examination. You just have to accept it or else you'd sink with the weight of the pressure.

All I knew is that I wanted to be in a pennant race, to be in a tough situation, even playoff games. I wanted to be there, be up. Every year I wanted to be the guy coming up in the ninth inning of the playoffs to either win or lose the game. And I won more than I lost. I absolutely loved that situation.

I had similar feelings in the All-Star Game, even though I complained about going because I wanted those days off, particularly when I got a little older. In my late thirties and early forties it was a struggle to keep up my weight. I constantly ate to keep it at a playing level. I had to eat huge meals, even when I didn't want to. I used to ask Mr. Yawkey to get me out of the All-Star Games, tell them I'd hurt my back. But when I played, I came to play. I had a high intensity level because of the opposing pitchers, whom I knew were the best in the National League.

So the clutch and I were old friends, even though I wish there had been a few more chances. The *Globe* once figured how I did in what it called the twenty-two biggest games of my career, with a pennant or championship on the line: the last two days of the 1967 season, when we had to beat Minnesota; the World Series against the Cards; the two games at the end of 1972 that we played in Detroit; the 1975 playoffs and World Series; the 1978 playoff game against the Yankees.

In those twenty-two games, I batted .417. My slugging percentage was .702. I drove in 25 runs and scored 19 as I hit 6 homers.

Imagine how good I felt in the first inning of the first game against the A's. Ken Holtzman—whom I had hit a grand slam off of in May—was on the mound. My mom was there, thanks to Mr. Yawkey's arranging for her to be brought in a wheelchair. With two out in the first, I singled off Holtzman. It started a two-run rally. Fisk hit a chopper to third that

Sal Bando misplayed. Claudell Washington, in left field, charged the ball. I didn't stop when I reached third. I headed home. The cutoff play was messed up and we opened the scoring.

Tiant nursed a 2–1 lead into the seventh, when he put two runners on and Billy Williams came to the plate. Williams hit a drive toward the Wall. I wasn't afraid of running into the Wall. I had learned to pace off the number of steps from the warning track to the Wall, even on a dead run. So I never had to take my eye off Williams's drive. If you had to think about the Wall behind you, it would play on your mind and probably stop you from running up against it. Instead, I counted as I ran, and when I knew I couldn't run any farther—that the Wall was right there—I leaped and caught the ball.

In Game 2, Reggie Jackson gave them a 2–0 lead. In the third, Bert Campaneris walked with two out. Bando drilled a ball off the Wall, with Campaneris running on the hit. There was only one play in my mind as I faced the Wall and waited for it to come down: *Throw to third.* I knew that's where Campy was headed. I wheeled as the ball hit my glove and I gunned him down. Instead of having two on with Reggie batting, they were through for the inning.

Like I said, I could play left field in my sleep. But hitting was something else again. My stance during the power years had me holding the bat up high. That was impossible now with the shoulder problems. For two days before the opening game, I had worked with Pop and Johnson on a new stance, holding my hands low, then gradually raising them up as the pitcher got ready to throw. It was a difficult and awkward adjustment. It wasn't made any easier by the fact that in Game 2 we were facing Vida Blue. But in the fourth, Denny Doyle singled. I wasn't thinking long ball, just contact with Blue's fastball. I made it—better than I thought I would. I stroked the pitch and drove it over the fence in left center.

We were tied at 3–3 in the sixth when Bando hit a ball off the Wall. He stopped at first, though. Lynn then ran down a drive to the gap on a hit from Joe Rudi that halted the A's

YAZ

• • •

from breaking the tie. We broke it in the bottom of the inning when I doubled and scored on Fisk's hit.

From the beginning of the playoffs, there was speculation whether I'd play left field when we moved to Oakland. At first, Johnson was concerned about the wide-open spaces there, and how difficult it could be for me. After the first two games, though, he didn't have any doubt. I'd be in left again.

We had a 1–0 lead in the bottom of the fourth when Jackson lined a ball down the left field line. I was playing him off the line and had a long sprint to run the ball down. As I grabbed it, I saw him headed for second. I spun and got off a good throw to second. We cut him down. I couldn't resist telling Reggie, as he was dusting himself off and I was running to the dugout, "You don't do things like that on me."

In the eighth, Reggie came up again, with two runners on and the score 5–2. Rick Wise, our starter, was getting shaky after a strong seven innings. This time Reggie really lashed the ball, a liner to left center. It probably would have been a triple. I never thought I'd have a chance to cut it off. I figured, *What the heck, I'll dive for it,* but it was just a desperation move. I remember my body flying after it, fully extended, and I caught the damn ball in my webbing. I got up and threw it to second. That held Reggie on first, Washington to third, and the score 5–3. Dick Drago came in and threw one pitch to Rudi. Because Reggie was held to a single, it made possible the double play that followed.

We won the pennant and for the first time in eight years, Tom Yawkey, who hated the stuff, drank a glass of champagne.

The Cincinnati Reds had the best record in baseball. They won the National League West by twenty games over the Dodgers. But we had Luis and you know what? I think we should have won the Series in five games.

Luis was so sharp in the first game that they only got five hits. I helped him earn the shutout when I made a diving catch off Dave Concepcion with a runner on first. We took a 2–1 lead into the ninth of Game 2 behind Lee. They got a couple of hits, they got a "safe" call on Concepcion's steal of second when Burleson tagged the guy, and they won.

Instead of leading, 2–0, we were tied at 1–1 and going to Cincinnati. More umpire trouble. In the bottom of the tenth, with none out in a 5–5 game, Ed Armbrister was sent by manager Sparky Anderson to bunt with Cesar Geronimo on first. He laid it down, but then the son of a gun just stopped instead of running. He was between Fisk and the ball. Carlton collided with Armbrister but got to the ball and winged it to second to try to force Geronimo. The throw landed in center and there were runners on second and third. We walked the next batter to fill the bases. And then Joe Morgan lined a pitch over Lynn's head. As that ball took off, Pudge took his mask and flung it into the screen behind home plate.

Luis kept us in it the next game with the kind of performance that another ballplayer appreciates. The big guy threw 163 pitches, he held on when they took a 2–0 lead in the first, he held on when the Reds put two runners on in every inning from the fifth through the ninth and he was nursing a 5–4 lead. And he got the final out by serving a pitch that Morgan popped up. That tied the Series at 2–2. We couldn't handle Don Gullett the next game, though, and we returned to Boston, trailing 3–2 in games.

We never did win the 1975 Series. But in the minds of many people, they have one picture: Fisk waving his ball fair, then jumping, then skipping around the bases and they think, *Hey, what a way to win a World Series!* But it was only Game 6.

Only? I suppose you could rightly call it the greatest Series game ever played. I know I wasn't ever in a better one.

Because of three days of rain, Luis was able to start again. Lynn's homer gave him a 3–0 lead in the first. But he crashed into the wall and was shaken up in the fifth when Ken Griffey tripled. The Reds went ahead in the seventh on a double by George Foster, and when Geronimo led off the eighth with a homer, we trailed by 6–3 and Luis was gone. Still, the crowd gave him the standing ovation that had become his theme song as they chanted "Loo-eee! Loo-eee!"

That set up the first of our theatrical comebacks. In the bottom of the eighth, we got two on and the Reds brought in Rawley Eastwick. He led the National League with 22 saves. We sent up Bernie Carbo, a great character. He once stormed into O'Connell's office minutes before a game, demanding to play. And even in this Series, he had belittled Johnson for not using him. In Game 3, he hit a pinch homer.

To take Bernie seriously, you had to get over some of his quirks, such as traveling with a toy stuffed gorilla. He was a hotheaded kid who always started the season well, but then tailed off. This was as tail end of the season as you could get. Eastwick got the count to 3–2. Bernie fouled off the next pitch. The one after that? He drilled into the center field bleachers to tie the score.

We thought we had it won the next inning. Doyle walked and I singled him to third. Fisk walked and the bases were loaded, none out, and Lynn up. Fred popped it up behind third, maybe eighty feet down the line. Foster ran in and had an easy catch. Zimmer, the third base coach, shouted to Doyle on third, "No! No!" But Denny, of course, thought Zim was saying "Go!" He was out by half a mile. Rico grounded out and we were in extra innings.

It wasn't going to go easily. Pete Rose led off the eleventh inning and was hit by Drago's pitch. Griffey tried to bunt Pete to second but forced him. Now Morgan was up. He hit a drive to right that was headed for the seats. Evans wouldn't let it. He raced over for it and caught it on the warning track. He spun into the short wall in right. I was playing first base, having moved there after Carbo remained in the game and went to left. Griffey, thinking the ball was never going to be caught, had already rounded second. Evans wheeled after running into the stands and threw the ball back in for the double-play attempt. It was wide, and I had to get it between first and the dugout. But Burleson ran in all the way from shortstop to cover first. When I saw that, I simply threw him the ball to double up Griffey. For a moment, seeing Dwight's catch, I thought of Willie Mays and his catch in 1954 World Series against Vic Wertz.

When a game like that goes into extra innings, I had the certain feeling it was going to end only with a homer. You're too tired, it's too late, and you have too many things to do right to push across a run any other way. Too many things can go wrong.

Pat Darcy, the eighth Reds' pitcher, faced Fisk in the twelfth. Pudge tagged the second pitch.

Stay fair. Stay fair, I said to myself. I knew it had the power to go out, but when you pull a ball that sharp, sometimes it hooks on you all of a sudden. I was just hoping it would hit the foul pole before it hooked. Everyone stood and Fisk looked at it, took a step, and then started waving it fair to the right with two hands, as if he was pushing it. The wind caught it—and it hit the foul pole netting for the homer that won the game. Dramatic? You bet. The Series was tied at 3–3.

Now for Game 7. The Red Sox had not won a World Series since 1918, when Babe Ruth pitched two victories. We gave Lee a 3–0 lead in the third inning after I singled in a run, and then we pushed across two more on bases-loaded walks. They chopped away, though. In the sixth they had a runner on with two out (after we threw away a double-play ball) and Perez came up. In a meeting with Lee before the game, he had been told, "Don't throw off-speed to Perez. He'll cream it." But Bill did things his own way. He had a pitch he called "the bloop," and he threw it just then. Perez knocked it over the Wall. The Reds got another run in the seventh after Lee developed a blister and it was a tie game. Here's one of the little things that happen to change history. Maybe it doesn't, but things are never the same. Jim Willoughby was pitching for us, and he had been effective against the Reds. He put them down one, two, three after coming into the game in the seventh and getting Bench with the bases loaded. Evans led off the bottom of the eighth with a walk. Burleson was trying to sacrifice him to second. Instead, after failing twice, he had to swing away and grounded into a double play. Now Johnson pinch-hit for Willoughby with two outs and nobody on base. Cooper, who had been in a 1 for 18 slump, fouled out.

So Jim Burton was pitching the ninth for us and started it by walking Griffey. He was sacrificed to second and got to third on a groundout. Rose walked and Morgan came up. Burton got two strikes on him and Morgan was thinking of protecting the plate. The pitch came in and Morgan obviously wasn't crazy about it. But he swung and he broke the damn bat, but the ball looped over second. Fred tore in after it from center, but couldn't get to it. Griffey scored and they took the lead, 4–3.

Will McEnaney pitched the final inning for the Reds. He set down Juan Beniquez and Bob Montgomery and there it was: my dream. Bottom of the ninth, two outs, last World Series game, down by a run, and I'm up.

Pride. I was thinking, *Home run.* I wanted to tie the game. He was a left-handed sidearmer with a sinkerball. I thought, *Wait until the last possible second before swinging.* You've got to do that with a sidearming left-hander. You have a tendency to open too quickly to pull the ball. I waited. He did make a little mistake. He kind of got it up. But I just got under the ball. I dropped a little too quickly, and instead of driving it I got underneath it, hit the ball to center field, got it close to the warning track. Geronimo caught it. If I didn't drop quite as much, I might have hit it out. But I probably thought wrong in going for the homer.

That was my last Series. The Sox waited eleven years for another one. But this was the one I thought we should have won. Sure, it hangs over me that we hadn't won a Series since 1918. We were all aware of it. Everyone in a Red Sox uniform knows the record. But the 1967 Series . . . well, we should never have been there. What bothers me still about 1975 was that I thought we'd go on from there, I thought we had the makings of a fine team even more than I did after 1967.

Look, you have Lynn and Rice. Baseball's a funny game. You don't know about 162 games, and what will happen. That's why it's such a great game. I didn't think we'd win the pennant every year after 1975, but I thought we'd be going right down to the wire every season, certainly be contenders for some time to come. At the age of thirty-six, that gave me a big boost, having the talent of a Rice, a Burleson, a Fisk, a Lynn, me. *Now,* I thought, *every game is going to mean something for some time. For the next five years, six years.* I was thinking, *Jeez, from now until I retire we're going to be in a pennant race.* I was walking on air. I had seen the 1967 club dissolve the next year with injuries, but now from a selfish standpoint, I saw myself getting better opportunities to hit as well. It makes it easier when you've got hitters in front of you and hitters behind you, and to have a shot at the pennant every year.

But then we got caught in the crap that surrounded free agency. It affected the attitude and the future of the Red Sox.

16
BREAKUP

It was like a nightmare. I couldn't believe it was happening. After 1967 we came apart because of injuries. But now, in 1976 and the years afterward, we came apart for a different reason. After the 1975 season, the courts ruled in favor of free agency. It meant that players could make their own deals when their contracts expired. It meant that Lynn, Fisk, and Burleson hired Jerry Kapstein, an agent who understood the power that players now had. Because all this was new, and there wasn't an agreement in place, all the players who were unsigned for 1976 would be free agents at the end of the season. The three players held out during training camp. It was probably the most serious challenge the Sox had ever faced—certainly under Mr. Yawkey's ownership. And it changed the club around. Things only got a little better when they finally showed up for spring training—late. As long as they were unsigned, there was a cloud over the team. It lasted more than half the season, until a new bargaining agreement was in place and the three players signed.

Everyone knew it was affecting our club, but we didn't talk about it much. The thing was, the fun had gone out of the game, not only that year but in the following seasons as well. Everything became more serious. Imagine what it was like for us when you'd walk into the clubhouse and there were agents standing in the hallway, talking to the players.

When the three were going through their troubles, Kapstein would telephone them in the locker room on the road. They'd talk to him while they were in the clubhouse, which is a no-no.

That was just one symbol of how the game changed, how everything changed. Baseball went from a team orientation toward an individual situation. Nobody kidded around. It became . . . I guess the word is "businesslike." In the next few years, we had an ownership crisis after Mr. Yawkey died and Haywood Sullivan and Buddy LeRoux, our trainer, who became an owner, ran the club like a business. People would be talking about contracts during the middle of the season.

Figure you lose something when you've got three key players holding out. That's understandable. But the free agency thing turned us upside down. We pulled fewer and fewer pranks. And when Luis Tiant went to the Yankees after 1978, well, that about killed it. Nobody would do anything to anyone anymore because a guy would get ticked off. Players would sit in front of their lockers, figuring their batting averages instead of how to help the team win. All of a sudden, it became a quiet clubhouse. After the 1978 season, nothing ever happened again. You'd sit in front of your locker and that was it. The guys didn't realize what silly things like pranks had done for us. A prank could bail you out. Say you'd lost a couple of games in a row, and someone pulled a hotfoot, you'd be loose when you went home. So when you came in the next day you wouldn't be worried about losing four straight. It was fun to go to the ballpark. You'd have to be here 4:45 in the afternoon, but everyone was at the clubhouse at 4:00, waiting for something to happen, Luis coming in, or some prank on someone.

Instead, new guys were coming in and the old guys were leaving. It wasn't that they were retiring. They were having contract problems or they were unhappy over the way they were being used, and these things would linger. Lynn was actually traded at one point, but Kapstein was able to void the deal over the length of the contract. Eventually, of course, Lynn did go, and so did Fisk and Burleson and Lee and Luis. We even had guys join us who weren't allowed to stay. In June of 1976, shortly before his death, Mr. Yawkey approved the purchase of Rollie Fingers and Joe Rudi from the A's. We paid $1 million each for them and I remember how happy they were when they posed in their new Red Sox uniforms. They actually worked out with us that night, since we were playing in Oakland. Finley was trying to get money out of his ball club before he lost the players to free agency. He also sold Vida Blue to the Yankees. But Bowie Kuhn voided the deals. "Not in the best interests of baseball," he said. It got so bad that you couldn't tell from week to week who your team-mates would be. We had heard that Mr. Yawkey was so miffed at the contract dispute with Lynn and Burleson that he wanted them traded before the June 15 deadline.

Sure, I was old-fashioned. Some other players accused me of being anti-union and of being part of a privileged few. I took a stand against strikes and against the Curt Flood ruling, but that didn't mean I was against the union. I didn't agree with everything that happened. Did my relationship with Mr. Yawkey affect my thinking? I'm sure it enabled me to see both sides of the situation.

When I came up, you'd join fellows you had played with in the minors. You grew up together, came up through the ranks with them. In spring training you'd have forty guys you were pretty sure would still be in the organization when the season ended. You got to know them. That was one of the things I'd talk about with Mr. Yawkey constantly—the minor league report. When you heard about a trade, it was terrible because you followed those guys from the time they were kids. When Reggie Smith and Mike Andrews came up in 1966, I knew inning by inning what had happened in their playoffs in the minors when Dick Williams was managing their club.

When Johnny Bench and I got together for our news conference in 1989 to announce our induction into the Hall of Fame, we realized we each had played our entire careers with the same clubs.

"Well, at least we know which uniform will be hung up for us," we said.

I thought about Pete Rose leaving Cincinnati while he was still playing. I couldn't believe it. I was a player at the time, and I wondered, *What the hell's he going to Philadelphia for?* Then he went to Montreal. When you're a person who's become an idol, like Rose, you don't start traveling around. There couldn't have been that much difference in money, for God's sake. With taxes, what's the difference?

There was an informality to life in baseball just a few years before. All I knew was that on our team, it had taken years for us to get a good attitude in the clubhouse, and now it was changed again drastically. It went from twenty-five guys traveling together, and seeing one another's families—to wives arguing over whose husband should be earning more money once all the salaries became public. That's something that just drove me nuts. Baseball is a team game and takes a whole team thinking and playing together to win the pennant. Some people don't think so because baseball seems to be a game of individuals. It looks as if teammates aren't involved in what you do when you come to bat, say like a quarterback in football or a guard in basketball.

But I always looked at it as a team game, even when I stepped in the batter's box. Sure, I loved the one-on-one competition: me against the pitcher. But there are situations that batting is a team game, when you have to do things for the team. Say there's a man on second, with none out. If you're going to get a hit, it's got to be a ground-ball base hit, past the second baseman or first baseman, on the right side. Even a groundout to the right side moves the runner along. So when I'd step in I'd be thinking, *I've got to get a low pitch and it's got to be a ground ball to the right side. It can't be up the middle because the shortstop or second baseman can get there and throw to third.* So they're really taking that at-bat away from you. You can't put the ball in the air. That's when it becomes a team game. Or: left-handed hitter, runner on first, one out or no outs. You've got to get a ball to pull inside to get him to third base with one out. So are you willing to get in that batter's box and say, *I'm giving this at-bat away?* You're hoping you'll get a base hit, but a ground-ball base hit. But what if you're facing a power pitcher who throws the ball up? You're saying to yourself, *I've got to try to make him bring it down in the strike zone, chop the ball to get it down to the right side.*

Not a team game? Sure it is, at least the way baseball is supposed to be played.

It was surprising, then, that we put up a pretty good fight in 1976, considering what was going on. In May we lost ten straight. A television station sent a witch out to batting practice to change our luck. The witch (and a double I hit in the twelfth inning against Cleveland) worked.

We then went on a streak, capturing four out of five. Going into Detroit, I warned the guys, "This is the most important week of the season." We had the Tigers, followed by four games against the Yankees, who were tearing the league apart. I knew if we didn't stay close, especially after meeting the Yankees head-to-head, it would be a long season.

I was honored at a ceremony in Detroit, where I played in game number 2,293, which broke Ted's Boston record. I acted like it, too. I was hitting .198. We won the game, our second straight there. But I just wasn't feeling right at the plate, and I came out the next day at three o'clock to get forty minutes of extra batting practice. I figured I'd try raising my hands again and see if I couldn't get some power back, even though it hurt like hell. It felt good being able to drill the ball, though. Even the ones I fouled off, I could tell I was swinging right. I just had to keep the guys moving.

Well, I did something I had never accomplished before—a three-home-run game. It was a beautiful evening—I put us ahead with a two-run shot off Dave Roberts in the fourth. Then I hit one the next inning off Steve Grilli (to left center) and then in the ninth, with John Hiller pitching, I hit an upper-deck job. How I loved that park! It completed a 4 for 4 night. I even scored from first on an infield out after they threw the ball away.

This was the getaway I wanted us to have as we faced the Yankees. We had won seven out of eight and were going to Yankee Stadium, where we'd had great games and great brawls over the years. We had done well against the Yankees in the 1970s and I thought that maybe all the internal stuff was behind us.

Something else happened in the opener instead. For the third time in my career, we had an all-out brawl with the Yankees. When it was over, Bill Lee had a separated shoulder and his year was ruined. We did win the game, though, as I tied a big league record by hitting two more homers—for five in two games.

The newspaper pictures the next day showed Piniella and Fisk on the ground, rolling around. It happened in the sixth inning after Lou tried to make it home on a ball hit to Evans, the best right fielder in baseball. Piniella collided with Fisk, who was waiting for him, holding the ball, and Pudge whacked Lou across the face with it. Lee rushed in, but Nettles caught him and threw him down. We all dashed out, as you're supposed to do in these things. Usually, not much happens. A lot of running around, you grab some guy on the other team and hold his shirt. But we all got into this one. Someone whacked me in my knee and it hurt like heck. It seemed to be quieting down, but Lee got up and tried to get Nettles and someone tossed him on his shoulder.

It reminded me of the 1967 free-for-all at the Stadium with Rico's brother, the security cop, pulling guys off. In 1973 we had one in Fenway when Thurman Munson and Fisk went at it. In that one, Gene Michael missed the bunt on a suicide squeeze and Thurman was barreling into home. He was out by a few feet, but he went into Fisk anyway. They shoved each other. It seemed to be over, but just then Michael started swinging at Pudge. Fisk and Munson were tossed out.

When this latest brawl all settled, we were tied going into the eighth. Fisk led off with a walk and Billy Martin brought in a lefty, Tippy Martinez, to face me. People in the stands still were riled and they were tossing beer cans around. Zimmer, coaching third, wore a batting helmet. With two strikes, I hit a slider into the stands. For effect, I stood at the plate an extra second so it could sink into them what I had done. Then, in the ninth, they brought in a rookie named Ron Guidry.

I didn't know anything about him and asked Johnson what he had on the kid. "Good fastball," I was told. Fisk was on first. I hit the fastball into the seats. We started off this big series with a victory.

That was as good as it got that season. Lee, our only southpaw starter, was finished. Rice and Lynn had some injuries and we just about played .500 ball the rest of the year, a year in which every other day brought new trade rumors. If only those three players had signed during training camp.

Contracts had always been such simple things. At least to me.

I signed one-year contracts because I was always confident that in the coming season I'd do better than I had in the last one. In 1969 I signed a three-year deal, but that was open to negotiation if I had a good year. This may strike people as strange, but from the 1970s on, all my contracts were done on handshakes, first with O'Connell and then Sullivan, as I did with Mr. Yawkey.

I'd go to lunch with Dick in the wintertime, usually at the private Algonquin Club. We'd agree on this and that. After a few beers, when he heard what else I wanted, he'd say to me, in exasperation, "What? Now, what do you really want?" and that's how it was. After we'd get close to an agreement, O'Connell would look very pleased and call the waiter over and say, "Get him a dozen stuffed lobsters to go." That was fun.

Oh, we'd haggle. But I knew I'd never be a holdout. I

never was, but when it came down to Opening Day I'd rarely have a signed contract. We were always on the road somewhere and they'd have to fly in and sign me. If not, the commissioner's office wouldn't allow me to play. The contracts I signed included special things for me that were never written in, such as bonuses and deferred payments. I signed a lot of blank contracts over the years, deals that never had any figures in them. But I signed so I could play on Opening Day.

I even used to forget about payments I was supposed to be getting. So when it came to the last week of the season, a check would come down—for $25,000 or $50,000—and I'd call the front office and say, "What the heck's this for?" and O'Connell would remind me, "Don't you remember? For 100 RBIs" or for a batting title.

Our relationship was at such a level that I don't recall ever asking specifics for bonuses if I reached a certain level.

"You be the judge," I told Dick. I knew he'd be fair.

The last seven, eight years, when salaries escalated and I was in the mid-to-upper six figures, I'd call Bob Woolf before negotiating. It had become more complicated. But I'd still go in myself to make the final deal.

You know where else I got advice from? Mr. Yawkey's man in New York, Joe LaCour. And John Harrington, who ran the Yawkey affairs in Boston. Talk about how different it is now. I was using Mr. Yawkey's people for advice on writing my own contract—that *he'd* have to pay for.

It wasn't so simple under the new rules, though. Darrell Johnson never could get feeling right about 1976. Midway through the season, he was gone. We were in Kansas City right after the All-Star break, and had just lost a couple in a row. He was alone in his office after everybody had left for the bus. He called me in.

"I'm calling Dick O'Connell and I'm quitting," he said.

"What the hell are you talking about? We won the pennant last year," I told him. "We may be having a little bit of a rough time right now, but don't get carried away because we lost two straight." We were just under .500.

"I've lost control of this team," he said.

"Darrell, it's the same team we won with last year," I said, trying to reassure him. I talked to him about half an hour. Then later that night, he called me and said, "That's it, I'm quitting." Only three months into the season after he won a pennant.

We played much better ball after Don Zimmer took over, but we were too far behind to catch the Yankees in Billy Martin's first full season as manager of the team. A couple of unusual things happened for me, though.

On my thirty-seventh birthday on August 22, the fans serenaded me. I responded with four hits against the A's, and I even threw a runner out at the plate. But everyone made a big deal over a non-hit. In the ninth inning, with the score tied at 6–6, I laid down a sacrifice bunt. It was my second bunt since 1967 and the ninth in my sixteen seasons. Reggie Cleveland and Rick Wise presented me with the ball after the game. They got one thing wrong on it, though. They wrote: FIRST CAREER SACRIFICE.

It was a bunt situation, I guess. Lynn got a one-out single. As I moved to the plate from the on-deck circle, Zim trotted down the line from third to talk to me. I knew the bunt was on, but I wondered if maybe he wanted me to slap at it and double-cross the A's. I figured their infielders would be charging.

"No, I don't think so. None of them have ever seen you bunt," Zim said. "They're not going to expect it and they won't charge."

So I bunted to first, and moved Fred over. It didn't help. He stayed there and the A's won in extra innings.

By the end of the season, we were so far out of the race that I was able to start thinking of some personal goals. One was to drive in 100 runs, which I hadn't done since 1970.

I had injury problems as the season wound down—a bad thigh, a pulled groin. I could barely walk. We were out of it, about to finish third behind the Yanks and Orioles. We had our final road trip in Detroit, when Zim suddenly fell ill and was hospitalized. Pop took over. I had 91 RBIs, with only a handful of games remaining, when we faced the Tigers.

"How about it?" Pop asked. He wanted me to get the 100. "Can you play?"

He put me in at cleanup. I knocked in a run in the first and another in the third, but I reinjured my groin running to first. He put in Lynn to run for me. Now I had 93.

Pop knew I was having trouble just standing up and said to me the next day, "I'll start you as the DH. I'm giving you one shot in the first inning. They're starting a right-hander today. Maybe there'll be a couple of guys on, and you'll have a shot to hit it out of there."

Well, sure enough, two guys were on, Vern Ruhle was pitching, I got up, and—*bang*—I hit the ball into the upper deck. A three-run shot. It took me five minutes to run around the bases. The Tigers were really ticked because here was a guy who couldn't even walk, for cripes sakes, and he hit a home run off them. In the third I singled and drove in another run. Pop took me out and sent Jim Rice to run for me. Now I was up to 97 RBIs.

The next day they started a left-hander against us, and Popowski told me to rest. But we had runners on second and third in the eighth, one out, and he called "time." He sent me up to pinch-hit. The guy on the mound was so mad that I was going for 100 RBIs at his expense that he threw four pitches right at my head. He didn't want me to drive in any runs, so he wild-pitched in both runs. All four pitches hit the backstop. When I got to first, Pop put in another interesting pinch-runner: Bill Lee.

In the fourth game, I walked with the bases loaded to force in a run. So in the four games, I had picked up seven ribbies and needed only two. In the last two games back home, I drove in four runs, including three against the Yankees. By then, Zim had returned and told me, "That's enough, Yaz, take the rest of the season off." So I didn't play that final weekend, but wound up with 102. The team also finished streaking, and with Rice and Lynn healthy, why shouldn't 1977 have been a great year?

Except that for a while I wasn't sure it would be with Boston. Or maybe I just wanted to see what someone else thought I was worth. Or maybe I was just going along with Bob Woolf, who loves to see how much one of his guys can command.

Baseball decided to expand in 1977 and added Seattle and Toronto to the American League. After the 1976 season, each of us who had played ten years received a form to fill out. The league wanted to know if we would allow ourselves to be drafted by one of the expansion teams or whether we insisted on being in the pool of players protected by our clubs. I never even filled out the form. I threw it away.

Mr. Yawkey asked me if I wanted to be protected. If not, the Red Sox could protect a younger player.

"Tom, I'm not going anyplace else," I told him.

A few days before the draft, though, Toronto called me, then Bob called me, everyone called me. Toronto had a deal cooking. They were going to draft me and then trade me—I heard to either the Yankees or the Mets—for some younger players, a four-for-one deal. And Toronto told me that whatever kind of contract I signed—even if, going on thirty-eight, I wanted a five-year deal—New York would honor it. Five-year deal? That meant I could be guaranteed a paycheck until I was forty-three.

I called Bob and asked whether I should talk to them. They were going to fly in the next day. As soon as I got off the phone, Seattle called—they had a different proposition. They wanted to draft me, and keep me. Could they fly in tomorrow, too?

"What do you want to do?" Woolf asked.

"I don't know, Bob," I replied, sounding confused, I guess. Deep down, though, I had other thoughts, just as I had four years before in Japan.

"I've been sitting here thinking about it. I've given my

word to the team that I wouldn't be drafted." But Bob was also thinking as my agent as well as my friend.

"Yaz, at least you've got to consider it. You don't have to sign anything. You never know where it's going to lead. You can sign whatever you want to sign for, and for as long as you want. I don't know if that's ever happened before in the history of baseball." That confused me even more.

"Let me think about it," I told him.

One of the things that ran through my mind, believe it or not, was: *Cripes, I know how to drive my car around Boston.* That's right. I knew my way around. And it's a great city. I know the people. And leaving Boston—not just leaving the Red Sox—weighed on my mind. It became a factor in my decision. For two hours I was on the phone to Seattle or Toronto or Bob, we had conference calls, and everyone was getting worked up.

Finally, I said, "Bob, I just can't do it. I gave my word to the man." Mr. Yawkey didn't have to protect me. So the next day I told Toronto and Seattle, "Forget it." Anyway, Seattle had never really been a consideration. As for Toronto . . . well, the idea of playing in New York had stirred something in me, something I hadn't felt in almost twenty years. But it came down to this: I had given my word. I called the commissioner's office and told them I wasn't going to be drafted. That was the year the Yankees went after Reggie Jackson.

• • •

It was also one weird year for us. It was either home run or nothing. We hit 213 because we had to. Not one starting pitcher won as many games as the 13 by Bill Campbell, a reliever who led the league in saves as well.

If we had won the division that year, we would have gone down as one of the most interesting teams in history. We belted 6 in one game against the Yankees—4 off Catfish Hunter alone in the first inning—and we had a stretch of 33 homers in ten games, we had a nine-game losing streak, we had an eleven-game winning streak (which we followed by losing seven straight). But that's what happens when your pitching staff can't come through consistently.

You can sense sometimes how a season will go by what happens in the spring. I hoped we were over the contract problems that hung over us in 1976. We weren't. Luis was sulking over his 1977 contract and didn't get to spring training until only a couple of weeks remained. Then, we were going to Bradenton to play an exhibition game against the Pirates. Lynn, who had some physical problems, was supposed to be our DH. Instead, the Pirates insisted on National League rules. Lynn got in as a pinch hitter, and as he was rounding second base he jammed his left ankle. He tore ligaments and missed the first five weeks of the season. Rick Miller replaced him in center, but got hit by a pitch early in the season and broke his left thumb. Dwight (Dewey) Evans moved over to center, but he hurt his knee after rounding third in a game. Lee still was recovering from his shoulder problems in the Yankee brawl. Luckily we used free agency ourselves when we picked up Campbell for the bullpen.

We walloped 16 homers against the Yankees in a three-day span in June, but Jackson got more attention than anything we hit out. That came in a game we ripped them by 10–4. We hit 5 homers. I hit 2 as I had a 4 for 5 game with 5 ribbies. Jackson and Martin had to be separated by Elston Howard after Martin yanked Jax out of the game. He hadn't run very hard to field a broken-bat hit by Rice that became a double. That teed off Martin, who pulled him out. I was sitting in the dugout, watching Billy go to the mound to replace Mike Torrez. I don't think I'd ever seen a player pulled off the field for a poor play, though. But all of a sudden I saw Paul Blair grabbing a glove and going to right field and Reggie coming in. This was hot stuff for the network television cameras. Then, when Reggie got to the dugout, he waved his arms, as if he was saying, "Why me?" Then Billy rushed him and Howard had to keep them apart.

We swept the Yankees the next day with 5 more homers. Talk about hot. That was 16 against them to set a three-game record. This was fun. In the series I had 9 hits in 14 at-bats, with 4 homers and 10 RBIs. We were in first place by two and a half games. But those Yankees . . . it's got to be the greatest rivalry in any sport. One team thinks it's got the other team down, it's the bottom of the ninth and you're killing them . . . and *boom,* something happens that wouldn't happen against anyone else. It's the Yankees-Red Sox, that's all. You don't even have to explain it. In fact, you couldn't explain it.

So a week later we went to New York, took a lead against Hunter, but they came back to start us on a nine-game losing streak.

Before that series began, we had almost wiped Martin out of the picture. After we had ripped them with our homers in Fenway, George Steinbrenner called a team meeting and told the players that he had come close to firing Billy, and that if they wanted their manager to remain, they had better get in gear. Then he gave them the clincher: "The series this weekend against the Red Sox is our most important series of the year."

So we blew a 5–3 lead when Roy White hit a two-run homer with two out in—you guessed it—the bottom of the ninth against Campbell. The Yankees won in the eleventh on a base hit by Reggie, and they were off and we were heading down. We had come into the Stadium with a five-game lead. After we had lost our first, Zim responded defensively to questions by saying, "Hey, we're still two games in front."

I always got along fine with Zim, especially when he was the third-base coach. We'd go out for dinner all the time. But it became a little different when he became the manager, I suppose because you have to have that distance. Zim's problem was that he took newspaper articles to heart. I'd go in his office, and he'd be infuriated at what Lee had said to a reporter.

"Zim, he's a pitcher, who gives a crap what he says?" I'd tell him, try to soothe him. But he was the type of guy who

couldn't read anything negative about himself. He'd listen to
the talk shows on radio and it would drive him crazy.

"You can't let it get to you," I explained. "That 'Sports
Huddle' would kick the crap out of me and Bobby Orr every
Sunday. But I don't even think about it." Zim was a good
manager, but he let it get personal with writers and players he
didn't like mouthing off. I had been around long enough to
love it when Lee was talking and no one bothered me for
comments. I mean, he'd be talking about the direction of the
moon. And when Hawk was on the club, he'd tell the writers
about his one hundred suits and two hundred pairs of shoes.
I'd be laughing. A guy like Zim, though, it would drive him
nuts.

A lot of that 1977 craziness fell on him. As the manager,
he had to take the heat and he had to last through all the ups
and downs. We had gotten back to a three-and-a-half-game
lead by the middle of August, but then we went into another
tailspin. Now, in the middle of September, we were back in
New York for a three-game series. The Yankees were leading
by one and a half games. We came in with five guys who had
more than 20 homers. Rice and Scott had over 30. We also
had a five-game winning streak. But Ron Guidry, by now an
established star, stopped us in the opener in an atmosphere
that felt like a playoff game. Kids were throwing Frisbees,
bands were playing, and Steinbrenner even introduced celeb-
rities before the game, as if this was something special. When
Guidry struck out the last batter, they mobbed him as if it was
the seventh game of the Series. The next night we started
Reggie Cleveland, who had beaten them seven straight times.
But Jackson came up in the ninth inning of a scoreless game.
He hit it out. We salvaged the last game, but we couldn't
make up the difference. For me, it marked the closest I came
to .300 again, finishing at .296. There were other aspects of
that season that, just in a personal sense, were rewarding: I led
the league's outfielders by not making an error. I stole 11
bases and was thrown out only once. I scored 99 runs and hit

28 homers. I also drove home 102 runs for the second straight year.

Something strange was going on. I was becoming an object of curiosity and affection. Someone pointed out that, at the age of thirty-eight, I had become one of the five oldest players ever to drive in 100 runs in a season. When I made an out, even in a key situation, I'd get polite applause instead of the sort of booing or an "Aw, shucks" reaction other players might get and that I used to hear regularly. But I never thought of each succeeding season as one in which I had to prove something. After all, Dad had played until he was forty —with all his aches and pains.

If I needed any incentive for 1978, it was to be for Mom's memory. She died that January. I dedicated myself to having a great season, just as I had wanted to do exceptionally well in 1976 after Mr. Yawkey died. Their memories hovered over me, spurred me on, and brought me up whenever I was down.

My mom was an exceptionally strong woman, the cornerstone of two families: the Yastrzemskis and Skoniecznys. She ran the show. If there was a party, Mom was the one who got everyone together. She was the disciplinarian. My dad would just give me a look if he didn't like something. You didn't want to get him angry. But she was the one who made sure I did the right thing. When I was in my junior year of high school, and my folks said it was okay to get in by eleven at night, I would usually get home a little later. I'd try to sneak in, take off my shoes. But she'd be hiding in a closet and come out and nab me. It got to be a game. I'd try to see how late I could make it back, but she was always waiting for me.

Mom loved baseball and it became a part of my parents' lives. My first few years in Boston, Mom and Dad would drive up on weekends for the Friday, Saturday, and Sunday games, then make the five-and-a-half-hour drive back home on Sunday nights. In 1967 they moved up near us to a house in Andover. Dad got a job working at the airport and they made the Red Sox—and Boston—part of their lives. Even after she got sick, Mom tried to take care of others. While she was stricken, her brother Jerry also got cancer. And so did my aunt Jean. The three of them died within a short time of one another. My grandmother was still alive, but saw three of her children dead.

I visited Mom during her last days. They said she'd be going at any moment. She opened her eyes and saw me there and said, "I'm hungry." She hung on for days afterward. Mom was the type who never gave in. Then Dad called me and told me, "She said the rosary in Polish, closed her eyes, and died."

My memory of her was strong when I left for spring training. Like everyone else, I thought 1978 was the year that Boston was meant to have since 1967. This, finally, was the coming together of hitting and pitching. In the off-season we had picked up Mike Torrez and Dennis Eckersley and we bolstered our bullpen to give Campbell some help.

On July 19, we held a fourteen-game lead over the Yankees, who were far back in the division. Eck was something. With Cleveland, he had never beaten the Yankees. But he stopped them three times in a two-week stretch. We were nine games ahead of the second-place Brewers. It was a gala day, our biggest lead of the year, with Torrez winning his twelfth game. Of course, you never know when you've reached the top in a season because it's so long. I mean, if you lead a club by fourteen games before the season's half over, you figure you could just as easily make it twenty games. But because of the length of the season, the other club can turn around and produce as much as you had.

When you hold a lead like that, you can have some fun. After I had gone through 1977 without an error, Burleson bet me $100 that I couldn't do it again. "You're on," I told him. That was one of the quickest $100 I ever lost. In the first week I dropped a fly ball hit by Jorge Orta at Chicago. My streak ended at 201 games, including 167 in left field going back to 1976.

The day in late July that we had a fourteen-game edge,

we overpowered the Brewers while the Yankees blew a 5–1 lead against Kansas City. The Yankees, as usual, were in turmoil because Jackson had disregarded a "hit" sign by Martin and had bunted instead. Reggie was suspended for five days. A few days later we beat them and increased our lead over them to nine and a half games.

Once again, things unraveled. But in a way that not even the most pessimistic Sox fan could have imagined (or could he?).

The Yankees began streaking. They dismissed Martin and brought in Bob Lemon. Injured players came back, particularly Catfish Hunter and Thurman Munson. Meanwhile, we got some injuries and Torrez went into a slump—knocked out in eight straight starts without a victory. We got tight and began making an error—and more—a game. Every starting pitcher except Tiant, who slumped through most of July and August, was sent to the bullpen at some point.

Still, when we played the Yankees in a four-game series in early September, we brought a four-game lead over them into Fenway. Four games later they had outscored us 42–9, swept all four games, and were tied for first. It was so bad we had to use a rookie who started the season in Pawtucket, Bobby Sprowl, in the fourth game. Luis actually wanted to pitch, but Zim didn't want to use him with three days' rest. Sprowl walked four Yankees and pitched one third of an inning. When that game ended, we were in a stretch of losing fourteen of seventeen games, committing thirty-three errors. After 113 days, we were out of first.

The next weekend they beat us in two games and now, with fourteen games remaining, had a three-and-a-half-game lead. Confused? Angry? I had never felt this way. *How can a team with so much talent play this way?* Sure, the Yankees played great after Lemon took over. But all we had to do was hold up our end of things, and we hadn't been able to do it.

This was the point when it would have been easy to collapse, to just let the season dissolve. But I hope people remember how we made a comeback. We won twelve of our last fourteen. And with eight to play, we were down two. We captured our final eight games. That 1978 club came together all of a sudden down the stretch. We said to one another, "The hell with everything. We're gonna get back in this thing." And we did. It was different from the 1967 team, which played on emotion. In 1978 we became very tough, very businesslike, and we said that nothing was going to stop us. On the final weekend, we were a game back, with a series against Toronto, while the Yankees faced Cleveland. It was scoreboard watching and listening. We had a radio in the dugout and in the clubhouse and in the bullpen. Bob Stanley had a no-hitter against the Blue Jays, while Cleveland was stopping the Yankees, 1–0. Bob lost the no-hitter, but we won. In the top of the ninth, the Yankees tied their game then went ahead. Fisk kicked a chair as he listened. We both won on Saturday, and it came down to the last game of the season.

Excitement? This is how crazy Boston was again. After one of our victories, a radio personality told listeners, "Pope dead, Sox alive, details at eleven."

That last Sunday was something. We were a game out and sent Luis to the mound to face Toronto. The Yankees were winding up with Hunter pitching against the Indians. The Yankees were streaking themselves, with six straight. I respected Catfish, and some of our guys thought he was the best clutch pitcher in the league, along with Tiant. Considering Cleveland didn't have much of a club, a few of our guys conceded the game to Catfish. I don't know whether 1967 had taught me something, but baseball is special in that, unless you're mathematically out, time never runs out on you. Good old Luis came through for us. Meanwhile, while I was out in the field, I heard the crowd roar. I didn't have to turn around to look at the scoreboard. I knew that meant the Indians had scored some runs off Catfish. They did, they knocked him out and Rick Waits beat the Yankees.

"It's a playoff!" someone shouted. Of course, we knew about that possibility for a week: one game to decide it all. Thirty years before, the Sox were in the first playoff in baseball history, losing to the Indians. Nothing, though, could be more perfect than this: Red Sox–Yankees. Torrez vs. Guidry. Mike looked at this as a game that could redeem him. He was one of the players who symbolized the new free agent era. Just the year before he had been a Yankee, but then he had joined us. When you came to a new club as a free agent, everyone expected immediate results. Fans looked at you as a hired gun who was supposed to come in right away and help. There wasn't time left anymore for a player to break in, to make mistakes on his new job. It often meant fans made instant judgments on you, and no matter how well you did after a while, you were made or broken by your first few appearances.

By October 2, 1978, I was thirty-nine years old. My wrist had bothered me since early April, when I got hit by a pitch. For a while, my fingers were numb. You get revived with stretch runs, and once again I found myself remembering the early years when September and October didn't mean a thing. There was something else about this day: I thought it would be my last shot at a pennant. I could see that the Fisk, Burleson, Lynn situation was going to end with their leaving. Tiant was unhappy because he couldn't get together with the new management over a contract, either. I just knew it was now or never. Maybe I shouldn't have been guided by emotions like that. I had seen too much over the years. But I also knew that the days were numbered for our young guys of the future, as well as the fellow who was a key element to our pitching staff and great fun around the clubhouse.

I was in the clubhouse after we tied the Yankees, absorbing the victory, thinking about tomorrow, when Zim sent someone for me. I looked at Dewey Evans and said to myself, *What does he want? He hasn't spoken to me in three months.*

Zim's coaches were in his office, meeting over the playoff game. He wanted to come across as very definitive and precise. He would ask you a question and then give you the answer before you replied. He actually had made up his mind whom he was going to play against Guidry. The coaches were going along with anything he said. Fine, I understood that, since he hired and fired them. You had to know that Zim ran his own game and didn't want anyone even seeming to intrude. Johnny Podres was a good friend of his. They had played together with the Dodgers, and Podres had become his pitching coach. One day a Sox pitcher had control trouble and started walking players. Podres called the bullpen and got two pitchers up. Zimmer saw them throwing and said, "What are they doing up?" Podres said, "It looks like he's getting tired." Zimmer snapped, "I'm the manager. I'll say when we get pitchers up."

We knew Guidry was going to pitch and we had Jack Brohamer playing third, but batting lefty. Zim platooned him and Frank Duffy, who batted right-handed. Zim's first question to the coaches: "Guidry's pitching tomorrow, so who's going to be playing third base?"

Then he answered the question by saying, "Brohamer's doing a hell of a job for us the last few weeks, and I think he should play. What do you think?" He went down the line and all the coaches said, "That's right, Zim."

"Wait a minute," I said. "You've got a guy who's 24–3, the best left-handed pitcher in baseball right now. Brohamer's never faced a left-hander like this and, besides, he hasn't faced a left-hander the last month because he's been platooning. Duffy might get his bat on the ball and scoot one into right field. But Brohamer's not going to have a chance against this guy. If they bring in Gossage, then you've got Brohamer to pinch-hit."

"No," said Zim. "We're playing Brohamer. That's it."

Then he said we were starting Torrez. *Fine,* I thought. "If he gets in trouble, who do we go with from the bullpen?" Zim asked. Before anyone could answer, he said, "Stanley's been having one hell of a year for us. I think we ought to bring in Stanley." Everyone said, "Yeah." Then it came to me again, and I said, "I agree with you on Stanley, but it all depends. They've got two, three lefty batters in a row—Nettles, Jackson. Andy Hassler has had a hell of a last two months." He was a big left-hander, wild, but for that two-month stretch he got the ball over. He reminded me then of Sudden Sam McDowell. He'd never throw at you, but you never knew where the ball was going. I had been playing first and watching him with that sidearm delivery. Lefty hitters didn't want to face him. If they got a walk, it was a big deal. Jackson got a walk in one game, and when he came to first he said, "Jeez, I'm glad I got that against this guy." I told Zim left-handed hitters are happy just to get a walk against him, that "I'd go with Hassler if you've got these left-handed hitters coming up and go to Stanley for the right-handers."

"No," Zimmer replied, "We're going to Stanley and that's it."

Zim liked to project the image of being tough, but I think that he was a sensitive guy underneath it all. Lee drove him nuts when he called him names, and I think the reason Zim took it so hard was because he really was sensitive. He put on an act that he wasn't, even in the way he'd take a pitcher out, as if it didn't matter, but I think it did.

There wasn't much to think about early in the game. In the first, Jackson stung a Torrez pitch to left, but the wind was blowing in and I caught it against the Wall. I got up in the bottom of the second and smacked a Guidry fastball for a home run down the line in right to give us a 1–0 lead. We made it 2–0 in the sixth when Rice singled home Burleson.

Then the famous Bucky Dent incident. Roy White and Chris Chambliss singled with one out in the seventh. Jim Spencer pinch-hit for Brian Doyle, which concerned me. Spencer could hit it out. But he hit a fly ball for the second out. I was a little uneasy in left because the wind had shifted, and now was blowing out to me. In April or May, or in late September, that wind could change at any time. Still, Dent was a slapper, a .240 hitter with 16 extra-base hits all season and only 4 homers—the least likely Yankee regular to hit one out in that situation. I wondered why they weren't pinch-hitting for him. Torrez got two strikes on him, including a foul off his foot that sent him hopping and searching for a new bat.

The way he hit the next pitch, high, with not much on it,
I could have expected it to come down to me on the warning
track—on any other day of the year, in any other inning of the
year. Except on that fall day, because he had gotten it so high,
because the wind had shifted. I didn't think I'd catch it, but I
thought it would hit the Wall. At first, I thought I had it. I kept
drifting back and even when I got to the warning track I
expected it to come down. Then I expected it to hit the Wall. I
was shocked when it didn't. It landed in the screen. A three-
run homer for Bucky Dent.

After Torrez walked Rivers, Zim brought in Stanley to
pitch to Munson, who doubled and scored Rivers. I still didn't
think much of that two-run lead. Guidry couldn't get his slider
over that day, and we had been getting a lot of hits off him.
We knocked him out in the seventh when Scott singled. We
couldn't score off Rich (Goose) Gossage, though. In the
eighth, Stanley, the righty, faced Jackson, the lefty. Reggie hit
the ball into the center field stands for a 5–2 edge.

Goose couldn't get his pitches over. He was behind in
the count. In the eighth, he gave a double to Jerry Remy. I
singled him home. It was 5–3. Fisk and Lynn then singled and
I scored and was confident that we had Gossage on the ropes.
But Goose got the next two batters. In the ninth, though,
Burleson got a one-out walk off Gossage. Then Remy hit a
hard liner toward right, where Lou Piniella was playing. It
was obvious that Lou didn't know where the ball was. I had
been out in right often enough myself to know that with the
shadows from the stands in the late afternoon, you can lose
that ball and never find it again. Eddie Yost, our third base
coach, knew it, too. "Run!" I screamed. Yost waved Burleson
toward third, but Rick wasn't sure whether or not Piniella was
trying to outfox him or not and stopped between first and
second. And then, after the ball hit the ground, it practically
bounced right into Lou's glove, just as luck—or bad luck—
would have it. Rick had to stop at second and Remy at first.
Rice hit a fly to center and Burleson tagged up and went to
third.

That left it up to me: bottom of the ninth, two outs, tying run on third, winning run on first. I had always hit Gossage well. I loved the fastball, after all. That year Goose's fastball exploded on the hitter. It really moved. If it was up, it would rise. If it was down, you wouldn't know what it would do. It could sink or it could come in on you. I was thinking of the at-bat before, when I got the base hit to center field, the pitch was out over the plate. Now I had a different situation. I had a hole between first and second because they were holding the runner on first. I made up my mind. I don't know whether it was the right way to think, but I said to myself, *I'm going to go for the hole. I'm going to look for an inside pitch, just to tie the score.*

With his fastball, I probably should have just thought of hitting the ball hard somewhere instead of placing it. Right away in the count, the first pitch was a ball, and he made up my mind for me. I could give him a strike and still look for a low ball that I could pull. But if it was low and inside, I'd swing at it. It was my option now. The pitch came in, on the inside, just at the knees. My pitch. I swung, but just as I got the bat out, the ball exploded on me, coming in quicker than I thought. I tried to turn on it, but I got underneath the ball and that's where the pop-up came from. To Nettles at third base. Third out. Season over. My last best chance at a pennant and World Series.

I look back at that pitch, that at-bat. If he had thrown the first pitch for a strike, I probably would have used the whole field. I wouldn't have been as selective and try to hit it just in a certain spot. But I tip my hat to him. Goose made the pitch. I did exactly what I wanted to do. Ah, maybe I should have used the whole field against him because of how live his ball was. Maybe I shouldn't have been so aggressive in my thinking that I could take the ball and yank it on him. In the seventh, my thoughts were just to hit the ball and I got it up the middle. Who knows? Percentage-wise, I guess I was thinking the right way. I guess if I had to do it all over again I would have thought the same way. I always loved to use that hole. Anytime anyone was holding that runner on, I loved that open hole. Just get that bat out in front, make contact, and you've got a base hit. I don't know what he was thinking, probably just to throw strikes because his ball was so alive. I'd love to know what he thought. Did he wonder if I was going to go for that open hole? Ah, he probably thought he'd just throw the hell out of the ball. I wouldn't have liked it if he thought that I would try to pull the ball. Because that would have meant he had outthought me.

• • •

Later, after a cigarette and beer, when I looked up at the crowd around me, their tape recorders spinning and lights flashing and pencils moving across paper, I tried to explain what this meant to me, to us, to Boston, to New England. It was very important at this moment for me to put into perspective where we were and what we had done.

"We have everything in the world to be proud of," I said. "The only thing we don't have is the ring."

17
HEADING
HOME

Sometime that year, a reporter told me that I could become the first player in the history of the American League to hit 400 home runs and total 3,000 hits.

Is that right? I thought. *The first player?*

As I approached my fortieth birthday, I became aware of other personal milestones ahead. There were things I could do, goals within reach, that had eluded most of the other players who had ever put on a uniform.

I went into the 1979 season with 383 homers, needing 17 for 400, and 2,869 hits, needing 131. The only other players who had reached that double career total were all in the National League: Aaron, Musial, and Mays.

And the nice thing was that I felt good enough to continue playing.

Pitching was what the Red Sox always fell short of, even in our good years, and pitching was what we didn't have during my last five. Lee was gone after one run-in too many with Zim, and Tiant, whom I believed was the heart and soul of the Red Sox, was now a Yankee. He came to us when he was in his thirties, but he was 122–81 while wearing a Boston uniform. Who could win 15 or 20 games for us? In my last four seasons, no one.

Still, we got off to another fine start in 1979, and I had a ball the last day of June. I came up in the ninth inning against Luis in Yankee Stadium and I took him downtown. But in my at-bat before, I knew I had hurt myself badly. I pulled an Achilles tendon. It ruined the rest of the season and made chasing the 400/3,000 thing a chore, requiring as much mental and physical energy as I had ever spent. Rice and Lynn were full-fledged stars, though, and Torrez and Eckersley had outstanding first halves and we were well over .500 and staying close to Baltimore, which had the best pitching in the league. It was another season in which I wondered what I might have been able to do if I was healthy. I went into July with a .306 batting average after hitting 9 homers and driving in 25 runs in June. My shot against Luis was number 16, in less than half a season, and gave me 53 RBIs.

Once the publicity about the 400 homers and 3,000 hits steamrolled, they became a focal point of our season. At first, I didn't even give them a thought. I charged out of the box. *Hey, this getting to be forty business is going to be fun.* The chase for records was just part of it, and not much pressure. With the start I had, I thought I could have homer number 400 by late June or early July, and hit number 3,000 certainly by July. But I wound up tearing the Achilles tendons in both feet.

The injuries forced me to wear two different shoes when I batted. I wore spiked shoes on my left foot, because that was my drive foot, the one I used to dig in. But on my front foot I wore a sneaker painted black to match my spikes. Those tendons were so bad that when I'd get up in the morning I had to crawl out of bed until I got to the tub. I had a little Jacuzzi in there, so I could put my feet in and get them to where I could walk around.

Charlie Moss, our trainer, tried all sorts of tape jobs to get the pressure off the heel. I'd go to the plate taped all the way to my thigh. When you're taped up that heavily on both legs, it's hard to stand in the batter's box. I had no feeling in my legs. When I got set in the box, I had to look down at my legs to see if they were positioned properly because I couldn't feel them. It was a struggle.

After I hit the homer off Tiant, I went sixteen games before number 400. It made me think of the Triple Crown year. I always believed that if we hadn't been in a pennant race, I wouldn't have won the Triple Crown. But because I wasn't thinking of individual honors then, I just played. But now I was thinking of the numbers. And when I was going for hit number 3,000, we started to slip out of the pennant race, so all the pressure was on me individually. Strangely enough, hitting 400 home runs and getting 3,000 hits were the toughest things I ever had to do. Winning the Triple Crown was easy. That season, every at-bat I thought, *How can I help the Red Sox win the ball game?* That last month I made up about twenty points in the batting race after Frank Robinson had been far ahead of me.

I often think about why the 400 and 3,000 almost over-powered me. I guess it became so important because of who *didn't* do it: Mantle, Ruth, Williams, among many other super-stars. As I've said, a person could analyze all the reasons why no one in the league had done it. Someone got injured, or didn't get as many at-bats, or any one of many things happened. Many players had the same potential I had to accomplish that, but I managed to do it.

In a Sunday game in late July, I tagged one to left, but it hit high off the Wall for a double instead of number 400. That night we went out to dinner at Felicia's, a restaurant in the North End, and people came over and told me I had missed it by this much. Their next statement was: "When are you going to hit it?"

Then on Tuesday, July 24, I did it. It was the seventh inning, and we were tied with the Oakland A's at 3–3. Mike Morgan was pitching. He was a nineteen-year-old rookie. In my last at-bat, I had worked him to 3–0 and he threw me a high fastball. I tried to muscle it and all I got out of it was a fly to right. This time he came in with another fastball on the first pitch.

As soon as I hit it, I knew it was gone. Or should be. *If this doesn't go out,* I said to myself, *I'm in trouble.*

At that moment, I was aware of the crowd roaring and of the right fielder backing up. But he wasn't going to get this one, 390 feet into the A's bullpen. Craig Minetto, one of their pitchers, caught it on the fly. God, the noise those thirty thousand fans made as I rounded the bases. When I got into the dugout, they wouldn't let me stay there. They kept standing and cheering until I came out. I waved my arms and went back in, but still they pounded and applauded. I had to take another curtain call.

There was only one person in the place who didn't realize what was going on: Morgan. After the game reporters asked him about it and he said, "So that's why there was all that cheering. I didn't know why he kept coming out of the dugout. I was about to tell him to sit down." But the kid was nice about it. He said I was a hero of his.

The crowd around my locker was thick. But on the fringe of it I saw my dad. "Hello, Pop," I said. "It's about time, huh?"

The 400 was nice. It allowed me to break a tie with Al Kaline and go into eighteenth place on the career homer list. But I also knew the key thing was the combination of 400 and 3,000. I still had to tie the two of them together. So after the 400, I immediately began thinking about the 3,000. If you look at the films of me hitting that year, especially when I got close to 3,000, I looked ten years older. I was drained. I was in a slump that seemed to last for the rest of the summer.

When I was a few hits away, I invited twenty-six relatives and friends along for the ride. Every day and every night we were surrounded by Pop and uncles and aunts and cousins, and Carol and the kids seemed to spend all their time just making sure there was enough to eat for everyone in the house. It became a sort of show in itself, with cameras recording our daily lives, film crews, microphones. The Yankees were in when I reached 2,999. To make it perfect, Tiant was pitching. Would I have loved to have whacked it off him. Can you imagine his reaction? That would have been some practical joke. But when I faced him in the second inning and walked, poor Luis got booed. I was hitless that game and I was sure it was *never* going to happen. It was the first time I had walked in 90 at-bats, which gives you some idea of the bad pitches I was swinging at. I was 0 for 7 and in my last 79 at-bats I only had 13 hits.

I was in a slump, one of my worst.

And I was doing something I had rarely—maybe never— done before, except for special situations when the game was on the line. I was swinging for a homer, just as I was when I was going for home run number 400. I wanted that hit number 3,000 to be special—and instead all I was swinging at was air.

Finally, Walt Hriniak came over to me. He had joined our club in 1977 in the bullpen and was also the hitting coach. He came to know me better than anyone else on the team. He'd do anything to try to help me hit. Sometimes, at seven-thirty in the morning, he would throw two hundred balls to me while I tried to get my swing just right.

"Goddam it, Yaz," Hriniak told me. "You've had almost 3,000 hits. But only 400-something of them were home runs. But now you're trying to hit a home run, aren't you?"

"Yeah, I am," I had to admit.

And he said something that I had to think about: "Well, if you do hit it out, you're not going to get the ball back. If you hit it in the stands, somebody's going to keep it. But if you get a base hit, they'll stop the game and you'll get it back on the spot."

That was interesting psychology, but it had the right effect. It made me think. *Sure, he's right. Only 13 percent of my hits have been homers.* The big thing now was reaching 3,000, getting that 400/3,000 combination, and then moving on from there. *Get this out of the way now.*

The jokes were starting because of how much trouble I

was having reaching the number. Someone said that I had gotten my first hit when John F. Kennedy was President, but I might not make 3,000 until Teddy was. President Jimmy Carter's press secretary had telephoned and wanted a private number to call to congratulate me. "We'll call within twenty minutes after the game," the official told Bill Crowley, our public relations director. Bill told him, "I can't keep the Boston press waiting for twenty minutes. They're more important to me than you are."

Meanwhile, I was paying $600 a day for my visiting relatives. The kids were missing school in Florida and had to get back. How many absence notes could Carol write? After the Yankee series, we were going on a long road trip, and Zim told me he was thinking of keeping me out of every game on the road if I didn't get hit number 3,000 in Fenway. This way, when we came back, I could try again before the hometown fans.

"This is a plot to kill me," Carol said before I went to the park. On Monday, when I was going to face Tiant, she got stuck in traffic on Storrow Drive, a mile from Fenway. She waved her arms at a passing motorcycle cop and he gave her an escort, with siren blaring, to the park and she made it just before I got up to bat.

Carol sat down with the kids, as she had done for a few games now, holding her rosary beads, and each of the girls clutched confetti and balloons, ready to let them go when I got the hit. There were other things on hold, too.

At Bob's office, calls were coming in: Suffolk Downs would name a race for me. Could the president of Aqua Velva get an autographed ball? Would I like a weekend with the family at the Concord Hotel in the New York Catskills if I answered questions from guests for an hour? Sun Life Insurance of Canada offered an endorsement deal. Someone was going to put out a commemorative envelope postmarked with the date of hit number 3,000. Bob had boxes in his office of badges that read: YAZ 3,000 and T-shirts, hats, and photographs. Someone was selling a color poster of me for $5.95.

Ray Herbert, whom I had gotten my first hit off of eighteen years before, called Bob and said, "Tell him to hit to left."

On Tuesday, September 12, Catfish Hunter started against us in what he announced was his last game. I walked against him in the first, then he got me out on a fly to the warning track in right center in the third. I hit a hard grounder to first in the fourth, and was out. When Catfish was lifted for Jim Beattie in the fifth, he got a standing ovation from the thirty-four thousand fans. They knew it was the last time they'd see him in uniform. Beattie got me out in the sixth, extending my hitless string to 0 for 10. When I grounded out, the pressure got to our youngest, Carolyn, who was ten. She began crying. Because we had a big lead, and wouldn't have to bat in the ninth, there was a good chance I wouldn't come up again in the game. The fans were looking ahead, though, and they gave Evans a big hand in the seventh when he singled. They knew it guaranteed me an at-bat in the eighth.

Little things put into perspective how long my career was, even at that point. I was playing for four years before Catfish came into the league, won his 224 games, and left. I was playing four years after he retired. Haywood Sullivan, who had become our key front office executive, was catching for Kansas City when I got my first hit. Their shortstop was Dick Howser, who became my son Mike's baseball coach at Florida State when I got number 3,000.

Wearing those two different shoes, I limped up to the plate to face Beattie in the eighth. The fans stood and started roaring. Carol stood, too. But she closed her eyes and never saw me swing.

It was Beattie's first pitch, a sinking fastball, and I hit a hard grounder between first and second. Willie Randolph ran a couple of steps to his left, put his glove down, but couldn't reach it. It went through to the outfield, where Reggie Jackson fielded it.

At last. And probably fitting, after all. Ground-ball singles in the hole between first and second were as much a trademark of mine as extra-base hits. When you get 3,000 hits, you're going to get your share of singles. None of those earlier singles ever resulted in horns blaring, balloons being released, fans yelling, "Yaz! Yaz! Yaz!" The scoreboard, the new scoreboard put up a few years before that now carried advertising, flashed 3,000 three times.

They stopped the game, and Mike and my dad came out. I stood there with my arms around both of them, when Reggie came over and hugged me and handed me the ball. Hriniak was right, after all. I got it back. Other Yankees congratulated me, including Martin. Then they set up a microphone near first base and I had to say something.

"I know one thing," I told the crowd. "The last hit was the hardest of all 3,000. It took so long because I really enjoyed all these standing ovations you gave me the last three days."

What else? I thanked Zim and my teammates, and Hriniak, of course ("particularly," I said). And then I concluded, "Finally, I'd like to remember probably my two biggest boosters—my mother and Mr. Yawkey. They deserve to be here." I started to cry, but there was nothing else to say.

When I drove home after the game, a funny thought crossed my mind. *Who's pitching tomorrow?* I wondered.

• • •

After the season, I was invited to the White House by President Jimmy Carter. We also were in a group that met the Pope. What do you bring to the President of the United States? I always wanted people to have something that belonged to me if I gave them a gift, something more than an autographed ball. If these things were just stored in a room in my house somewhere, not many people could see them. So I gave many gifts and trophies to people I knew and respected, to Senator Kennedy or Tip O'Neill or presidents. I knew that every President, sooner or later, gets a library where people could see the awards. Senator Kennedy kept mine in his office in Washington, and when people came in they could see the trophy, that beautiful clock.

I don't make big displays of affection, but in handing something to another person that's very personal to me, I've shown that person how deeply I feel. Also, it's an honor when someone asks me for something I've worn. I decided to give the President a Red Sox jacket.

"It's been worn a few times," I told him. He said, "That's great, I wouldn't have it any other way." I also gave him a T-shirt with the 3,000/400 memento and said, "You can wear this when you go jogging with the Secret Service."

When he met me, his first words were, "Yaz, congratulations on 4,000 hits—oops, that's what Ty Cobb got! He was from Georgia, too." The President started to laugh.

Since he was kidding me, I replied, "Don't worry, Mr. President. Cobb's record is safe with me."

You know what was nice? The reason he said I was being honored. "The whole country has great admiration and friendship for you," he said. He explained it went beyond the 3,000 hits and 400 homers. It was "because of your general attitude toward sports and competition."

Meeting the Pope was a different sort of special feeling. I felt a special closeness to him because he was from Poland. Someone told him that's where my grandparents came from. As I sat on the White House lawn next to Elizabeth Taylor, the Pope asked, "Did Yastrzemski get any hits today?"

It was an off-season of parties and honors. But the real world of baseball next year again showed what a tough game it is, and how fragile careers are. I saw still another manager fired. Zim was let go with a week remaining in the season. It was a year where hitting couldn't compensate for the fact we didn't have one pitcher with more than 10 victories who was over .500. Both Lynn and Rice missed a considerable part of the season with injuries.

On August 31, I played left field. The A's Jim Essian hit a shot in my direction. You'd think that in twenty years of playing the Wall, I'd know enough to stop before hitting it. I was concentrating so much on the ball, I lost track of where I was. I knew the number of steps from the warning track to the Wall and usually I'd pull up. But I thought I had one more step left. But I was moving toward left center instead of going straight back and that threw my stride off. I crashed into the Wall and felt a stab. *Whew, that hurt.* I stayed in the game, though, and I even got a hit later on. Then I found out I was playing with a cracked rib. I took a week off in Florida, then tried to play in parts of three games the rest of the season. When I swung, it took all the wind out of me. I didn't play the outfield again for almost two years. And I played left field only one more time— my last game.

Johnny Pesky mopped up for Zim and then Sullivan hired Ralph Houk, whom I had always respected, to manage the Sox in 1981. Unfortunately for Ralph, we also lost Lynn, Fisk, and Burleson as a result of the confusion and legal squabbling over the five-year contracts they had signed in 1976.

Houk was one of those steady guys you always have confidence in. He not only was able to make decisions, but a ballplayer felt secure with him. Here was a manager who cared, and who protected you, especially from the press if things weren't going well.

I would have liked to have had Houk at Fenway for ten, fifteen years. He was one hell of a manager. Ralph would have won a lot of pennants for the Sox. He put out a team that was very competitive and hated to lose, but he controlled himself. He reminded me—the way he kept it inside—of Mr. Yawkey. During a losing streak, Houk always tried to pump you up.

"Go out and play hard and don't cross me," he'd say to the team. "I'm going to treat everyone like a man and I expect the same from you." But he'd challenge a guy who gave him any crap. But Ralph did it the right way—in his office. I used to see that all the time because I was always the last one to leave. I'd notice that one player was still sitting around after everyone else left. I knew that guy was going in to see the Major. I could hear him behind the closed door yelling at the guy, but he wouldn't do that in front of everyone. And it was always after the game was over. One time Houk challenged a guy, took off his glasses, and shouted, "You want to fight? I'm sixty years old. Let's go." That's the type he was.

I learned quite a bit from him because when he was managing I was the DH most of the time, so I'd be on the bench next to him. I found that one of the toughest things to do was to keep myself ready for the game while sitting on the bench. In 1981, for the first time in my career, I was the designated hitter more than I played in the field. Until then, I never thought much about the moves a manager had to make. But that was something all the utility players loved to do. Jeez, what else did they have to do anyway? Just sit on the bench. A lot of the benchwarmers over the years would have liked to become managers—and some even did—so they were always second-guessing what the manager did. But until I sat next to Houk, day in and day out, I never realized how much thinking went into managing a ball club.

As early as the fourth or fifth inning, he'd start to think about the moves he might need to make later on. Here we would just have finished the heart of the order and he'd start writing. "What are you doing?" I'd ask. Ralph would explain, "Well, they got these guys coming up in the eighth, and maybe I should have one of our pitchers ready if they get a rally."

In my later years, I knew the other players were looking up to me as a leader. Even when I was hurt, I'd always play. They knew that. They'd see me getting taped up. Even when we'd come back from Anaheim, at five in the morning or some damn time like that, and we had a day game and everybody would be limping to the ballpark, they'd be looking for me to provide leadership. They were in their late twenties and I was in my early forties. I accepted that role and tried to use it to pump them up.

I'd always put on a little act, trying to look enthusiastic. "Come on, let's get 'em!" I'd say. And I really felt like crap. I did things like that. If they saw me bouncing around the club-

house, maybe it made them feel better. But it really got tough
for me the last four years. I couldn't rebound after a night
game if we had a day game. Houk was good to me. I was
honest with him. I explained to him I just couldn't do it at the
same level every day, especially with the Coast trips. I always
got up early, probably from my farm days. We'd get out to the
Coast, but I couldn't make the adjustment. I'd get two, three
hours sleep when we went West and I'd be up at Boston time,
which would be fourteen hours before a night game. My body
ached. The first few days of those trips out there, I was useless.
I'd go into the batting cage and the bat felt like lead. It used to
take me a couple of days just to feel normal again—and normal being a forty-year-old guy with bad shoulders who had
played 3,000 games. Even eating was a chore. I forced food
down, even though my body was in another time zone—all
these factors ganged up on me.

Funny thing, though, I didn't use a lighter bat then. I
went to a heavier one. I played with a thirty-five-and-a-half-
inch, thirty-three ounce bat most of my career. At the end I
went to a thirty-six-inch, thirty-five-ounce. That was a big bat.
In fact, I used the same-sized bat Rice used during my last four
or five years.

Ralph understood. If a left-hander was pitching, he'd tell
me, "You're not playing, but take batting practice if you want
to."

At night games I'd have problems with the tricky lefties
like Tommy John. I wanted the Guidrys, the power guys. So
Ralph wouldn't play me against a Tommy John. He'd give me
a few days off, which is what I needed when I got to be forty.

Ralph would call me in after game and he would have the
stats prepared by Dick Bresciani, the Red Sox vice president
of public relations. It would show what I did against a pitcher
throughout my career, and Ralph would say, "Okay, you've
got Guidry tomorrow and you've hit him pretty good. What
do you want to do? Want to play?" And I would.

If it was a Tommy John, he'd tell me, "Look, it's a day

game, and you don't hit him that good anyway, so I'll rest you, maybe use you as a pinch hitter, okay?"

That was another great thing about playing for Houk. He'd tell you a day ahead. So when I left the ballpark, I knew whether I'd be playing the next day. When I knew I wasn't, I'd come in, shag a few balls, and keep ready in case I had to play.

Ralph got the rest of us going, too, in his first year. We were the best come-from-behind team in baseball, at least in winning in our last at-bat. Torrez and Eckersley came back. We were playing decently when the players' strike hit after a third of the season. I was working on a new batting stance under Hriniak that would allow me to use more of the field. I think I was getting into a groove, but then the strike hit. When we finally got back to playing, after fifty games were lost, we came close to finishing first during the second half of the split season. That would have gotten us to a divisional playoff. But Milwaukee beat us out by a game and a half. Bob Ojeda, who had become a key pitcher for us, was sick at the end and missed key starts at a time when we might have been able to handle the Brewers. The front office, strangely enough, looked pretty good in the Lynn-Burleson trades since Carney Lansford, one of the players we picked up, led the league with a .336 batting average. Mark Clear, another player acquired in the trades, had an 8–3 record. That second-half record didn't conceal the fact that, overall, we were a fifth-place team.

In my own role as elder statesman, I was becoming a fixture in Boston. It was as if I was a must-see on an itinerary of New England. That was great with me. It increased my world. It gave me a chance to do things that people fantasize about, such as flying in Air Force Two.

I didn't play in the All-Star Game that year, but George Bush, who was the Vice President then, called and said he was up in Kennebunkport, Maine, for the week.

"How'd you like to accompany me to the All-Star Game?" he asked.

I met him at an Air Force base and he led me onto the plane with Mrs. Bush. The whole first-class section was filled with electronics gadgets, consoles of computers, guys sitting there so they could keep in touch with President Reagan and any critical event anyplace in the world. Bush showed me his bedroom and sitting area. He had a chair on a track so he could slide across the whole "office" without getting out of his seat if he had to use the communications system during a bumpy flight.

He and Barbara were real down-to-earth people. I had bought a couple of Red Sox jackets and caps for the two of them. As I got on the plane, the Secret Service asked for the jackets, so I handed them over. I got into a conversation with Mrs. Bush and mentioned I had brought the jackets.

"Well, where are they?" she asked excitedly. She went over to the Secret Service people and got the jackets and put them in her compartment.

"These are for my boys," she said proudly. "I've got two of them living in Boston."

On takeoff, the Vice President and his doctor went into his private room. It's reinforced, and I suppose the doctor was there in case of any takeoff problems. Bud Wilkinson, the great Oklahoma coach, was aboard, too, and we discussed sports. But Mrs. Bush was interested in the Red Sox. "The boys in Boston love going to the games," she said. When I told her to have them call me if they wanted tickets to the games, she said, "Are you sure? I don't want to trouble you." That was funny, as if getting tickets for the Vice President's kids was a bother.

We landed in Cleveland during rush hour, about six-thirty, with an extra reason for traffic: the game. But because of our caravan of cars the expressway in both directions to Cleveland's Municipal Stadium was blocked. I thought, *Boy, there're some ticked-off people out there.*

Bush asked me to work for him in his presidential campaign against Michael Dukakis in 1988, but since a Massachusetts governor was in the race, I stayed out of it, even though I voted for Bush.

Throughout 1981, people wondered whether I would play another year. Well, why shouldn't I? Sure, I was getting more tired toward the end of each season, but I was also able to perform, overall, at a pretty good level. And I thought, *Maybe one more year will give me one more chance at a Series ring. A last chance.* But we continued to have the same problem: no pitching. In 1982, Mark Clear, our top reliever, won more games than any of our starters: 14. Our entire staff had only 23 complete games. Still, the bullpen was outstanding early in the season, and at one point in June we led by five games. By the All-Star break I had 13 homers and was hitting close to .280, with more than 50 RBIs. Ralph even had me start a game in center field in July after Evans and Reid Nichols were injured. I was forty-two years old, a month away from my forty-third birthday. Someone figured that I was the oldest man ever to play center field in the major leagues. I went 2 for 3 with a double and single. Of course, I couldn't continue at that pace or in the outfield. Still, we had a decent enough season, finishing third, only six games out.

We unveiled a player that year who impressed me the moment I saw him in the cage. The first thing I noticed about Wade Boggs was how long he kept his head on the ball before releasing it. I don't recollect any ballplayer keeping his head on the ball as long as he did. He gets that little extra look before releasing it on the follow-through. Wade could hit with any stance because of his head action. The way he sprayed the ball reminded me a lot of myself.

That was the way I had hit more than twenty years before. Now, as I approached 1983, I raised questions in my mind over whether this would be my last season. Even when I went to spring training, I was waiting to see what kind of year I was going to have. In the back of my mind, I thought that playing in 1984 was still a possibility. Listen, I was coming off a .275 season in 1982, with 16 home runs and 72 RBIs.

As usual, I did not relax in the off-season. Oh, I'd take a

few weeks off at first. But then I not only had to get in shape, I was also busy working for Hillshire Farm and Kahn's. They are a subsidiary of Sara Lee. I had been connected with them since the end of the 1975 season, when they called Bob and asked if I'd be interested in doing a commercial. Bob thought about it and then suggested, "Why not use Yaz even more, as a spokesman, have him get to know your company?" He knew that Milton Schloss, who was president then, was an avid baseball fan.

I not only did the commercial, but we started an association that became my full-time job once baseball ended. I told them I was interested, but only if I could learn the business and have input into decision-making. I had some knowledge of the meat business, since we had raised hogs and cattle on our farm in Bridgehampton. But this was going to extend to advertising and sales and the whole range of doing business inside a multimillion-dollar company that is part of a billion-dollar international conglomerate. For one week before spring training I went to their home office in Cincinnati and attended seminars, worked at the plants, learning every phase of the business, from buying cattle and hogs, to slaughtering, to packaging, to selling. My territory was New England and Florida, my two homes. After I quit the Sox, it became my full-time job. I'd meet with the meat merchandisers and their assistants and make decisions on how to spend our marketing money. There might be one program in Florida using television, but we might want to use radio in Boston, or newspaper coupons in another part of New England.

Bob worked out an outstanding contract with Kahn's. In the early 1980s, we made a big push and sales increased tremendously. I was comfortable enough with Kahn's to know that this was going to be my life when baseball ended. It made the transition easier.

Feeling secure in business, and feeling the aches and pains of being forty-plus, I thought deep down that 1983 would be the final season for me. Or did I? I thought so, then I didn't think so. Right up to the end. Right up to the speech I made. Right up to the trot I took around Fenway, shaking hands with people reaching out to me from the stands.

I'd feel great and I'd tell myself, *What do you want to quit for? You're playing better than 80 percent of the ballplayers out there.* Better, maybe, but in more pain: my heels, my shoulders, my knees.

Ted Williams used to tell me, "You're crazy to change your swing." But I had no choice. I couldn't get the bat up there anymore. I just couldn't raise it. Then I had to change my stance to go with it. One adjustment always led to another.

The years I should have been mellow weren't pressure-free. After my mom died, I tried to look at baseball as less important than life itself. To a degree I succeeded. But there was another level. Ironically, often the intensity became greater than it ever was. Everybody seemed to be watching me, and newspapermen were constantly speculating in the papers about when I'd retire. Or else they'd ask me about it. It wasn't that my production was off—at least not by standards of other players—it's just that in sports the public has a tendency to want its heroes to quit while they're on top, as if fading diminishes the accomplishments you've had. No downslide permitted. Funny thing was, I always thought that near the end of my career I'd be able to relax and enjoy baseball, and instead it became so much more intense because I had to concentrate so much harder. I had to get by on skills that were affected by injuries. If you look at photographs of me at the end of my seasons from 1976 to 1983, you wouldn't believe it was me. I was drawn and my eyes were sunken. I looked sick. Totally drained. It was the pressure.

I thought of all those things when I more or less decided that: *Yes, 1983 will be it.* The Red Sox planned a gala retirement for me on the final weekend of the season. Every city we played wanted some sort of celebration for my last appearance. Tip O'Neill even ran a party for me in Washington he headlined "Congress Welcomes Yaz."

Can you imagine a lineup of congressmen coming with bats and balls and caps, waiting for me to autograph all the items? But there they were in line: "Hi, Yaz, I'm Congress-man . . . , would you do this for my granddaughter?" Or "Here's a ball from 1975. Could you make it out to my wife?"

By the 1983 All-Star break, six weeks before I was going to turn forty-four, I was hitting .323. I told Sullivan and Houk, "Look, we've advertised this day for me, but I'm think-ing about playing next year."

"That's all right," said Sully. "Instead of a retirement day, we'll call it a Yaz appreciation day."

That was fine with me. Meanwhile, we told all the teams we were visiting that I didn't want gifts. If they wanted to have a pregame ceremony, that was fine. They could say something like "probably making his last appearance." But no gifts. I mean, how would it look for me to come back in 1984? Would I have to return all the things the other teams had gotten me? Also, I didn't want to distract our guys from the race if twice a week there'd be something going on and all the attention would focus on me.

But then we dropped out of the race, fell about twelve games back. My intensity left me. I realized that being in a pennant race had kept me hitting .300 and drove me. But now, as we continued to sink, my attention span would wander. When I made an out it didn't eat me up inside any-more. What was wrong with me? I didn't want to kill myself after making an out. I didn't feel like crap when we lost. When the game was over, I'd mentally replay the at-bats, but then I'd be able to walk out of the clubhouse and not worry about them again during the car ride home. This went on for a couple of weeks and then I knew it was time. It was mid-August.

I went in to see Houk before a game in Milwaukee.

"Ralph, baseball just doesn't mean that much to me any-more unless we're in a pennant race. I think it's left me," I told him. "It's just not there. Do we have a shot at the pen-nant next year?" I didn't wait for his answer. "I don't think so."

Ralph looked at me and nodded. He had played with the Yankees of Joe DiMaggio and Allie (Superchief) Reynolds and Vic Raschi and Yogi Berra, had managed Mickey Mantle and Whitey Ford. In fact, he was managing them twenty-two years before when I broke in. And he said, "Yaz, I managed and played with some great ones. Get out at the right time if that's how you feel."

So that's what I did.

The final weekend was a shower of memories and emotion. I worked and reworked my speech, and my friends Bob Woolf, Dave Mugar, and Will McDonough helped me to sharpen it. The whole weekend was like a giant civic happening, with proclamations, speeches, parties. I brought in 123 relatives and friends and put them all up at the Boston Marriott Long Wharf. The Sox planned a two-day celebration. On Saturday, October 1, 1983, the official goodbye, the ceremonies, the friends, the speeches, my speech. Then on Sunday, my final game.

When I picked up the *Boston Globe* on Saturday morning, the lead editorial was headlined: THE NUMBERS, THE GLORY, YAZ. It put an interesting perspective on my career when it said that I had come up to the plate 14,971 times, at that point, and asked how many people—carpenters or salesmen or editors—had to face 14,971 critical decisions? Well, that's how I had always seen myself: a workingman. Maybe that was why such a bond had developed between me and the fans, maybe that's why the fans in left had come to accept me, because they saw that, when all was said and done, I was just trying every day to do the best I possibly could.

I was the first player at the park on Saturday. Vinnie Orlando was there as I walked in, busying himself as usual, preparing the dozens of balls for us to sign, the ritual of daily baseball life that has been the same for, what, eighty, ninety, a hundred years? Certainly the same since I came in. My palms were sweating this time, as if it was Opening Day. I thought to myself, *God, I wish this thing was over with.* Or maybe I wished it wasn't even happening.

Steady now, I told myself. *Cripes, you're not going to back out now, are you? You're not gonna change your mind? What the hell's wrong with you?*

One by one the team came in, and when the room was nearly full, someone put a video tape on the machine showing hit number 3,000 and the guys ragged me about it. I watched from my locker and tried to smile along with them, taking the kidding. Once in a while I stopped and read my speech. It had to be perfect, as perfect as a swing. Speaking in front of more than thirty thousand people intimidated me. You have to work at things so they go off without a hitch.

Jeez, everyone was out there on the field waiting for the ceremonies to begin: Carol, the kids, Dad, Senator Kennedy, Governor Dukakis. President Reagan sent a telegram.

I began my speech with "This is a very special day for me." I could tell this was going to be a tough one. I barely got through the opening sentence and started to gulp and had to stop to steady myself. But I think it honestly summed up how I felt about the game and the people I played in front of:

> *This is a very special day for me. I am extremely honored that so many of you came here to share this day with me. One thing that I've learned over the years is that Red Sox fans are the greatest and most loyal. The spirit at this great ballpark makes it the best place to play baseball in the world. I am proud to have worn only the Red Sox uniform for my entire twenty-three years. It was a privilege to have worn it longer than any other player. I will miss you. And I will miss my teammates, past and present. The clubhouse people. The bat boys. And all the terrific people who work at the park.*
>
> *I have been blessed with great parents and a wonderful family. And, I was given the ability to play baseball, the finest of all games. There is no other like it. In recent weeks, I have been asked how I would like to be remembered. I hope you will think of me as a*

winner, because I feel just playing one game at Fenway Park makes me a winner. I loved the competition. I always gave my best. I might not have had the greatest ability in the world, but I got the most out of it.

I don't have any regrets.

Again, thank you. And I hope I represented Boston and New England with class and dignity.

Ladies and gentlemen, there are two people who are not here today, but they are the reason that I am.

I would like to ask you to please join me in a moment of silence for my mother and Mr. Tom Yawkey.

The bell sounded in their memory, and when it ended, and the place was still silent, I said, "New England, I love you!"

No one expected it, but I decided to touch as many people as I could. They were all standing and I ran to the stands behind first and people reached out to me and I touched them and said, "Thank you." And then I continued running along the edge of the stands toward right field, people on their feet and cheering and I thought how wonderful it was that, after all these years, I could show them some emotion, how I felt about them. In right field they waved at me, someone shouting, "We love ya, Yaz," and I waved back. I continued running toward center and to left. I ran along the Wall that had been my backdrop and I ran alongside the stands in left where the fans there had been my closest and best critics. I knew there were tears in my eyes, but it didn't seem to matter anymore. *Let them know how I feel.* I wanted to let them know how I felt, and what this really meant to me.

My emotion was running so high, I started to think about leaving all this and I almost dashed back to the microphone and said, "I'm coming back."

I don't know how I stopped myself from doing that. But I did. I went 0 for 4 against the Indians, grounding out each time. I had a shot at some dramatics when I came up in the bottom of the ninth with two out. Another grounder.

For my final game, Ralph said to me, "You're back in left field, Yaz." Left field. I hadn't started there since cracking my rib. But where else should I really be this final Sunday? Of course, I got to the park early.

"One last time, Charlie," I said to our trainer as he taped my wrists.

"Well, the Red Sox are going to save a hell of a lot of money on tape, now that you're retiring," he replied.

Some of the players wanted their pictures taken with me and Vince said, "Better make it good, it's $25 a shot." I was sitting at my locker when all of a sudden I noticed all the guys starting to come around.

"Could I have your attention?" Evans said, and everyone got quiet.

"For the good times you've given us . . ." he began. "And the bad," interjected Rice with a laugh. "For the great career you've had and all you've done for baseball, we'd like to give you this." It was a beautiful rod and reel, inscribed from the guys.

"And you've got no excuses now," said Dewey. "Go get 'em."

I swallowed hard. *How much more of this can I take?* I told them, "Thanks," that I'd miss them, even if I might not miss playing the game anymore. But I was going to miss their friendship.

"In twenty-three years, I've been with some wonderful guys," I told them. "The last few years have been tougher on me. I appreciate all of you who worked with me and supported me."

Funny how I still thought of the details while all this was going on. In these final weeks, stuff had begun to disappear from my locker no matter what city I was in. I knew that people wanted mementos. I even used a different bat for each plate appearance on that last weekend so I could give them to friends as souvenirs. I had each bat mounted. Before the last game, I asked Bob Woolf to meet me in the locker room. I emptied the locker of balls and bats, I handed him all the gifts and plaques, including a piece of the Wall that the Jimmy Fund had made into a plaque for me. "Put this in your car, Bob," I told him. "I don't want to lose any of it." He made a few trips to his car. After everything was in, I asked him, "Is that it?" When he told me he was finished loading, I said, "Okay, it's all yours. If you want to put some of them on a wall, I'd be honored." That's what he did. In his office he's got a Yaz Wall. So now I've got a Wall of my own.

There was just supposed to be a short Sunday ceremony. I came out of the dugout before the game and turned to the fans. I faced each of them while the organist played "My Way." Then I stepped to the microphone to introduce my teammates. We patted one another on the back and shook hands and hugged.

"One of the signs I saw said: SAY IT AIN'T SO, YAZ. I wish it wasn't," I told the crowd.

"Today marks the last day of my career as a Red Sox player. I want to thank all of you for being here with me today. It has been a great privilege to have worn the Red Sox uniform for the past twenty-three years, and to have played at Fenway Park in front of you great fans. I'll miss you, and I'll never forget you. Thank you very much."

There was one thing I wanted to do that last day more than anything else—throw a runner out at the plate. And, yeah, in the back of my mind was what Williams did in his last at-bat: hit a home run. But jeez, throwing a runner out, that was a big deal to me. It would say that I was more than a hitter. I was proud of every phase of my game.

Well, I didn't throw anyone out. In the seventh, Toby Harrah lined a hit off the Wall. The carom almost fooled me, but I reached for it, spun around, and fired to second. I held Harrah to a single. The fans got such a kick out of it that they gave me a standing ovation.

My only chance to get a runner out at home came in the second. Ironically, it was on a hit by Essian, whose shot I was chasing when I cracked my ribs three years before. This time, he singled to left with Alan Bannister on second. The field was wet. It had been raining the entire weekend. I charged the ball and got to it as he was rounding third. I could have had him. I came up with the ball cleanly, but because the field was wet, when I threw it the thing slipped and I got off a low throw. That really teed me off. I wanted to throw a guy out at home so bad. I was beside myself.

Ah, what the hell. If I threw the guy out at home, I might have wanted to play another year.

My last at-bats were kind of funny. Someone told me that Rich Garcia, one of the umpires, had told the Indians' pitchers, "If he doesn't swing, it's a ball."

In the third, Bud Anderson threw me a fastball and I stroked it into left for a single. In the seventh, I was up again. I knew—and everyone else knew—that this was it. My final turn. Dan Spillner was on the mound. Boggs was on first with two out. Vic Voltaggio, the home plate umpire, called three balls. Spillner's next pitch was a little high and I tried to jerk it out of the park. All I got was a pop-up. That gave me a final average of .266 for the year. Oh well, it closed the circle. That's exactly the average I had as a rookie twenty-three seasons earlier. I went back to left field to start the eighth, but Ralph and I had agreed that after my last at-bat, he would send someone out for me. This way, I could trot off the field in front of the crowd. They stopped the game and announced that Cleotha (Chico) Walker was playing left field for me.

I loped in and when I got near the dugout I stopped to wave to the crowd, turning again to see every one of the fans. As I headed for the dugout I noticed a boy, maybe seven or eight years old, about my age when I began to think of hitting like Musial or Williams. He was sitting in a box with his parents. I took off my cap and handed it to him and saw him beaming as I went down the steps of the dugout for the last time.

THE CAREER OF CARL MICHAEL YASTRZEMSKI

Born August 22, 1939, at Southampton, N.Y.
Height, 5-11. Weight, 185.
Throws right- and bats left-handed.
Attended University of Notre Dame, Notre Dame, Ind., and received bachelor of science degree
in business administration from Merrimack College, North Andover, Mass.

Signed as free agent by Boston Red Sox organization, November 29, 1958.

Named Carolina League Most Valuable Player, 1959.

Established major league record for most years leading league in assists by outfielders (7), 1977.

Tied major league records for most seasons, one club (23), most consecutive seasons, one club (23); most home runs, two consecutive games (5), May 19 and 20, 1976; highest fielding percentage by outfielder, season, 100 or more games (1.000), 1977.

Became first American League player to total 400 home runs and 3,000 hits, lifetime.

Established American League records for most games, lifetime (3,308); most seasons, 100 or more games (22); most at-bats, lifetime (11,988); most plate appearances, lifetime (13,990); most intentional bases on balls, lifetime (190); most consecutive seasons, 100 or more games (20).

Won American League Triple Crown, 1967.

Hit three home runs in a game, May 19, 1976.

Hit for the cycle, May 14, 1965.

Led American League in sacrifice flies with 9 in 1972.

Led American League in total bases with 360 in 1967 and 335 in 1970.

Led American League in slugging percentage with .536 in 1965, .622 in 1967, and .592 in 1970.

Led American League in bases on balls received with 95 in 1963 and 119 in 1968.

Led American League outfielders in assists in 1962, 1963, 1966, 1969, 1971, and 1977, and tied for lead in 1964.

Tied for American League lead in sacrifice flies with 11 in 1977.

Tied for American League lead in double plays by outfielders with 4 in 1971.

Named Major League Player of the Year by *The Sporting News*, 1967.

Named American League Player of the Year by *The Sporting News*, 1967.

Named American League Most Valuable Player by Baseball Writers' Association of America, 1967.

Named outfielder on *The Sporting News* American League All-Star Team, 1963, 1965, and 1967.

Named outfielder on *The Sporting News* American League All-Star fielding team, 1963, 1965, 1967 through 1969, 1971, and 1977. Winner of Gold Glove Award in each of those years.

Named to Hall of Fame, 1989, with 94.6 percent of ballots cast. (First former Little Leaguer to enter Hall of Fame.)

Year	Club	League	Pos.	G	AB	R	H	2B	3B	HR	RBI	B.A.	PO	A	E	F.A.
1959—Raleigh	Carol.	★2B-SS	120	451	87	★170	★34	6	15	100	★.377	★255	284	★45	★.923
1960—Minneapolis	A.A.	OF	148	570	84	★193	36	8	7	69	.339	243	18	5	.981
1961—Boston	Amer.	OF	148	583	71	155	31	6	11	80	.266	248	12	10	.963
1962—Boston	Amer.	OF	160	646	99	191	43	6	19	94	.296	329	★15	★11	.969
1963—Boston	Amer.	OF	151	570	91	★183	★40	3	14	68	★.321	283	★18	6	.980
1964—Boston	Amer.	OF-3B	151	567	77	164	29	9	15	67	.289	372	●24	11	.973
1965—Boston	Amer.	OF	133	494	78	154	●45	3	20	72	.312	222	11	3	.987
1966—Boston	Amer.	OF	160	594	81	165	★39	2	16	80	.278	310	★15	5	.985
1967—Boston	Amer.	OF	161	579	★112	★189	31	4	●44	★121	★.326	297	13	7	.978
1968—Boston	Amer.	OF-1B	157	539	90	162	32	2	23	74	★.301	315	13	3	.991
1969—Boston	Amer.	OF-1B	●162	603	96	154	28	2	40	111	.255	427	★38	6	.987
1970—Boston	Amer.	1B-OF	161	566	★125	186	29	0	40	102	.329	816	64	14	.984
1971—Boston	Amer.	OF	148	508	75	129	21	2	15	70	.254	281	★16	2	.993
1972—Boston†	Amer.	OF-1B	125	455	70	120	18	2	12	68	.264	498	43	8	.985
1973—Boston	Amer.	1B-3B-OF	152	540	82	160	25	4	19	95	.296	979	119	18	.984
1974—Boston	Amer.	1B-OF-DH	148	515	★93	155	25	2	15	79	.301	806	46	6	.993
1975—Boston	Amer.	1B-OF-DH	149	543	91	146	30	1	14	60	.269	1217	88	5	.996
1976—Boston	Amer.	1B-OF-DH	155	546	71	146	23	2	21	102	.267	922	55	4	.996
1977—Boston	Amer.	★OF-1B-DH	150	558	99	165	27	3	28	102	.296	344	★22	0	★1.000
1978—Boston	Amer.	DH-OF-1B	144	523	70	145	21	2	17	81	.277	523	49	5	.991
1979—Boston	Amer.	DH-1B-OF	147	518	69	140	28	1	21	87	.270	529	56	4	.993
1980—Boston	Amer.	DH-OF-1B	105	364	49	100	21	1	15	50	.275	225	13	4	.983
1981—Boston	Amer.	DH-1B	91	338	36	83	14	1	7	53	.246	353	34	3	.992
1982—Boston	Amer.	DH-1B-OF	131	459	53	126	22	1	16	72	.275	119	10	0	1.000
1983—Boston‡	Amer.	DH-1B-OF	119	380	38	101	24	0	10	56	.266	22	1	0	1.000
Major League Totals—23 Years			3308	11988	1816	3419	646	59	452	1844	.285	10437	775	135	.988

★ Led league.

● Tied for league lead.

†On supplemental disabled list, May 10 to June 9, 1972.

‡On voluntary retired list, October 25, 1983.

CHAMPIONSHIP SERIES RECORD

Year	Club	League	Pos.	G.	AB.	R.	H.	2B.	3B.	HR.	RBI.	B.A.	PO.	A.	E.	F.A.
1975—Boston...........Amer.			OF	3	11	4	5	1	0	1	2	.455	7	2	0	1.000

WORLD SERIES RECORD

Year	Club	League	Pos.	G.	AB.	R.	H.	2B.	3B.	HR.	RBI.	B.A.	PO.	A.	E.	F.A.
1967—Boston...........Amer.			OF	7	25	4	10	2	0	3	5	.400	16	2	0	1.000
1975—Boston...........Amer.			OF-1B	7	29	7	9	0	0	0	4	.310	35	1	0	1.000
World Series Totals—2 Years				14	54	11	19	2	0	3	9	.352	51	3	0	1.000

ALL STAR GAME RECORD

Tied All-Star Game records for most hits, game (4), July 14, 1970; most one-base hits, game (3), July 14, 1970; most home runs by pinch-hitter, game (1), July 15, 1975.

Year	League	Pos.	AB.	R.	H.	2B.	3B.	HR.	RBI.	B.A.	PO.	A.	E.	F.A.
1963—American		OF	2	0	0	0	0	0	0	.000	1	0	0	1.000
1967—American		OF	4	0	3	1	0	0	0	.750	2	0	0	1.000
1968—American		OF	4	0	0	0	0	0	0	.000	0	0	0	.000
1969—American		OF	1	0	0	0	0	0	0	.000	1	0	0	1.000
1970—American		OF-1B	6	1	4	1	0	0	1	.667	8	0	0	1.000
1971—American		OF	3	0	0	0	0	0	0	.000	0	0	0	.000
1972—American		OF	3	0	0	0	0	0	0	.000	3	0	0	1.000
1974—American		1B	1	0	0	0	0	0	0	.000	5	0	0	1.000
1975—American		PH	1	1	1	0	0	1	3	1.000	0	0	0	.000
1976—American		OF	2	0	0	0	0	0	0	000	0	0	0	.000
1977—American		OF	2	0	0	0	0	0	0	000	0	0	0	.000
1979—American		1B	3	0	2	0	0	0	1	.667	5	1	0	1.000
1982—American		PH	1	0	0	0	0	0	0	.000	0	0	0	.000
1983—American		PH	1	0	0	0	0	0	0	.000	0	0	0	.000
All-Star Game Totals—14 years........			34	2	10	2	0	1	5	.294	25	1	0	1.000

Member of American League All-Star Team in 1966; did not play.
Named to American League All-Star Teams for 1965, 1973, and 1978 games; replaced due to injury.

BOOK MARK

The text of this book was set in the typeface Garamond and the display was set in Futura Medium Condensed by Berryville Graphics, Berryville, Virginia. It was printed on 50 lb Glatfelter, an acid-free paper, and bound by R. R. Donnelley, Harrisonburg, Virginia.

DESIGNED BY DIANE STEVENSON/SNAP·HAUS GRAPHICS